THE OLD SHRUB ROSES

*With eighteen subjects in full colour
and twenty-one in monochrome*

Rosa Gallica Versicolor. *Rosier de France à fleurs panac...*

A reproduction of the portrait of 'Rosa Mundi', by Redouté, from his famous work published in 1817–24. This rose is reputedly named after Henry II's 'Fair Rosamond'. Description on page 151. See also plate 7.

THE OLD
SHRUB ROSES

Graham Stuart Thomas

O.B.E., V.M.H., D.H.M., V.M.M.

Gardens Consultant to the National Trust

WITH CHAPTERS ON THE

EVOLUTION OF OUR GARDEN ROSES

by Dr C. C. Hurst, SC.D., PH.D., F.L.S.

FOREWORD BY

V. Sackville-West

C.H.

J. M. Dent & Sons Ltd

London   Melbourne

In association with the Royal Horticultural Society

To all those who have
helped me in the
Quest
&

to all other lovers of
THE ROSE

Printed in Great Britain
by Garden City Press Ltd, Letchworth, Herts
for J. M. Dent & Sons Ltd
Aldine House 33 Welbeck Street London W1M 8LX

First published 1955
Second impression 1956
Second edition 1957
Third edition 1961
Fourth edition 1963
Reprinted 1966
Revised edition 1979
Reprinted 1980
Reprinted (with revisions) 1983
Reprinted 1985

ISBN 0 460 04345 5

Foreword

by V. Sackville-West, C.H.

I REMEMBER THAT many years ago, in the bazaars of Constantinople, we used sometimes to spend a fabulous, Arabian-tale of an afternoon, not propped on banks of amaranth and moly, but on divans and cushions in the warehouse of a great carpet merchant, sipping sweet-thick Turkish coffee from cups with filigree containers, while the treasures of his collection were rolled out at our feet by innumerable servitors, picturesque in their blue blouses, broad red sashes, and baggy blue trousers.

Those were the days of extravagant leisure. Looking back on them it seems as though they had occurred centuries ago, instead of merely in 1913, just before the first of two world wars. There was no need to hurry; rush and speed had scarcely entered into man's conception of the desirable life; flying machines were still something to bring housewives out on their doorsteps to stare at; statesmen and politicians had not yet begun to dart backwards and forwards between America, Europe, and the Far East, descending on Delhi and touching down somewhere in Australasia on the way. Expressions such as 'breaking the sound barrier' would have been incomprehensible to our ears. How soon we forget!

But what has all this to do, you may ask, with the old roses which are the subject of Mr Graham Thomas's book? Perhaps not so very far removed. Mr Thomas swept me quite unexpectedly back to those dusky mysterious hours in an Oriental storehouse when the rugs and carpets of Isfahan and Bokhara and Samarcand were unrolled in their dim but sumptuous colouring and richness of texture for our slow delight. Rich they were, rich as a fig broken open, soft as a ripened peach, freckled as an apricot, coral as a pomegranate, bloomy as a bunch of grapes. It is of these that the old roses remind me.

It may be true, as Mr Thomas with his downright honesty remarks, that some of the old roses demand an acquired taste before they be properly esteemed and appreciated. Not everybody likes oysters. I have myself observed, with some amusement, a look of dismay coming over the faces of visitors to my own garden where I grow many of the roses dear to my heart and to the heart of Mr Thomas. 'Surely, surely, that's not a rose as we understand roses?' No, perhaps it isn't. It bears little resemblance to the highly coloured Hybrid Teas and polyanthas and floribundas of the modern garden. It is a far quieter and more subtle thing, but oh let me say how rewarding a taste it is when once acquired, and how right is Mr Thomas when he implies that they have all 'the attraction that sentiment, history, botany, or association can lend them'.

The first essential is to regard them as *shrubs*, the name which Mr Thomas boldly gives them. It is a temptation to describe the great foaming bushes, but Mr Thomas has done it in the following pages. The next need is to discard the idea that roses must be limited to certain accepted and accustomed colours, and to welcome the less familiar purples and lilacs, and the striped, flaked, mottled variations which recall the old Dutch flower-paintings; to approach them, in fact, with open and unprejudiced eyes, and also with a nose that esteems the true scent of a rose warmed by the sun. They have one major fault, and Mr Thomas does not evade it: their flowering period is limited to one glorious month of midsummer. Personally, I think that they are more than worth it. A glance at the illustrations should suffice to convince the sceptical; the already converted will find the text of this uniquely authoritative book of the deepest interest and value.

Contents

7

Illustrations

9

Acknowledgments

MY OWN small library of books on roses has enabled me to check many names and descriptions of roses at my leisure, but on frequent occasions I have had recourse to the Lindley Library, of the Royal Horticultural Society, where the Librarian and Staff have always given me the greatest courtesy and assistance. To them my very real thanks are due, for frequent access to Redouté's volumes alone has in great part enabled me to write the following chapters with some feeling of confidence.

I also want to record much valued help and advice from Mr Gordon D. Rowley, and for the preparation of the Family Trees of Roses on pages 94-7. My thanks are due to Mrs Rona Hurst for her very kindly interest and help in several ways, and more especially for allowing me to republish her late husband's writings, permission which was also generously accorded to me by the Council of the Royal Horticultural Society. The inclusion of Dr Hurst's notes provides an opportunity for their increased circulation, and adds immeasurably to the value of this publication. I should not have felt happy about writing the chapter on Roses in Pictures without the knowledge that Mr Wilfrid Blunt would be good enough to read it through, and I must record my indebtedness to him for his help and several suggestions. Mr Bennell has proved a most patient and painstaking photographer and has earned my deep appreciation. Permission to quote from Edmund Blunden's 'Shells by a Stream' is gratefully acknowledged to Messrs Macmillan & Co. Ltd.

And to all those who are not mentioned in this brief list I add my warm gratitude for all kindness, help, and the shared enthusiasm which has enabled me to tread this thorny path and to bring to print these notes.

It was roses, roses all the way.

Robert Browning.

G. S. T.

Woking, Surrey

PART I

The Development and Cultivation of the Rose

While by the rosebed gay you stood, and
    revelled in the multitude
Of blooms with unfamiliar names, and tints
    and folds new-found, new sweet,
We wondered much at the rich power which
    breeds so many and many a flower
Not like the myriads known before, and
    each one lovely and complete.

Edmund Blunden, Shells by a Stream

Chapter I

· ·

A Personal Approach

His talk was like a stream which runs
with rapid change from rocks to roses.
Winthrop Mackworth Praed

IN THE PROGRESS of horticulture every plant has a place or use
to which it is most suited. To maintain such a position it must be
worthy in some way of the space usually given to it in cultivation.
Some plants linger for ever at the ground level of popularity,
while others rocket quickly to the top. Again, some may dis
appear from general use only to be revived again when conditions or fashions alter. I think the reasons are not difficult to
find.

Plants appeal to us in many ways, and most of them have considerable beauty, even when they are artificially created, and they
may also have the attraction that sentiment, history, botany, or
association can lend them. They may be easy or temperamental to
grow but, at this stage of horticultural history at least, their
garden value is paramount. We all desire as much beauty, colour,
fragrance, longevity, and annual goodwill as possible from our
plants, and it is the purpose of this book to try to shew how a
great group of neglected roses can add to the list of shrubs available for general garden use.

In singling out these particular roses for examination, I feel I
am fulfilling a kind of mission, since they appeal in an increasing
way to a widening circle of gardeners. I find them fascinating, and
not only does this fascination apply to the summer months, but
also to the winter evenings spent in culling historical details from
old books and catalogues, and associating the many historic
figures with the period flowers whose names they bear. The only
apology, therefore, with which I write these notes is that my
knowledge of these roses is still incomplete, though yearly growing, thanks to what has been written in the past and to the steadily

17

increasing circle of friends, whose enthusiasm and interest are continually pooled in furtherance of our quest. And so I am going to write what I hope may be considered as a gardener's rather than a botanist's approach to a few roses which we will term 'old', and to extol their value in the garden—although perhaps in the course of the following pages history or botany or reminiscence may occasionally expel the horticultural aspect.

I think the rose must hold a high place in our early affection for flowers. I can distinctly remember delighting in the fragrance of the Hybrid Perpetual Rose, 'Mrs John Laing', at the age of 8; in fact 'Mrs Laing' and 'Alister Stella Gray' have been my constant companions since those early days, and never fail to give plentifully of their beauty, year by year. There was also in our Cambridge garden another very fragrant rose; it was a big bush of the plant used frequently as an understock, *Rosa multiflora* 'de la Grifferaie', although I was not aware of this until many years later. This is often found in old gardens, having outlived the rose budded upon it, and few roses have a more delicious scent in the fully double, almost pompon-like, magenta-pink blooms, borne in clusters along the arching sprays.

Well remembered, too, is the day on which I purchased my first rose—'Caroline Testout', followed by other Hybrid Teas, now outclassed; they were recommended by an uncle who was something of a connoisseur, and in whose garden every rose bore, to my great satisfaction, a cast metal label. At the age of 14 or 15 I added 'General McArthur' and 'Mrs Aaron Ward'—a new colour note to the garden—to my little collection, together with 'Mrs Herbert Stevens', 'Madame Édouard Herriot', and 'Madame Abel Chatenay'. Most of these stay in general cultivation.

At this period alpine plants claimed my full attention, Reginald Farrer's pen working upon my imagination so much that rocks and alpine plants absorbed all my spare pocket money. On leaving school I spent some years at the University Botanic Garden at Cambridge. In those days Dr H. Gilbert-Carter and Mr F. G. Preston were there to guide my advancement in botany and horticulture, with Mr J. Blades filling in all the details that my enthusiasm needed. I was ripe for the wider appreciation of all classes of hardy plants that may be acquired in that unique Garden

—Alpines, Herbaceous plants, Conifers, Shrubs, Trees, and Roses. *Rosa gigantea* flowered well, and also such diverse plants as *Rosa Banksiae lutea*, the 'Old Blush' China, *Rosa Hardii, Moyesii, rugosa*, and *moschata*; Dr C. C. Hurst was busy in frames and houses with his genetical experiments; *Rosa cantabrigiensis* was soon to appear as a chance seedling and to be given an Award of Merit and also the Cory Cup in 1931.

It was while at the Cambridge Botanic Garden that I met Thomas Blythe, a fellow student, whose often repeated eulogies of Irish luxuriance prompted me to visit him in Ireland in 1937. I shall never forget the spectacle which his kindness unfolded for me at Rostrevor and Rowallane, while other excursions took us to his uncle's nursery at Daisy Hill, Newry, and to the Botanic Garden at Glasnevin, Dublin. At this famous Garden some most beautiful roses happened to be in flower: *Rosa Paulii* and its pink form *rosea, R. macrophylla*, and several other species of note, while at Newry the rather sad remnants of Tom Smith's once magnificent collection were also in full bloom. The several 'old' roses grown here did not immediately appeal to me, their mauve-pinks and purples being so unexpected that, like many others newly approaching this class of rose, I was almost repelled. I could only single out the rose known as *R. gallica* 'Vivid' and the *rugosa* hybrid 'Vanguard', both of which I now look upon with considerable coolness.

At the outbreak of war Brian O. Mulligan, at that time Assistant to Mr Harrow at the Royal Horticultural Society's Gardens at Wisley, drew my attention to the great collection of old roses gathered together by Mr E. A. Bunyard, which was shortly to be sold. This awakened me to the treasure stored by this enlightened man, who was so great a loss to us all in his passing. And then shortly afterwards the only other big commercial collection of shrub roses fell upon the market, that of Messrs G. Beckwith & Son of Hoddesdon. Although this collection was mainly composed of species, many of which were of doubtful horticultural value, the entire collection was acquired in the spring of 1940, and it was with much interest that we awaited flowering time the next year. There were several nuggets among the dross, such as 'Nevada', whose portrait in the *New Flora and Silva* [1] had fired my

[1] Vol. 8, p. 245.

enthusiasm, some good Provence and Moss roses, and the exquisitely fragrant Gallica Rose 'Belle de Crécy'. This perfectly shaped old-world rose, in its extraordinary mixture of cerise, violet, and lilac-grey, happened to be planted near to the incomparable white hybrid Damask Rose 'Madame Hardy'. I lost my heart to them during the first flowering week, and have found no better types among the old roses since. It was my first real appreciation of these exquisite florist's creations.

To the few enthusiasts of those days the sale of these two collections and complete disappearance of such roses from commerce seemed to be the death knell, I have been told, of the little cause that had been growing. The war dragged on, and a hayfield sprang up through our plantation of roses, but they survived, being tough and hardy and thrifty. A little later the Daisy Hill Nursery changed hands, and a few roses reached us safely; among them were 'Tuscany', 'Commandant Beaurepaire', 'Alain Blanchard', 'Coupe d'Hébé', and a striped rose that has since proved to be *Rosa centifolia variegata*.

Meanwhile, in 1941 I was lucky enough to find my way to Nymans, the late Lt-Col L. R. C. Messel's beautiful home at Handcross, Sussex. It was my special privilege to be taken round the remarkable collection of old roses by Mrs Messel, whose particular hobby it was to collect these delights before the war. Here was my first introduction to them as garden furnishings, and I recall the great beauty of 'Charles de Mills' in all its glory, 4–5 feet high on that rich Wealden soil, with several dozen flowers well open. At Nymans these roses were grouped in formal beds, set in grass and interspersed with apple- and mulberry-trees, in a pleasing cottage garden style. It was a great experience to see them and hear all the delightful names of these rare old varieties from so knowledgeable and enthusiastic a gardener as Mrs Messel.

There was not much time during the war to look out for roses, but an occasional visit to Nymans and Wisley, where there were several interesting varieties, to Kew and Cambridge, kept my interest alive though suppressed and subordinate to matters of moment. Towards the end of the war my interest was greatly quickened by a visit from Mrs Constance Spry. The long French names flowed from her, enthusiasm was at bursting point; a few glances at the little lot we had collected drew forth some remarks that, while they were not disparaging, made me realize I had little to shew. There were no half measures with Mrs Spry—a long and growing friendship proved this over and over again—and she had assiduously collected her roses from French and American nurseries, and from gardens here and there, in days before the war. It was necessary for her to move them. Could I propagate them meanwhile in order to ensure their perpetuity in case the old bushes died? This was a problem in those days, but we managed it somehow. There was nothing for it but that I must up and away to Kent and see her roses, and this I did, and was once more thoroughly convinced that, not only was there nothing like them in horticulture, but that they were good and fascinating garden material, neglected by just that generation that could make the best use of them. A few prophets of pre-war days had been crying in the wilderness, and a few keen spirits had preserved these beauties for our later enjoyment; this is a fact that will become the more apparent as the story unfolds. Messrs Pajotin-Chédane of La Maître École, Angers, France, had given up their collection when I wrote to them after the war, but Constance Spry had their most sumptuous varieties in Kent. Messrs Bobbink and Atkins of New Jersey, in America, still grew a number of good varieties, but how fortunate that many of their best were already in this country, again in the Spry collection. And also the roses from Messrs Bunyard's had found their way through Mr E. A. Bunyard to Nymans, and there were roses there and at Wisley from Daisy Hill Nurseries, Newry.

Another noted preserver of these plants, my old friend and mentor Mr A. T. Johnson, of Bulkeley Mill, Tyn-y-groes, North Wales, sent me a special invitation to see his garden in June, when he found that I had become an ardent admirer of the old groups. It was indeed a joy to find 'Tuscany' suckering strongly in the poor shaley soil, the Alba Roses growing to 6 feet high, and many a Gallica showering their blossoms over the borders. A great find was 'Félicité Parmentier', which A. T. J. had imported some years previously from the German nurseryman Peter Lambert of Trier. Not only had A. T. J. preserved numerous old roses from various sources, but his writings—in various journals and in his books about his enchanting small garden— did much to foster interest in these splendid garden shrubs.

With petrol again available in small quantities a few other visits became possible in 1947, one being to Sissinghurst Castle, where Sir Harold and Lady Nicolson (V. Sackville-West) grow some unique old roses, including the one we call 'Sissinghurst Castle', and the rare purple Hybrid Perpetual 'Souvenir du Docteur Jamain'. Another journey was to Colonel F. C. Stern's garden at Highdown, Goring-by-Sea, Sussex; good bushes of old-fashioned roses grow strongly in his chalky soil, and fine examples of hybrid Musk Roses and many species thrive amazingly well. The Oxford University Botanic Garden had one or two rare varieties with cast-metal labels, including *Rosa gallica conditorum*, and on the same day I went farther, into Buckinghamshire, to Chetwode Manor. In this quiet country garden Mrs Louis Fleischmann had preserved another collection of roses; these had been mostly gathered from old gardens in England and Ireland, and 'Tour de Malakoff' was one of the great bushes, loaded with huge blooms, that greeted me. One of the rarest roses in her garden was the Autumn Damask, a precious heirloom from the days when a few late blooms were greatly treasured. I described her garden at some length in *Gardening Illustrated* for July 1951. On the way back I called on Miss Nancy Lindsay and was delighted to find several ancient roses which she had collected in Persia, together with some most beautiful French kinds, and to compare notes with her. Another garden I visited on the same trip was that belonging to Mr and Mrs Nigel Law, High Trees, Chalfont St Peter, Bucks. Some very scarce varieties are to be found carefully preserved in their garden, several of which I had not seen before, and among them was the pompon variety 'Cramoisi Picoté'.

I had been in correspondence with the Hon. Robert James of St Nicholas, Richmond, Yorks, and was keenly interested to see his renowned collection. Accordingly, when our roses were over, with my friend James P. C. Russell of Windlesham, who had become infected with my enthusiasm, I decided to visit some northern gardens, and our first call was at St Nicholas. Mr James had preserved numerous splendid roses among other plants in his delightful garden, and I was particularly interested to find beds of the single pink *Rosa gallica*, apparently a wild type, and also the so-called 'Empress Josephine', which proved to be a form or hybrid of *Rosa francofurtana*; both were running through the soil and thriving. We also went over the Pennines to Penrith, where magnificent bowls of purple roses and other floral decorations awaited us at Crossrigg Hall, the home of Mr Cornish Torbock. Roses do well in these gardens, and also at Sir William Milner's, at Appletreewick, near Skipton. One of the best things in Sir William's garden was the skilful framing of the view from his terrace, but on the more sheltered side of the house a good collection of old roses grew. Here we found numerous choice varieties, including a most exquisite White Rose, which has since proved to be 'Mme Legras de St Germain'. Our fourth call was at Weston Hall, Towcester, where Mr Sacheverell Sitwell grows another splendid collection, the most striking variety being the sumptuous crimson-purple Moss, 'Maréchal Davoust'. We felt greatly elated on completing this little northern tour, and to have seen four excellent collections in such good condition, carefully preserved by these keen and discriminating gardeners.

The year 1948 was spent mostly in consolidating my own plants and getting to know the numerous varieties I had collected; comparing them with old books and sorting them into botanical groups, and writing short descriptions of each. It was therefore with some little knowledge stored that I went to Ireland again in 1949; the story of my travels from one wonderful garden to another is written elsewhere,[1] but I will recall here two most interesting places, Old Conna Hill, Bray, where the late Colonel and Mrs Riall used to tend a wide variety of plants in a beautiful setting, and Mr and Mrs Salmon's *multum in parvo* at Larchfield, Dublin. Here were a thousand or more roses closely grown in mixed borders, and Mr Salmon proudly produced a family treasure, 'Le Roi à fleur pourpre'. Also in their collection were two roses which I have, I think, traced successfully since: the pink sport or parent of 'Léda', and 'Blush Hip', the climbing pink *Rosa alba*. It was a great pleasure, too, to visit Lady Moore, at Rathfarnham, Dublin, for she has specially preserved some interesting old Scots Roses, and that new rose of ancient lineage, 'Souvenir de St Anne's', a sport from the Malmaison Rose.

I was no sooner back from Ireland than Gloucestershire called

[1] *Journal of the Royal Horticultural Society*, June and August 1950.

me. The season is later there than in Surrey, and while our roses were going over, those at Hidcote Manor—Major Lawrence Johnston's garden of consummate taste and constant surprises—and Mrs J. B. Muir's garden at Kiftsgate Court, both near Chipping Campden, revealed a display of old roses flowering in the wildest profusion and of the greatest luxuriance. Mrs Muir's garden received a share of its due from my pen elsewhere,[1] but I cannot pass on without recalling once again the satisfaction I received, and yearly regain, in going from one border to another, each of a different character and colour, and culminating in the splendour of the double 'Rosa Mundi' hedges, and the supreme touch, the white garden. These two gardens, Kiftsgate and Hidcote, display the old roses in much of their natural state, while at Abbotswood, Stow-on-the-Wold—the home of Mrs Harry Ferguson—there was a splendid group of old-fashioned roses carefully pruned to produce the maximum number of beautiful blooms by Mr F. Tustin. I need hardly say more than that a visit to Abbotswood immediately proved that the rose, old or new, has no peer for scent and colour among all the brilliant denizens even of that superb colour garden.

Meanwhile I had not been idle in regard to correspondence, and was in touch with Bobbink & Atkins, of New Jersey, and the Lester Rose Gardens in California. Both firms had collected and propagated many old roses from all parts of that continent, and my collection was very considerably enriched by their generosity. The Morton Arboretum, Illinois, and Mr G. D. Greene of St Louis, Missouri, have also added to our collection, and Herr Wilhelm Kordes in Holstein and Mr O. Sonderhousen of Denmark have both sent me many varieties of merit. Through the great kindness and co-operation of Mr André Leroi of the Conservation des Parcs et Jardins in Paris I was fortunate to receive a complete catalogue of all the roses grown in the re-nowned German National Rose Garden, at Sangerhausen. This amazingly complete list includes hundreds of old roses, and I managed to get the majority safely over for comparison. The Moss 'Général Kléber' and *gallica* 'Cosimo Ridolfi' stand out as two most desirable varieties from this collection. It has indeed been most interesting comparing notes and descriptions,

[1] *Journal of the Royal Horticultural Society*, May 1951.

and also the living plants, side by side, from these many keen and co-operative donors. Many times does one find a name completely and utterly wrong attached to a beautiful rose, and occasionally by careful searching through old books one finds a clue to its correct name. More often than not, unfortunately, this becomes impossible, the great majority of descriptions being too vague to enable one to do more than check the colour and group.

The collecting of these roses over a number of years has not been the only aspect of the work. Together with a large range of species a comprehensive collection of Old Shrub Roses has been established at the Trial and Display Gardens of the Royal National Rose Society, Bone Hill, Chiswell Green Lane, St Albans, Hertfordshire. At Mottisfont Abbey, Romsey, Hampshire, the National Trust has assembled my entire original collection of Old Shrub Roses with numerous old climbers and ramblers, in an old walled garden. There are also considerable collections in other gardens of the National Trust, particularly at Hidcote, Chipping Campden, Gloucestershire; Nymans, Handcross, Sussex; Sissinghurst Castle, Cranbrook, Kent, and West Green House, Hartley Wintney, Hampshire. The Northern Horticultural Society's Garden at Harlow Car, Harrogate, Yorkshire also has a good number, likewise Castle Howard, York. These collections can be utilized for study, to unravel the history and guess the future conduct of a glorious race.

Can I term them, also, the popular roses of the future? I do not feel it would be wise to do so. That these roses find favour with many is very true; admirers have come from America, Tasmania, New Zealand, Australia, South Africa, Tangier, Cyprus, Italy, and many other countries of Europe, and those desiring to grow them in this country are increasing in numbers yearly. But they are, apart from all this, an acquired taste: at least I have found this very true in my own approach to them. They have, as I have stated before, a colouring and form unique in the realm of horticulture, and they are easy to grow, but they do not satisfy all the modern preconceived ideas, either in colour or in their limited flowering season, and so they can never be 'popular' within the present meaning of the word. They are 'a heady subject, and like wine they go to one's head', as Mr Selwyn Duruz says in the chapter devoted to them in his book *Flowering Shrubs*. How very true this is can be proved by the enthusiasm which they arouse in people in all walks and stations of life, including artists, fortunately, for where should we be without those capable of depicting these treasures on paper?

Some of the most pretentious horticultural works have been devoted to the genus Rosa, and a great band of artists has contributed from time to time in painting the favourites of the period, and in the descriptive list of varieties later in this book I have endeavoured to indicate where reasonably accurate portraits may be found. This will, I hope, save others from hours of searching, and will also serve to shew how popular certain varieties were in years gone by, when roses were still classed as flowering shrubs.

Chapter II

· ·

The Rise of the Old Roses

Oh, no man knows
Through what wild centuries
Roves back the rose.

Walter de la Mare

THE BOTANISTS enumerate 100–200 species of roses, according to
whether they feel that small and possibly inconstant characters
are sufficient to separate one species from another. It is amusing
to read in Bean's *Trees and Shrubs* that one botanist was known to
have separated the species so finely that the characters of two
could be found on one bush! The genus is found throughout the
temperate and sub-tropical regions of the Northern Hemisphere.
Practically all, except a few from the warmer parts, are deciduous,
and are bushy or trailing or climbing shrubs of varying dimensions. A number of learned works may be found in libraries dealing with them in a botanical way, but since we are concerned with
so few species in these pages it will not be of any advantage to
enter too deeply into a general botanical discussion. Suffice it to
say that a mere handful of species have given us all our highly
bred roses of today, and many are in what the botanists term the
group 'Gallicanae'. These form the bulk of the 'old' roses which
are our concern. But there are a few other species, to some of
which my concluding chapter is devoted, which were also
quite popular in the past in Europe, judging by the fact that they
are enumerated in nearly all the old books on roses. They are the
European species *Rosa rubrifolia*, whose soft plum-coloured leaves
are its main attraction; *Rosa canina*, our native Dog Briar; *Rosa
glutinosa*, so strongly and strangely redolent of pines; the Sweet
Briar, *Rosa eglanteria* or *rubiginosa*, and *Rosa pomifera*. These all
belong to the Caninae section and have pink flowers, while *Rosa
foetida* and *Rosa hemisphaerica*, from Western Asia, the so-called
Austrian Briar and the Sulphur Rose respectively, bear yellow

27

flowers. *Rosa pendulina* (R. *alpina*), also European, and *Rosa moschata*, a native in its many geographical forms from North Africa, Southern Europe, and Western Asia to the Himalayas and China, bring this little list nearly to its close.

A few of these species were grown in cultivated forms, and *Rosa foetida* has in more recent times altered the colours of our roses almost beyond recognition, but otherwise they have remained on the verge of horticulture, and have not been absorbed by it, nor have they ever entered the main ancestral popular group of roses, apart from *Rosa moschata* and *canina*.

The Gallicanae, which I have referred to as 'main' and 'ancestral', form a closely related group, descended, it is reasonable to suppose, from *Rosa gallica* (R. *rubra*), *Rosa moschata*, *canina*, and *phoenicea*. *Rosa gallica* has had predominance, and in general horticultural feeling may be considered the common ancestor of the Gallicas, the Damasks, the Provence and Moss Roses, and the White Roses. These are examined in more detail in the next chapter, and they formed the foundation of our present popular races of roses. When we read (in Hurst's notes) that *Rosa gallica* was a religious emblem of the Medes and Persians in the twelfth century B.C. it is small wonder that it has united with other wild roses in the cradle of our present civilization, and that the hybrid progeny, all fragrant presentable roses of bushy habit, should have been favourites with the Southern European peoples for thousands of years. They have been preserved mainly for their beauty, as their only economic products are scent and conserves, comparatively of little importance to the survival of the human race. Nobody knows, of course, how these old races of roses developed in the first place, but one can visualize certain tribes delighting in one form or another and spreading them over limited areas where they may have become hybridized by chance with the few other species concerned.

Our roses went on in a small way, being loved and tended by the few who could devote time to such a trifling pursuit, until the general awakening of the Renaissance. In spite of the knowledge of tricky vegetative propagating—for even the grafting of fruits on various root-stocks was current in Virgil's time—roses did not profit except by limited selection of a few forms. The production of new forms by seed was not understood. And thus

one finds in very old works the same old varieties again and again
—the bullate or laciniate leaf, the double or single or striped
flower which in those days were sufficient spice and variety to
ensure the protection of these plants.

But when the new desire for beauty, the new use or possible
use of spare time, and the new awakening to the cultivation of
plants arose, apart from the vegetable garden, we find a steady
stream of varieties appearing. Seed began to play a part later, and,
once unleashed, the rose gave forth its potentialities, stored in a
complex hybrid group for these thousands of years, and became
one of the most prolific of the favourite races of plants.

It is interesting to delve into some of the noted gardening
books of the past to see the development of the rose. In Gerard's
Herbal, 1597, 14 roses are enumerated; Parkinson, in his *Paradisi
in Sole Paradisus Terrestris* (1629), mentions 24; in 1663 Mollet
mentions 6 roses only for the ornamental garden, but the 'Rosier
de Provins' (*Rosa gallica* or *rubra*) is relegated to the kitchen
garden. Lawrance in 1799 produced 90 coloured plates of roses;
Roessig, between 1802 and 1820, depicts 121 varieties in colour.
These are extremely valuable works from our point of view, many of
the roses being still in cultivation, and they are accurately depicted.[1]

From 1817 to 1824 Redouté was producing the monumental
work *Les Roses* with the text by Thory, and this really marks the
beginning of our present appreciation of the rose. The three magnificent volumes are a delight to handle owing to their sumptu-
ousness and spacious pages, and every plate shews a masterly
hand delineating a fine, and, in many examples, a recognizable
rose. The volumes immortalize not only Redouté and Thory but
also the Empress Josephine, at whose behest there was such a
gathering together of roses at La Malmaison as had never before
been seen, and to Redouté was given the task of conveying their
beauties to paper.[2] Bunyard, in his *Old Garden Roses*, mentions that

---

[1] Georg Dionysius Ehret (1708–70), a great painter of plants, has left us some
superb portraits of the roses of his time. Originals may be seen in the Victoria and
Albert Museum, and they include Rosa Mundi, Common Provence, York and
Lancaster, Red Provence (*R. gallica officinalis*), and Common Moss. An excellent
reproduction of twelve of his pictures was published in 1953 with an introduction by
Wilfrid Blunt. (Traylen, Guildford.)
[2] There have been several reproductions of Redouté's rose portraits, perhaps the
best being the set of twenty-four published in 1954, with an introduction by Eva
Mannering. (The Ariel Press.)

an English nurseryman, Kennedy, was employed by her—war or no war—and between him and Dupont, the director of the Luxembourg Gardens at Paris, the world was ransacked to furnish her famous collection. 'There was also a rival,' Bunyard remarks, 'the Countess of Bougainville, to spur to further efforts, and under such auspicious impetus the rose became the most important flower in France.' Seed-raising on a grand scale had begun, and he records that Descemet, the nurseryman at St Denis, had some ten thousand seedlings when the Allies prepared to march into Paris in 1815, and that these were rescued by Vibert and taken to safety on the Marne.

Roses from then onwards were very much in the hands of nurserymen, and their erudite and comprehensive little volumes give one cause to wonder how they found the time to do their botanical and classical research, and what is almost more to the point, what sort of public it was that could regularly purchase their works. Take, for instance, Prévost, Pépiniériste à Rouen, *Catalogue descriptif, méthodique et raisonné des espèces, variétés et sous-variétés du Genre Rosier*; his list embraces 880 names. Our two famous English nurserymen specializing in roses at that time were Thomas Rivers and William Paul, and both made their contributions to the growing library devoted to the rose. Rivers's *Rose Amateur's Guide* (1837) is a discursive and delightful small book devoting a hundred pages to a pleasantly written enumeration of varieties, together with details of cultivation. It is a catalogue of his roses presented in a most readable fashion, and many old varieties are traced to their origin in its pages. Paul's *The Rose Garden* (1848) ('to the Rose Amateurs of Great Britain this work is most respectfully inscribed by their humble servant the Author') is a much more pretentious work, the first half being devoted to an exposition of the rose in the Arts, and its requirements in cultivation. The second half contains many chapters, each devoted to a special group of roses, all given careful descriptions, which I have found very useful and helpful; among hundreds of roses of many other groups it is wonderful to find descriptions of 87 Damask, 76 Provence, 84 Moss, and 471 French (Gallica) roses.

To these two books I must add Max Singer's *Dictionnaire des Roses, ou guide général du Rosieriste*. This was published in 1885, and, apart from fifty pages at the beginning devoted to a few species and small groups of roses—including, rather strangely, over five dozen varieties of *Rosa alba*—this is an alphabetical enumeration of six thousand varieties, in many instances with long descriptions. His descriptions do not always tally with those of Paul, but between them there is much to be learned.

Singer's *Dictionnaire* was followed in 1906 by another French work, *Nomenclature de tous les Noms de Roses connus, avec indication de leur race, obtenteur, année de production, couleur et synonymes*, by Léon Simon and Pierre Cochet; their list extends to 10,953 entries, from 'Abaçon' to 'Zulmalacareguy'. What an intriguing name for a rose! It was a Provence, and is also mentioned by Paul.

Many of the most shapely and sumptuous of our old roses were raised during the nineteenth century: 'Madame Hardy', 1832; 'Félicité Parmentier', 1836; 'Cardinal de Richelieu', 1840; 'La Ville de Bruxelles', 1849; and 'Tour de Malakoff', 1856. Their heyday of popularity was perhaps around 1810 to 1830, for the later introductions mentioned above were only isolated examples of a doomed race. Had they not been very vigorous and thrifty shrubs they would probably not have survived for a hundred years, ready to be collected together again to serve a type of garden changed beyond recognition from those which in bygone days they graced. For the rose was to suffer a great revolution in common with its most ardent admirers of that time.

Chapter III

· ·

Revolution

Then in that Parly all those powers
Voted the Rose the Queen of Flowers.

Robert Herrick

THE REVOLUTION that had taken place in the genus Rosa was due
to the introduction in 1789 of the China Rose, *Rosa chinensis*.
The White, Damask, Provence, Moss, and Gallica Roses, to
which these pages are mainly devoted, were with few exceptions
capable of flowering at midsummer only. The exceptions were
the Autumn Damask Roses. Throughout the centuries a few
forms had been evolved of these hybrids (supposedly between
Rosa moschata and R. gallica), and as far as I am aware no satisfactory solution has been offered whereby their autumnal flowering habit arose until my rediscovery of the original R. *moschata*,
flowering from August onwards. This is set forth at length in my
Climbing Roses Old and New (1978). Today the production of an
odd bloom or two in the autumn would not be counted of much
importance, but two hundred years ago this character was
greatly appreciated. Although these old 'Quatre Saisons' Roses
are not of great value now, it was with considerable interest
that I observed a white unnamed Moss Rose producing a pink
sport without Moss in 1949. Until then I had not realized that
this Moss Rose was a Damask, but have since found references
to it in old books, as 'White Perpetual Moss'. It had sported
back to the Autumn Damask from which it originated, and it
doubled my interest to hear from Miss Murrell at Shrewsbury of
a similar occurrence at about the same time, and also to find that
the resultant pink Damask was identical with one at Chetwode
Manor, and with one received from California. (Pls. IV, 19.)

The China Rose is almost alone among roses (*Rosa rugosa* is
another notable exception) in being able to produce flowers from
May to October in this climate. In warmer countries it has no

resting season at all. The Chinese have records as far back as
A.D. 900 of double China Roses on their pottery, and it is a preg-
nant thought that this rose, preserved and evolved by their
ancient civilization, should have been transported to our younger
Western civilization at a time when it would most make its influence felt. It was small wonder that this rose was used for
hybridizing by devoted rosarians in this country and on the
continent of Europe. Whether those early raisers realized what was
about to happen has not, I believe, been recorded; but the fact
remains that the frail China Rose, with its smooth twigs and few
translucent thorns, its smooth, delicate, pointed leaves, and loose
silky blooms with little shape or variation in colour, was fused
gradually with our coarser roses, resulting first in the Bourbons,
Noisettes, and Boursaults, and later giving rise to the Hybrid
Perpetuals.

All of these newer races were selected for their capability to
give flowers from June to October, some plentifully, others only
sparsely. Many gained their 'remontant' habit at the expense of
hardiness and scent. And so we can visualize two races of roses:
the one, composed of the old summer flowering kinds, being
raised in decreasing numbers and lingering mostly in cultivation
in the gardens of the poorer classes, while the new remontant
roses were being produced increasingly by nurserymen, and being
taken up by wealthy garden owners. It was indeed a revolution,
not surpassed in rose history for a hundred years, when our
modern roses began to develop flame and yellow tints due to the
influence of *Rosa foetida*. Mr N. P. Harvey very aptly refers to this
matter in his book *The Rose in Britain*. This is an excellent and
enlightened modern treatise shewing the development and future
trends of the rose; in it he says, 'to introduce a single new quality
into Hybrid Teas generally, without losing those virtues it is
desired to retain, may take as long as a generation'.

That something of this kind did happen to the rose with the
infusion of the China Rose's characters is obvious from the books
that appeared from about 1830 onwards. Increasing numbers of
Hybrid Provence Roses, Hybrid Damasks, and the like appeared,
along with numerous Bourbons and the early Hybrid Perpetuals.
In fact the bulk of the names in Singer's and in Simon's books are
of these classes. In 1872 Paul published his third edition—it lacks

the coloured plates of the first—enumerating no less than 538 Hybrid Perpetuals and 142 Tea Roses, not to speak of long lists of Bourbons and similar classes. His Moss Roses have shrunk to 53; the Gallicas to 18; he lists 10 Alba varieties; 10 Damask, and 7 Provence. The corresponding collections in his first edition in 1848 I have given on page 30; this first edition also contained the 106 Hybrid Perpetuals and 145 Teas. Other and smaller groups remained more static, since they were composed of roses of original and distinct types. It is only in the artificially created and all too numerous productions of man that fashions change in any genus, apart, of course, from fundamental changes in the flow of horticulture.

A contemporary picture is provided by *Les Roses* by Hippolyte Jamain and Eugène Forney, published in 1873. This is a fine, well-illustrated work figuring almost exclusively Hybrid Perpetuals and roses of related classes. It is quite evident which way fashion was developing.

The evolution of the various hybrid races of roses and their popularity can be compared in a rather interesting way with the evolution of plants on this planet.

Thus we have whole races developing and becoming paramount for a period, such as the Giant Club-mosses and Tree Ferns of the Coal Age, only to give place to some other groups later, such as dicotyledons (including roses). In a similar vein one might compare the temporary popularity of certain small groups of roses with the occasional rise of the Moss Roses. In the Coal Age example the plants gave way to others which were better suited to conditions ultimately prevailing; the Moss Roses have remained static because they represent a finite perfection in their own class. The Hybrid Perpetuals were an achievement on the way to a perpetual, fragrant, hardy, and attractive rose, and lost their popularity when something better began to appear, just as they had usurped the pre-eminent position of the Gallicas because these flowered only at midsummer. On the other hand, still recalling our fanciful simile, the Scotch and Austrian Briars remained static because they bred only among themselves, each group forming a little entity of related forms, and did not take part in the general move towards the Hybrid Teas. And unless my critics take me to task I must repeat here that the Austrian

Briar, having been mated with the popular rose of the period, eventually has changed the colour of the Hybrid Teas beyond recognition.

This is the third revolution we may record in the artificial evolution of our favourite flower—first, the French Revolution, which indirectly produced Josephine's great collection at Malmaison; secondly, the advent of the China Rose into the breeder's capable hands; and thirdly the similar advent, but much more gradual and limited, of the Austrian Briar. Its first results were the Pernetiana Roses, which have since been merged into the many-hued modern roses. Just where and when the next revolution may occur remains to be seen, but I suspect and predict it is going to be some great perpetual flowering shrub rose which will produce numerous progeny. Up to the present such a rose does not seem to have been raised, for 'Nevada' remains obdurate to the hybridizer.

To return, we may take up another English nurseryman's book, John Cranston's *Cultural Directions for the Rose*, whose fifth edition was published in 1875; a book full of sound practical help and good points about cultivation, in which he describes many pages of Hybrid Perpetuals and numerous other groups. He says, 'The fearful havoc which was made amongst roses, especially the tender ones, during the severe winter of 1860 and 1861, will, I trust, be the means of bringing about a more hardy race. . . . This delicacy has doubtless been produced by crossing the hardier Perpetuals too freely with the Tea-scented and other tender sorts.'

The stigma of tenderness could never be applied to the old groups, but in our modern roses can almost always be traced to Tea and sometimes to China parentage.

So far the chronicles of the rose have largely fallen to nurserymen; now begins what I like to term the clergyman's period. Dean Hole, and the Rev. Shirley Hibberd and the Rev. Foster-Melliar, wrote books between 1870 and 1894; they are all charming in their way, but shew the trend of artificiality in gardening and particularly in the use of the rose, and reflect very forcibly the ubiquity of the popular groups. By 1900 things had reached a more enlightened peak, and from this date onwards the Hybrid Teas have marched forwards, themselves now being by far the

most numerous and popular group, thanks to the addition of the
Pernetianas.

That is, however, not the end of the story. Having allowed old
roses with iron constitutions to fall into obscurity, it has been
natural that in time their very longevity and sweet scent should
bring them once more into favour as *shrubs*—not as 'roses' in the
modern sense—while just those very roses which proved their
undoing, have, in their turn, been neglected, and indeed have
mostly vanished. The hordes of Hybrid Perpetuals have gone,
except for a handful of tried favourites like 'Mrs John Laing' and
'Ulrich Brunner', 'Frau Karl Druschki', and the Dicksons; the
unique 'Reine des Violettes'; 'Souvenir d'Alphonse Lavallée';
'Souvenir du Docteur Jamain', and a few more.

It was at this time that Gertrude Jekyll, ever to the fore in
sensible use of garden material, produced a book, *Roses for English
Gardens*, in collaboration with Edward Mawley; it is profusely
illustrated, mostly with photographs. 'The time having come
when there is a distinct need for a book that *shall not only show how
Roses may best be grown, but how they may be most beautifully used*, and
that will also help the amateur to acquire some idea of their
nature and relationships, the present volume, with its large amount
of illustration, is offered in the hope that it will fit usefully into a
space as yet unfilled in garden literature.' The date was 1902, and
the italics are mine. Such a book was certainly needed to call the
rose enthusiasts from their greenhouses and pots, their show
benches and artificialities, and to shew them how the queen of
flowers could grace the garden, giving colour and fragrance and
charm, in her less sophisticated forms.

Two beautifully illustrated rose books appeared in 1908 and
1913; they were Rose Kingsley's *Roses and Rose Growing* and H. H.
Thomas's *The Rose Book*. Both show a wider insight into the
rose than their immediate predecessors. The former stresses the
extreme beauty of old and new types, with portraits excellently
reproduced in colour; the writer is well informed, although she
confuses Rosa Mundi and York and Lancaster, but intrigues me
with her mention of the Single Crimson Damask raised in 1901.
This is a rose I should much like to acquire; Damasks are always
the most elusive of roses. Mr Thomas's book shews mostly
Hybrid Teas in colour, but devotes much subject-matter to old

and species roses. Meanwhile another important work had appeared.

From 1910 to 1914 Ellen Willmott was producing *The Genus Rosa*, having secured the services of no less an artist than Alfred Parsons. This work, just falling short of the word 'great' in view of its mistakes, inconsistencies, and limitations, is packed mostly with information gathered from many earlier works, and is superbly illustrated in colour. The plates are exquisitely drawn and shew the grace of the living plant, from an artist's point of view rather than a botanist's. Many of the portraits are of species, but several are devoted to the old roses. *Rosa centifolia* and its variety *albo muscosa*, are, I consider, depicted wrongly, and I have referred to this in my notes under these plants. The book shews the very real awakening of a great gardener to the manifold beauties of the rose, and is a landmark in horticultural history. Ellen Willmott very clearly envisaged the possible turn of the tide towards garden beauty, already suggested by Gertrude Jekyll, and this feeling was undoubtedly influenced by the increasing popularity of two lovely species, *Rosa hugonis* and *moyesii*, both introduced from China early in the century. These two roses have played a similar part in popularizing rose species to that played by *Lilium regale* among Lilies, and *Meconopsis betonicifolia* among the Blue Poppies. In any select list of rose species these two are sure to be found. They epitomize the beauty and charm of the species roses, and give us colours far removed from the predominating pink.

There is no doubt that these two renowned women, Gertrude Jekyll and Ellen Willmott, each the creator of a beautiful garden, left their mark on the genus, although this mark was more in the way of a pointer to the general trend of horticulture than might at first sight be apparent. From 1914 onwards we have seen book after book appear, but they are nearly all concerned with the popular varieties of the day, the Hybrid Teas and Polyanthas, and they are mostly written by enthusiastic garden owners. Two other publications appeared which were, however, of much wider interest. I have an old catalogue, dated 1912, by Tom Smith of Newry, one of the fine nurserymen of that time, containing a really amazing collection of roses of all kinds, but it is quite obvious that his first loves were the lusty shrub roses, the Rugosas, and the old groups, and he did his best to interest gardeners to try them. And then E. A. Bunyard turned his rare ability to the old roses, and the result, charming, readable, and erudite, *Old Garden Roses*, appeared in 1936. As far as I know this was the first book for over a hundred years which owed its inception to a deep-seated love for all the old roses. His life was prematurely ended, otherwise he would undoubtedly have corrected the several inaccuracies which are to be found in his book, but he gave new zest to the cause of old roses, and collected many varieties together. We of this generation owe much to his guidance. In days since the war the only publications on similar lines have been my own little booklets *Roses as Flowering Shrubs*, followed by *The Manual of Shrub Roses*; the latter has run to three editions. For the rose is at last, I believe, regaining its proper place, and when all its points are considered, it must certainly take a very high standing in our affection as a first-rate flowering shrub.

It is to my regret that a feeling of comparison between the old and the modern roses has crept in repeatedly to these pages. It may be inferred that I have no use for the modern roses, but nothing could be farther from the truth. To my mind the two types are not suitable for comparison. Modern roses are flowers *par excellence* for beds, providing colour throughout summer and autumn; they are also beautiful in the extreme when grown into large bushes and only lightly pruned. Their colours and scents are attractive, their shape and their poise appeal to all, and many good varieties of considerable stamina are on the market. It does, however, remain true that only in their less pruned state can they be called flowering shrubs in our present accepted sense of the word; more truly would they be described as small shrubby plants producing very finished florist's flowers. The Polyantha and Floribunda roses appeal in a different way, but have similar garden qualities.

It is encouraging to find that rose breeders of today are once again finding pleasure in full-petalled roses of the old form, and are also producing varieties of purplish and pastel shades. No new 'blue' rose, however, so far has surpassed 'Reine des Violettes', raised in 1860. Never were comparisons more odious than between the old and the new in roses. There is room for both in our gardens, and the next chapter will present a considered case for the old groups.

Chapter IV

. . . .

Appreciation

La Tulipe est une fleur sans âme; mais
il semble que la rose et le lis en ait une.

Joubert

IT IS ONE thing to make botanical descriptions for plants and quite
another matter to convey to a gardener an image of a given plant.
Let us be quite sure, therefore, that the right image is given for
the contents of this chapter. For the dust jacket of his *The Art of
Botanical Illustration* Wilfrid Blunt has selected a painting by
Johann Walther of Strasbourg, executed among many others for
Count Johann of Nassau. It depicts the Austrian Briar, a striped
Gallica, and some soft, purplish-pink Provence Roses. One shews
a full, open flower with its serried ranks of imbricated petals,
another the globular form of the half-open flower, and some buds
shew various stages of development. It is an excellent presentation
of our subject, and is available for all to see in shops and libraries
catering for such books. Other fine examples are to be found in
the little King Penguin *A Book of Roses*; this gem, in a series
sparkling with similar riches and published at a price within reach
of all, contains sixteen colour plates from the originals in Redouté's 'Roses', and particularly would I refer to plates VI, X, XI,
and XV. These beautifully portrayed flowers give the student at
once the essence of the floral qualities of the old roses.

Considering them as a whole, I would say that the roses that
are termed 'White' (*Rosa alba*), 'Provence' (*Rosa centifolia*),
'Moss' (*Rosa centifolia muscosa*), 'Gallica' (*Rosa gallica*), and
'Damask' (*Rosa damascena*) are forceful stalwart shrubs usually
from 4 to 6 feet in height, and from 4 to 6 feet in width in maturity.
A few are of lax or untidy habit, or of open growth, but there is a
decided shrubby similarity to be found among them. As a general
rule they are prickly, the White Roses bearing a few firm, large
prickles, while the Gallicas are at the other end of the scale, with

39

the prickles absent or changed to hairy thorns which rub off at a touch. Their leaves are of varying greens, thin and rough to the fingers, and a few bear small thorns on their leaf stalks. The majority have glandular hairs on the stalk below the flowers and on the incipient hep, and it is these glandular hairs, often present also on the leaves, that provide one of their great attractions: a warm fragrance that stays on the hands for long after picking a bunch of flowers. This is one of the characters I should most like to see bred into our modern roses again. The Bourbon Roses, included in these pages because they are in many ways only just removed from the old roses, are dealt with fully in Chapter XVII.

The old roses contain all those colours found in their parent species—white through pale to dark pink and light crimson—together with a tendency to purple tones. Many of the most sumptuous of the purple-tinted varieties prove to be the most popular among the devotees of these plants. We have become so used to thinking of roses in terms of brilliant carmine, scarlet, salmon, pink, flame, orange, and yellow that we are apt to forget that these colours can be traced to the influence of three species only, while all the softer tones are natural to a far greater number of species. The exquisite colourings found in 'Charles de Mills', 'Cardinal de Richelieu', 'Belle de Crécy', and 'Tour de Malakoff' —violets, purples, mauves, magenta, and maroon, enlivened by pale and cerise pink and blush white—represent a searching of the florists after novelty. The whites and pinks had held the field for hundreds of years, but when seed raising and other propagation came into vogue, these newer darker tones provided the perfect foil for the lighter colours while remaining all within a delightful sympathetic range. For any of these roses blends well with the next, and all the colours are soft; some are muted, while others are radiant with life without being hard. Carnations and lilacs give us similar tones. And yet one so often reads or hears the words 'a hard blue-pink'; disparagement is generally conveyed and inferred, but it seems incongruous to me that a blue-pink can be hard—at least not among the roses. Their colours are certainly 'hard' to use with our modern flaring flowers, but those in search of examples of floral colour grouping should make a pilgrimage to Kiftsgate Court and observe how Mrs Muir has introduced the modern tones of 'Albertine' and even 'Orange

Triumph', to add telling point to her glorious borders devoted
to pink and lavender and mauve, with the all-embracing softness
of grey foliage. Colour is, of course, only relative, and in the beholder's eye.
But in studying a group such as this, or a bunch of plucked
blooms, the harmonious softness of the colours, varying each
with the day and the hour, is very apparent. The richly coloured
varieties may display pink and magenta in cool weather, but the
hot sun develops their violets and purples and gives them an
incredible richness, enhanced by their velvety texture.

And their fragrance? Their fragrance is intense, intoxicating,
and delicious. The scent of a sun-warmed Provence Rose, or a
dew-cooled 'Maiden's Blush', is not surpassed for sweetness,
although it may be equalled in its intensity, by flowers of other
genera. The fragrance of typical varieties of each old group is
distinct—one could not confuse the examples cited above even
when blindfolded—but my senses have not yet found the means
of conveying to my pen their qualities. And yet this subtle distinction found in the groups has a relationship that has later been
fused by hybridization and is now misguidedly called 'Damask'.
Poets and horticulturists alike have used 'Damask' to denote
richness in scent (as well as in texture), whereas a glance at the
parentage of our modern roses will immediately prove that the
Damask fragrance cannot really be detected, for example, in
'Crimson Glory' or 'Red Ensign' at the expense of the Gallica
or Provence scents. This glorious fragrance of the old roses
comes in great part from *Rosa gallica*, but is enhanced by the infusion of the other species, notably by the heady perfume of the
Musk Rose. The Musk (*Rosa moschata*) and its relatives and
progeny, together with *Rosa rugosa*, are the species which in my
experience float their fragrance on the air with the greatest
abandon, sometimes for more than a hundred yards.

The old roses in their double forms are as a rule very well filled
with petals, and their various modes of opening have resulted in
certain terms being used in their descriptions. Like most other
groups of garden hybrids and forms such terms can only be
applied to a few very distinct varieties.

During the unfolding of the petals many roses may pass from
'cupped' to 'globular'; they may then open with all the petals on

one plane, when they are 'compact'. A fully open flower may reveal petals 'imbricated' (piled one above the other), and then they are usually divided into 'quarters'. Often a number of the central petals are tucked so tightly into the receptacle that they cannot open, and thus form what I term a 'button eye'. Again, these button eyes may shew a small green point in their centres, which is composed of abortive carpels. One rather concludes from remarks in old books that these green points were not approved; in coloured roses they may be disfiguring, but I always feel that in white roses such as 'Madame Hardy' and 'Madame Plantier' they give a delightful finish. Eventually many roses reflex, often almost into a ball, and in doing this their petals may have their edges rolled backwards.

Some sketches shewing these various styles are given in Mrs Frederick Keays's *Old Roses* (New York, 1935). Her book reveals a generous wish that her readers may share in her delight in re-discovering some of the old roses still found in Maryland and elsewhere in America. These old styles are also carefully described and figured on page 29 in *Les Plus Belles Roses au début du Vingtième siècle*, published by the Société Nationale d'Horticulture de France (see opposite).

To review our findings, I think we can justly claim that in the old roses we find stalwart, thrifty shrubs, able to fend for themselves, bearing fairly good foliage; their flowers are borne in the utmost profusion at midsummer in colours from white through pink to violet, fragrant to an unbelievable degree, and shewing a perfection of form evolved by skilled florists of the past; they thrive on a variety of soils and need little pruning.

Their faults, from a garden point of view, are that their flowers are mostly over by 15th July except for the Bourbon and other races shewing some affinity to the China Roses; that some of them retain their dead petals long after they should have fallen; that some of them suffer from 'black spot' in certain districts, and that their foliage in dry districts assumes a dusty appearance by August.

The first point we can readily forgive, considering the prodigality with which they produce their flowers at midsummer; the second is greatly obviated by pruning at the right time, namely, immediately after flowering; the third, black spot, scarcely impairs their strength or flowering capabilities, and is a common symptom of unhealthy conditions in all roses, and careful attention to the plants' needs in the way of mulching and cultivation will help to rid the plants of this disfigurement; the poor late summer foliage, our last point, is unavoidable, but interplanting with suitable plants for later display will obviously help.

The shapes of Old Roses in the early years of the twentieth century. Reproduced from *Les Plus Belles Roses*.

Above left: A double flower with quartered arrangement of petals. *Above right:* Semi-double cupped. *Below left:* Double flower with reflexed petals, but in this drawing they are shewn twisted as well. *Below right:* Semi-double or double globular.

Chapter V

. . . .

Old Roses in the Garden

Roses, the garden's pride,
Are flowers for love and flowers for Kings,
In courts desiréd and Weddings.

Thomas Campion

FROM EARLY SPRING onwards we watch our favourites appear; how keen we are to see the snowdrops, and to grow six or more varieties to prolong their flowering season; then the daffodils—what flower more expressly trumpets the coming of spring?—the tulips, giving off redoubled energy when the sun's rays rebound from their richly hued cups; and later the glistening crystalline irises; each new flower of the year more abundantly endowed than the last in colour and form. We pass, too, from the sudden awakening of forsythia to the sweet fragrance of *Viburnum carlesii*, and before we are fully aware of it the great family of rhododendrons is upon us, imparting grandeur to the scene. The flowering cherries and crab-apples give way to may and laburnum, and the whole horticultural world is ablaze with colour and fragrance. I await these arrivals every year with intense delight, but the coming of the rose is to me the very crown of the year. From the first delicate-flowered pale yellow species and Scots Roses that open, in company with the Cherokee and Banksian Roses, on warm walls, to the last poignant autumn blooms, the rose gives unequalled beauty. There is a rose for every taste. Whether we are newly awakened to flowers and delight in the dazzling display of Floribundas, or the more exquisite blooms of the classy Hybrid Teas; or whether our senses have developed still further and embrace the perfect roses of a more refined and elegant age; or whether we go back to the exquisite grace and charm of the original species, there is, I repeat, a rose for every taste.

Roses have so much 'fullness' about them; they are full of

44

vigour if the most suitable kinds are planted and reasonably treated; they are full of contrast, their rounded flowers, sprinkled over the network of leaves, create a delightful effect; they are often full of petals, of a good texture of rich velvet or of shining silk; and they are full of scent. They are rich throughout in qualities which have been favourites with gardeners of all ages. Listen to M. Cochet-Cochet: 'Le Rosier est de beaucoup le plus important de tous les arbustes cultivés pour l'ornement des jardins.'

This paean of praise from a worthy French nurseryman may perhaps require a little qualification. Roses are certainly the favourite flowering shrubby plants of today, but with few exceptions they cannot form the framework of a garden. Evergreens are needed for such positions. Roses are more suitable for foreground colour-work, the filling-in of bays between heavier material, the covering of stumps, hedgerows, and banks with their long trails, and for growing near to the eye and nose, that their beauties may easily reach the senses. Apart from their loss of leaves in winter the Rugosa Roses and the new hybrid 'Nevada' are flowering shrubs of the heaviest calibre, and can be used in important positions governing the design of beds and borders. Most species are more airy, with a dainty refinement that I feel prompts one to place them well away from buildings. The modern and the old florist's roses are more suitable for use in conjunction with formality, whether it be of wall, path, or hedge. When the wall can be of grey Cotswold stone, or the hedge of a blend of holly and box and copper beech, the contrast is superb. A visit to Hidcote will convince intending hedge-planters of the tapestry background that can be obtained from mixed hedges. For informal hedges the roses themselves present several varieties and species of great value.

It cannot be denied that a garden full of one thing can be boring to all but the ardent collector himself. While we are all entitled to do as we like with our gardens I would suggest a careful disposal of the old roses, so that the eye may not tire of their qualities in perspective. The old roses create a delightful pattern of flower and foliage at six yards' distance, but at a greater distance give a rather spotty effect. (Pl. 1.) This is due to their small leaves and the regular dotting of flowers along the branches.

I feel they very much need the foil of other foliage and the contrast of other flower shapes and styles. Particularly successful with these old roses are foxgloves—just the common wild type and the white, with a few of 'Sutton's Primrose' placed near the dark purple forms. Their spikes give the right contrast in form, and their colours blend happily. Also I like to use *Lilium candidum* and some of the daintier delphiniums in light colours, and the tall irises of the ochroleuca section. The striking contrast of leaf and flower in these gives just the relief and 'uplift' that is needed. Foliage of *Iris pallida* and *Sisyrinchium striatum*; *Eryngium giganteum*, the silvery grey biennial 'Sea Holly'; sages, the ordinary culinary and the purple leaved form; Hosta or plantain lily of which the best is *Hosta sieboldiana*; *Stachys olympica*, and *Santolina neapolitana* and *chamaecyparissus*—all are splendid subjects for underplanting and mixing with the old roses. The blatant yellow blooms of the Santolina or 'Cotton Lavender' need never interfere with the colour scheme if the plants are clipped over in February. For bold corner-work, especially against paved paths, the Megasea Saxifrages (*Bergenia*) provide the very best of materials, their big broad leathery leaves of dark green matching the stones' solidity.

These foliage plants can blend an otherwise jumbled mass of flowers and leaves into an harmonious and satisfying whole. The use of white flowers with the roses cannot be too strongly emphasized. For this purpose I have already mentioned foxgloves and *Iris ochroleuca*, and to them will add Philadelphus or Mock Orange. A great range of these is available from small shrubs of 2–3 feet to giants up to 15 feet, and the blend of their fragrance with that of the roses can be almost overwhelming on a still summer evening. A quantity of pinks—a seed-raised garden strain is the best, embracing all the tones that are found in the 'Highland Hybrids'—'White Ladies' and others will provide the most ideal display at just the right time, and their fragrance again enters into the scheme. White flowers will intensify the purples and enrich the pink roses; pale lilac, as may be obtained from *Campanula lactiflora*, will purify pink roses. Various contrasts, such as the clouds of greenish yellow stars and velvet leaves of *Alchemilla mollis* with 'Tuscany', will be found, and over them all a solid garden quality should reign. Flimsy annuals and ordinary daisy-flowers, so often the body of the average herbaceous border, may well be avoided.

It will be apparent from the above that I like my old roses mixed with other plants, rather than arrayed in beds by themselves. They can be very pleasingly grown in this way, but the general blend of flower and foliage which is apparent in a mixed border is to my mind more satisfying and appealing. In addition to creating a glorious picture at midsummer, many of the foliage plants will produce flowers earlier or later; a suitable grouping of spring bulbs, followed in late summer by Galtonias (summer hyacinths), the hardy *Agapanthus campanulatus* (*mooreanus*) and hybrids, and the free flowering dwarf *Yucca flaccida* and *Y. filamentosa* will provide interest through the year. Over my more stalwart roses I have just planted some of the small hardy *Clematis viticella* varieties. These can be cut to the ground every February and will provide a canopy of glorious maroons, mauves, and whites to blend with fuchsias and agapanthus in late July and August. With the old roses, therefore, may I suggest a generous blend of flowers and foliage, to create a 'cottage garden' mixture, to give colour and interest from April to October.

Rose Kingsley, in *Roses and Rose-growing* (1908), sums up the matter very well: '. . . to my mind, the Cabbage, Moss, Gallica, and Damask Roses look most thoroughly in place in the old-fashioned mixed border along the walk in the kitchen garden, where they flower after wallflowers, daffodils, and polyanthus, with lilies and pinks, stocks and carnations, and all the delightful and fragrant odds and ends that, somehow, make it the spot in the whole garden to which all footsteps turn instinctively.'

Chapter VI

· ·

Cultivation

Unkempt about those hedges blows
An English unofficial rose.

Rupert Brooke

THE OLD ROSES are tolerant of neglect. Their very survival in face
of the thousands of varieties that have been raised since 1850
proves this. It is their immediate successors, the Hybrid Perpetuals, that have virtually disappeared. The old roses are, with
few exceptions, long lived, especially when grown on their own
roots. Although most roses produced in nurseries are budded on
to a different rootstock (generally our native English Briar Rose,
or Laxa Rose), when planted with the union 3 inches beneath the
soil, the Gallica Roses in particular speedily throw out under-
ground shoots of their own and develop into a thicket in just the
same way as they would if grown from cuttings. The Damasks,
Albas, and Centifolias are not so ready to do this, but suckers
from a properly budded rootstock seldom appear if it is not exposed to the air, nor when a good canopy of foliage is over the
ground. Many of the Provence Roses are by no means easy to
strike from cuttings, in fact, to put this in practice commercially
would be difficult. The resort to budding is therefore necessary,
and in many instances desirable.

There has been much written about growing roses on their own
roots, and I would not deter anyone from doing so. It must be
remembered, however, that *Rosa canina* is a very tough rose, far
more tough even than the old roses themselves. The roots of
Canina will stand being maimed and dried better than those of
most shrubs; they are deep-questing and vigorous, and will thrive
on a variety of soils. I have already described old roses growing
successfully on shale and chalk (see pages 21–2), and often the use
of Briar stock has helped.

There is another point to be considered. The growing of

Gallica and Rugosa Roses on their own roots—whether originally reproduced from cuttings or budding—is not altogether desirable in a small garden. Gallicas can and will run about with amazing prolificacy and a thicket of stems two yards through may be the result of four years of growth. This is the ideal where there is plenty of room, and for covering the ground, but something of a nuisance when a clump of bulbs or other plant is invaded in a mixed border.

When suckers from the rootstock do have to be removed it is best to uncover the root to see where they arise, and to pull the suckers off. This generally ensures a freedom from recurrence, and I find an ordinary claw-headed hammer an excellent tool for the job. The sucker, a foot or two high, can be grasped near the base and pulled; the more it is pulled the tighter it becomes clasped in the claw; the hand is well away from thorns, and with a tug the sucker comes out. It is no use cutting suckers off at ground level; this only acts like pruning, and two or three will spring from the one that was cut.

There have been many books published dealing with the preparation of the ground for roses, and their actual planting. I will simply say here, therefore, that deep digging is the finest preparation that can be given, providing undesirable subsoil is not brought to the surface, and that firming of the soil, after planting at the right depth, is the next essential. The most unsatisfactory results are generally obtained when a hole of about 1 foot square is made in an old and settled border or in grass. This kind of preparation is not accepted by the rose, nor by any tree or shrub. The ground where the roses are to go should be prepared and dug throughout, if possible, but where isolated plants are to be put in the ground should be dug to a depth of 18 inches, over an area 3 feet in diameter. The less cultivated the soil may be the greater the area that should be prepared. This is a counsel of perfection; I may add once again that the old roses are thrifty and give good results even in neglect. Provided the ground is not in a squelchy condition, the full force of the heel is needed to firm the soil round the roots. The admixture of well-decayed manure or rotted garden compost is helpful in poor soils, although roses are best left to fend for themselves in rich soils; the most important fertility rule to remember is to maintain a good humus content in the soil by

mulching. This helps to destroy summer weeds and thus to
minimize labour. Lawn mowings can be spread over the ground
as soon as cut, to the depth of 1–2 inches, and can be repeated
again later in the season. Much weeding is thereby eliminated; the
fertility of the soil is increased, and the soil will not bake and
crack so badly as when exposed to the sun. Roses are not particular in regard to soil, and all, apart from the few weak-growing
varieties, may be expected to thrive anywhere. Although they will
indeed grow on poor soils, and much beauty and enjoyment can
thereby be obtained from them, it is only fair to add that they are
incomparably more prolific, richer in colour, and more sumptuously bedight in a good, well-dug medium loam, for they are
worthy of the best we can give them. The Gallicas will not run so
fast in heavier soils, and in my opinion many of the old and other
shrub roses prefer a lighter soil, so long as it is deep and well
mulched.

Writing as I do of my experience with these roses in Surrey, I
must mention that they do not seem to approve of our climate in
south-east England. I used to look at Redouté's drawings with
amazement, wondering why he so exaggerated the length of stem,
the luxuriance of the leaves, and the size of the flowers. A visit to
Hidcote Bartrim Manor, in Gloucestershire, speedily proved that
the cooler climate and retentive soil in the Cotswolds produce far
better flowers than we can obtain in sunny Surrey. Sample blooms
which reach me for naming from the west and north are nearly
always of better quality than my own, and are, of course, some
weeks later. All this is rather surprising in a flower cradled in the
Mediterranean region, a flower commemorating 'Rhodes the isle
whose very name means rose', but it once again goes to prove
that coolness at the root will give rise to good growth, and a cool
atmosphere ensures the gentle development of the flower. Here
in the Woking area the temperature varies greatly from night to
day, extremes being frequent, and a scorching heat not unusual.
In very hot districts, therefore, I suggest a cool exposure for the
old roses, so that their blooms may develop slowly and their
beauties last as long as possible. They will not thrive under trees
although they will grow in such positions; they are essentially
children of the sun and revel in full exposure. Shade from a wall
is a different matter, and some of the best specimens of my

acquaintance grow where their roots are shaded and their flowers are in full sun.

The distance apart at which to plant will be a point often asked, and exact rules cannot be given; so much depends on the vigour of the plant, the type of soil, and the plant association which is intended. Except where plants are described as being of erect growth, or of wide lax habit, it may generally be understood that their width is two-thirds of their height. The Gallica Roses are mostly compact, and can be planted at 3 feet apart; the Centifolias and Mosses are of comparatively open growth, and although they are rather taller than the Gallicas, they need also to be planted 3–4 feet apart so that their arching branches may interlace. The Damasks are mixed in habit, and 3–4 feet will again serve, but most of the Alba Roses are stronger growing and may be given a space 4 feet in width, or rather more for 'Great Maiden's Blush', *maxima*, and *semi-plena*. Similar distances may be given to the Bourbons, according to their height.

When setting out a rose hedge very much will again depend on the variety chosen. Compact growing varieties are best and these are mostly found in the Gallicas; such as *Rosa gallica officinalis*, *versicolor*, 'Tuscany', 'Président de Sèze', 'Assemblage des Beautés', *conditorum*, spring at once to mind. At Kiftsgate the *versicolor* hedges ('Rosa Mundi') (Pl. 7) are trimmed every March with a pair of shears, and they respond in a wonderful way to this treatment. Larger hedges might well be composed of White Roses: 'Maiden's Blush' and 'Celestial', mixed with *maxima* would give a most delightful effect. Where something less wide than 3 feet is desired, some of the more lax varieties can be trained along wires, and 'Belle de Crécy', 'Gloire de Guilan', and 'Duchesse de Montebello' would adapt themselves admirably to such treatment, up to 4 feet in height. Varieties for similar treatment on wires up to 4 or 5 feet would be 'Ispahan', 'Comtesse de Murinais', and 'Capitaine John Ingram', 'Tour de Malakoff' would grow up to 7 feet on good soils, and this, together with 'Jeanne de Montfort' and 'William Lobb', would make a splendid screen on wires up to this height, taking up no more than 2 feet width even at flowering time. These strong-growing roses could be planted at 4–5 feet apart for this purpose.

These few suggestions indicate in a very small way how these roses can be used for the embellishment of the garden. A rose hedge is one of the most satisfying features of any garden, and a great wealth of fragrant bloom will result. In important positions Hybrid Musk Roses and Bourbons should be used to give colour for as long as possible.

Chapter VII

. . . .

Pruning

Every thing doth pass away;
There is danger in delay
Come, come, gather thou the rose
Gather it, or it ye lose.

Giles Fletcher

PRUNING IS A subject which has exercised rose-growers' minds very greatly for many years. A long chapter is given to it by William Paul in his first edition of *The Rose Garden* in 1848. Once again the old roses should be considered as 'flowering shrubs' rather than as roses in our modern conception. They do not need pruning during the first spring after planting, and many growers do not prune them afterwards, apart from removing old spent wood. The habit of the plants is to produce strong long shoots from near the base of the plant when established, which grow up in late summer. It is these shoots which form the foundation of the bush; and in the spring they send forth side-shoots up to 1 foot in length, which bear the best flowers. The following season these side-shoots break again, each bearing shorter flowering shoots, and this is repeated with waning strength every season until the branch dies. After three or four years have passed it is best to remove one or two of the older branches from the base, encouraging fresh growth to carry on the life of the plant, and this is all the pruning that need be given. Sometimes a strong young shoot will spring from half way up one of these old branches, and the old top twigs should be then removed to this point only. As these roses flower best on growth of the previous summer, this work should be carried out *immediately after flowering*. The Alba Roses need less pruning than the other groups, and old branches make a beautiful head of twigs which go on flowering well for many years. These pruning rules will produce what I would call well-furnished informal flowering shrubs.

If on the other hand the roses are grown in formal beds, a little more pruning may be given. In addition to the occasional and methodical removal of whole or portions of branches, the flowering side-shoots should be shortened *in the winter*. By cutting these shoots back to about 2 or 3 inches, a more limited number of short flowering shoots will again be produced, with a consequent better quality of bloom. In gardens where several plants of one variety are grown, it is useful to prune a plant or two quite severely every year; the result will be a few blooms of superlative quality late in the following season, and a great rejuvenation of the bushes for subsequent years.

The only other suggestion I have to make is that the long new shoots from the base may be shortened by about one-third to keep them within the bounds of the bush, and to prevent damage at flowering time. In windy seasons these long shoots, if left to their original length, will whip about, and the flowers and leaves may become lacerated, beating against other prickly stems. This work may be done at any time during the winter or early spring.

The above pruning is sufficient to keep the old roses in good flowering trim provided the soil is maintained in a healthy condition. Pruning will not make a bush grow unless the soil has nutritive qualities, and on poor soils pruning must be gentle. On very rich soils pruning must again be sparingly done, or loss of bloom may result.

The Bourbon Roses, producing flowers as they do throughout the summer, need to be pruned almost entirely in the winter. After the first burst of bloom is over in July some of the smaller twiggy growth can be removed, but all other pruning can be safely left till the winter, using the same rules as for the old roses. In Surrey the end of February is the latest time for winter pruning; and it need hardly be emphasized here that a sharp knife or really good pair of secateurs are the best implements. Very large wood may require a small saw.

Further details of pruning, relating to specific groups, are given in the introductory remarks to Chapters XII to XVI.

Chapter VIII

· ·

Old Roses for the House

You may break, you may shatter the
vase if you will,
But the scent of the roses will hang
round it still.

Thomas cMoore

THE TRUE OLD roses have one great advantage over the Bourbons
and all subsequent races when it comes to cutting for the house,
for removal of whole branches bearing many buds and flowers
will not spoil the bush. Rather will it be a good method of
pruning, for there is no second crop of flowers to lose.

Roses are not the best of flowers for cutting if lasting qualities
be the criterion, but at rose-time I like to have roses indoors as
well as in the garden, to revel for the six or eight weeks in rich
colours and scents, to meet roses on the table at meal times, and
to let their beauty register deeply in the mind. Just two or three
blooms at a time in a small vase, picked when half or fully open,
are best for a gradual deepening of acquaintance with these
gracious flowers. The pale colours, the whites and pinks, can
safely be picked in exquisite bud and be allowed to open in water,
but to savour the full tones of the violet and maroon roses they
need to open fully in the air, and be brought in just at their most
spectacular best. Their rich colours do not develop properly in the
shade of the room.

I shall never forget my first introduction to these roses in a cut
state. It was during my visit to see Constance Spry's collection in
Kent. Before being allowed into the garden I was taken into the
house, and on an oval marble table a satin cloth of palest spring-
green was spread. In the centre was an almost overwhelming bowl
of the most exotic violet, lilac, purple, and maroon roses spilling
over the edges on to the cloth. An indescribably rich contrast was
given by the dusky tones of the velvety petals, and the shining

satin cloth. A few buds of Moss Roses appeared here and there, adding a delicate touch to the gorgeous qualities of 'Tour de Malakoff', 'Charles de Mills', 'Cardinal de Richelieu', and other famous varieties.

Constance Spry devoted whole chapters of her books to the decorative qualities of these roses, and some good colour reproductions of them appear in her *Summer and Autumn Flowers* (Dent, 1951).

Once again the uses of contrasting foliage need stressing, and alchemilla and hosta leaves can play a successful part with roses of purple tones. Many roses have most decorative leaves, and *Rosa rubrifolia*—greyish green suffused with plum purple—comes at once to mind. Some have very dainty foliage, while the Bourbon 'Mme Ernst Calvat' produces in late summer the most handsome plum-coloured young shoots. Nor must we forget the decorative qualities of the heps; a few of our old roses, such as *Rosa gallica officinalis*, the Damask 'Gloire de Guilan', and *Rosa alba semi plena*, are very ornamental, but the pride of place in this character is given without hesitation to *Rosa moyesii* and its relatives.

When cutting roses for indoor decoration, it is advisable to cut in the evening or early morning, and to hammer or slit up the bases of the stems, as with all hard-wooded subjects. They will then last for several days in water, filling the room with fragrance. 'The air of June is velvet with her scent, the realm of June is splendid with her state.' [1] How very true are these words.

[1] V. Sackville-West: *The Garden.*

Chapter IX

. . . .

The Work of Dr C. C. Hurst

Yet, though thou fade,
From thy dead leaves let fragrance rise.

Edmund Waller

MY EARLIER, historical chapters have proceeded in a curious way;
each one has perforce gone a little too far, with the result that the
next has had to start chronologically earlier, and this will be no
exception. I have mentioned how Dr Hurst had been conducting
his research into the botanical and cytological evolution of the
genus Rosa at Cambridge University Botanic Garden, from 1922
onwards, and in Chapter III I have recorded various writings on
roses during the period between the two wars. With the very
greatest respect and pleasure I now want to write my little appreciation of what Dr Hurst has done for us.

C. C. Hurst (1870–1947) had already been engaged for some
years in pioneer work on Heredity when Mendel's papers were
discovered in 1900, and from that time he took a leading part
with Bateson, of the John Innes Horticultural Institution, in the
foundation of the new science of Genetics. His experiments
covered many plants and animals, including Man, and in 1909
he founded the Burbage Experiment Station for Genetics in
Leicestershire.

Among many other things he was working on the production
of pedigree rose stocks, resulting in some highly satisfactory
types. He also enthusiastically collected old-fashioned roses and
rose species, together with the many books, old and new, which
have been written on this very favourite genus.

Unhappily the 1914–18 war intervened. Hurst, one of the
leaders in the Leicestershire Territorials, was in the forces for five
years, and on his return he found it impossible to resuscitate the
Experiment Station, which had lost its working staff and experimental horses to the war, the poultry, rabbits, etc., for food, and

most of the plants from neglect, while the grants of money for the various projects had ceased to exist.

One of the few things left was the hardier part of his rose collection, which he now took up again with renewed interest. Since most geneticists were now feeling that little more could be done without co-ordinating the study of hereditary characters with that of the genes and chromosomes, he went up to Trinity College, Cambridge, in 1922, to work on the cytology of *Rosa*.

This new approach elucidated many of the difficult points in this genus, especially with regard to classification. Hurst planned to write a monograph of *Rosa* from this new angle, and much material was collected, but the 1939–45 conflict interrupted its publication. His war work as a member of the Royal Observer Corps brought on a severe illness from which he never fully recovered, and he died in 1947 with his work on *Rosa* still unfinished.

Fortunately his voluminous and careful notes are in the capable hands of his widow, and Mrs Hurst, who shared the burden of much of her husband's work, has a skill and knowledge which, when time permits, will I hope enable her to co-ordinate these findings into a book rich in rose lore and scientific charts. She has been good enough not only to furnish me with the above notes on her husband's life, but also to let me make full use of her library of Rose books, and has added considerably to my own knowledge of roses from her deep fund of experience.

Dr Hurst did not, however, die without having some of his writings recorded, and, in collaboration with Mabel S. G. Breeze, produced his 'Notes on the Origin of the Moss Rose' in 1922. These were published in Part I of vol. xlvii of the *Journal of the Royal Horticultural Society*, and make absorbing reading. In 1941, in the March, July, and August numbers of the same journal, a more exhaustive and comprehensive survey of roses appeared, entitled 'Notes on the Origin and Evolution of our Garden Roses'. These have been of the most inestimable value to me in classifying my collection, and I would like to feel that they are widely read and appreciated by all who grow roses. His style, at once pithy, lucid, and attractive, leads one on from one considered aspect to another, every paragraph well thought out and packed with historical detail. Since the Journals are not readily available to everyone I approached Mrs Hurst for permission to have these invaluable notes republished, and to my delight she readily agreed. It is, to me, a very happy thought that the work of Dr Hurst's most able brain is thus to be given increased publicity, and his notes will do much to foster that wider interest in *Rosa* that is needed to appreciate the genus as a whole, from a horticultural point of view. Even in this century some new Moss Roses have been raised, and who knows but that some of the older types may be revived and given a further chance to share in the future races of garden roses? At least we may well feel glad that cytology arrived just in time for this great pioneer to unravel many of the mysteries woven in the old roses, before they became too confused or even extinct. His work was far in advance of all other rose genealogists, and it is surprising how few writers on the subject have availed themselves of the theories he put forward and the work which he carried out.

1965: My rediscovery of the ancient Musk Rose, flowering from August onwards, is recorded in *Climbing Roses Old and New*, and will shed further light on the ancestry of the Autumn Damask Rose.

NOTES ON THE ORIGIN
AND EVOLUTION OF OUR GARDEN ROSES

by C. C. HURST, SC.D., PH.D. (CANTAB.), F.L.S.

I. ANCIENT GARDEN ROSES

2000 B.C.–A.D. 1800

THE INTRODUCTION of the China Rose to England towards the end of the eighteenth century caused a complete revolution in the garden Roses of Europe, America, and the Near East. The effects of this introduction from the Far East first became evident in the Noisette and Bourbon hybrids which appeared in the early years of the nineteenth century, so that we may take A.D. 1800 as a natural line of division between ancient and modern garden Roses.

The ancient Roses, for the most part, flowered only once a year, in the early summer, while the modern Roses bloom continuously from early summer to late autumn. In a favourable climate like the Riviera they may flower all the year round, since they are potentially perpetual. Recent research shows that this habit of continuous flowering is due to the action of a Mendelian recessive gene introduced into our modern Roses by the China and Tea Roses, already cultivated in China for a thousand years or more. A similar mutation was observed by the writer in the Botanic Gardens at Cambridge a few years ago in a batch of wild seedlings of one of the Chinese Musk Roses, R. *Helenae* Rehd. and Wils., from seeds received by Mr Reginald Cory.

There was one ancient Rose which under favourable conditions of high culture and special pruning often produced a second crop of flowers in the autumn. This Rose was known in England as the Monthly Rose, in France as Quatre-Saisons, and in ancient Rome as *Rosa bifera*. It was, however, uncertain and sporadic in its second flowering, and was in no sense a continuous bloomer like the China Rose. In the days of summer-flowering Roses a few scattered blooms in the autumn were highly prized.

A. THE RED ROSE OF LANCASTER (*Rosa rubra* Blackw. 1757).[1]

The Red Rose is the foundation species from which most of our garden Roses have been evolved. The species, in its dwarf wild state, extends from France to Persia and has produced many natural hybrids with other species. The history of the garden Red Rose is lost in the night of time. According to Gravereaux it was the Rose of the Persian Magi, and the Median Fire Worshippers of the twelfth century B.C., who cultivated it for their religious ceremonies. According to their sacred writings of the ninth century B.C. (the Zend Avesta) this Rose was dedicated to an archangel. In the fourth and third centuries B.C. the Red Rose was apparently cultivated by the ancient Greeks and also at

---

[1] Syn. *Rosa gallica* L., 1759 (*non* 1753). R. *gallica* L., 1753, was a species of the Caninae, near to R. *canina tomentella* (Léman), and it was not until 1759 that Linnaeus described the R. *gallica* of authors. In the meantime Mrs Elizabeth Blackwell had described and figured the species under the name of *Rosa rubra* (the Red Rose) in 1757.

[Mrs Blackwell's name *Rosa rubra* cannot be taken into consideration in matters of priority, as it is contrary to Art. 79 (4) of the 1952 Code of Botanical Nomenclature. Trew's edition of Mrs Blackwell's *Herbarium* does not consistently use Linnaean binomials, nor does it cite references to Linnaeus for R. *gallica* should therefore be adopted. G. D. R.]

Miletus in Asia Minor, whence it was imported by the ancient Romans in the first century of our era. Pliny describes it as vivid red in colour with not more than twelve petals. In the sixth century it appears as the Rose of the *Codex Caesareus* at Constantinople, which has been identified by Gravereaux as the Dwarf Red Rose known as R. *pumila*. In the twelfth century the dark Red Rose was cultivated by the Arabs in Spain with the tradition that it was brought from Persia in the seventh century.

The Apothecary's Rose of Provins (R. gallica officinalis Thory)

In the thirteenth century the town of Provins, south-east of Paris, became the centre of a great industry which persisted for more than six centuries, although its greatest production was in the seventeenth century. This industry arose through the discovery that a certain variety of the Red Rose had the peculiar chemical property of preserving the delicate perfume of its petals even when dried and reduced to powder. The apothecaries of the period developed this discovery by making conserves and confections of Roses, in various forms, which gave rise to a great industry in the course of centuries. Documents show that in 1310 the town was able to offer presents of conserves and dried Roses to the Archbishop of Sens on his solemn entry, to Charles VII and Joan of Arc in 1429, to Henry II in 1556, to Louis XIV in 1650, 1668, 1678, and 1681, to the Queen of Louis XV in 1725, and to the Emperor Napoleon I in 1814. In 1600 the historian of Henry IV remarked that the main street of the town of Provins was peopled with apothecaries, who make the famous conserve of Provins Roses which is sent all over France. The Provins Roses were also much appreciated in India and England, and in 1860, 36,000 kilos of Provins Rose petals were sent to America. This peculiar scented variety of the Red Rose grown at Provins for more than six hundred years became known as the Apothecary's Rose and was beautifully figured by Redouté in 1817. There is a particularly good photograph of this Rose in Edward Bunyard's book *Old Garden Roses*, 1936, Plate 25, under the name of 'Red Gallica'. For more than three hundred years this Rose of Provins has been known in England as the Red Damask Rose, although, as Bunyard points out, it is botanically a *gallica (rubra)* and not a Damask. It was called a Damask because it was believed to have been brought originally from Damascus by a Crusader. The original plant, from which many thousands of bushes have been clonally propagated and grown at Provins and elsewhere, was said to have been brought to Provins from the Valley of Damascus by Thibaut Le Chansonnier on his return from one of the Crusades. Thibaut IV was King of Navarre and also Count of Champagne and Brie, which explains his interest in the town of Provins. Born in 1201, he was the author of sixty-six poems, and evidently fond of Roses since he sings of them in his verses. In *Le Roman de la Rose*, written about 1260 (later translated by Chaucer as *Romaunt of the Rose*), there is a reference to the Roses from the 'land of the Saracens', and it is probable that we are indebted to the Crusaders for the introduction from Eastern gardens of superior varieties of the Red, Musk, and Damask Roses.

Rosa Mundi

At some time in its history, the date of which is at present unknown, the ancient Rose of Provins gave rise by a bud-sport (somatic mutation) to the old-fashioned favourite striped Rose, *Rosa Mundi*, which occasionally reverts to its bud-parent. *Rosa Mundi* is often mentioned and figured by the old herbalists (Clusius in 1583, Besler in 1613, Caspar Bauhin in 1623), under various names, and there is a drawing of it by Robert in Paris at the Jardin des Plantes dated 1640. There is a popular tradition that this Rose is intimately associated with the Fair Rosamond of Henry II, and in the older writers the name of the Rose is often written as one word, *Rosamonde*. The Fair Rosamond seems to have died in 1176, so that perhaps an earlier Crusader found the striped form in a Syrian garden, and on his return presented it to her after giving her name.

Both the ancient Rose of Provins and its bud-sport, *Rosa Mundi*, are tetraploid with twenty-eight chromosomes in their body-cells and fourteen in their male and female germ-cells.

Up to the seventeenth century only a few varieties of the Red Rose were cultivated in Europe; in 1629 Parkinson notes about a dozen; in the eighteenth century Dutch horticulturists, thanks to Van Eden and others, took up the breeding of the Red Rose on a large scale, and the dozen varieties of Parkinson soon became a thousand. Early in the nineteenth century, owing to the ardour and enthusiasm of the Empress Josephine, many of these were cultivated in France, England, and Italy, whereas hitherto their cultivation had been confined to Holland, Belgium, and Germany. Very few of these varieties of the Red Rose are now in cultivation, but owing to the courtesy and kindness of M. Gravereaux of La Belle Roseraie de L'Haÿ I have been able to examine the chromosomes of a large number of the old Roses which are preserved in his collection. It may be said that all the garden varieties of the Red Rose examined are tetraploid with twenty-eight chromosomes in the body-cells and fourteen in both the male and female germ-cells, while many of the hybrids are triploids.

B. THE DAMASK ROSE (*Rosa damascena* Blackw., 1757).

To the gardener the old Damask Roses are a very natural and charming group with their damask colouring, damasked pattern of the flowers and, above all, the damask fragrance of their perfume; he also likes to believe the old tradition of 1551 that they came originally from Damascus with the returning Crusaders.

The botanist is not so happy about the old Damask Roses, although he has always been willing to admit that they are a natural group and has usually given them the rank of a species; he realizes, however, that their characters are very near to those of R. *rubra* and that these are sufficient to prove the origin of the Damask from the Red Rose. At the same time he is aware that there are certain characters in the Damask Roses which are quite foreign to the Red Rose.

Analyses show that some of the Damask characters foreign to R. *rubra* are those of R. *phoenicia* Boiss, while the others are those of R. *moschata* Miller. It is evident therefore that the Damask Roses are all hybrids of *rubra*, but that some are hybrids of *phoenicia*, while others are hybrids of *moschata*.

Consequently the Damask Roses can be divided into two natural and distinct groups:

(1) × R. *damascena* (*rubra* × *phoenicia*). The Summer Damask Rose.

(2) × R. *bifera* (*rubra* × *moschata*). The Autumn Damask Rose.

(1) THE SUMMER DAMASK ROSE (× R. *damascena* Blackw.).

The York and Lancaster Rose

To this group belongs the old striped Damask, the York and Lancaster Rose, which has often been confused in our gardens with the striped Red Rose, *Rosa Mundi*. There should be no difficulty, however, in distinguishing these two striped Roses, since (apart altogether from the striking differences between them in habit, armature, leaves, and flowers) the pattern and colours of the striping are altogether different in the two Roses. In the *Rosa Mundi* the ground colour of the petals is pale rose-pink, irregularly but heavily striped and blotched all over with rosy-red. In the York and Lancaster the ground colour of the petals is white, irregularly but lightly marked or blotched with blush-pink or rose, the striping and blotching being only partial. This famous Rose was faithfully described by John Parkinson in 1629, and there is little doubt that it is the Rose mentioned by Shakespeare in *Henry VI*, in the scene of the plucking of red and white Roses in the Temple Garden. In Shakespeare's Sonnet XCIX we get an intimate picture of the York and Lancaster Rose which will appeal to the practical gardener.

> The Roses fearfully on thorns did stand,
> One blushing shame, another white despair;
> A third, nor red nor white, had stolen of both
> And to his robbery had annexed thy breath;
> But, for his theft, in pride of all his growth
> A vengeful canker eat him up to death.

These lines are of peculiar interest because they show that Shakespeare had more than a casual acquaintance with the York and Lancaster Rose; he must have had personal experience in growing the plant. My own experience is that this variety, in spite of its vigorous growth, has a poor constitution and does not last long without propagation and renewal.

The York and Lancaster Rose is a tetraploid with twenty-eight chromosomes in its body-cells and fourteen in its male and female germ-cells. The chromosomes show definite signs of hybridity, with irregular pairing and weakened affinity. In two cases whole sets of seven chromosomes acted independently of the others in somatic divisions. Such disturbances are likely to affect metabolism and weaken the plant's constitution. The young pollen-grains were not healthy, about one-half being degenerate. The embryo-sac formation was normal and healthy.

The Holy Rose

Another interesting but rather mysterious Rose, belonging to the first group of Summer Damask Roses, is the Holy Rose. Our knowledge of this Rose is somewhat scanty, yet it seems to go much farther back in history than any other garden Rose, and there are indications that it may have had a distant part to play in the evolution of our garden Roses. The little we know of its history is both curious and chequered. It was first found in Abyssinia, in the Christian Province of Tigre, where it had been planted in the courtyards of religious sanctuaries. It was described by Richard in 1848 in his *Flora of Abyssinia* under the name of *Rosa sancta*.[1] The Holy Rose forms a low erect bush, and is intermediate in its characters between the Red and the Phoenician Rose. Indeed, except for its single flowers with five or six petals, it would pass well for a dwarf Damask Rose. Since its *phoenicia* parent is not a cultivated plant, the Holy Rose is presumably a natural hybrid with its home in Asia Minor and Syria, where its two parents overlap, and the question arises how it came to be transported to Abyssinia. The story of St Frumentius may help to solve that problem. St Frumentius was born in Phoenicia about A.D. 300, and it is said that while on a voyage he was captured by Ethiopians, taken to Axum, the Abyssinian capital, and became the King's Secretary. He is said to have converted the Abyssinians to Christianity, and secured its introduction to that country. In 326 he was consecrated Bishop of Axum by Athanasius at Alexandria, and died in 360.

In view of the above facts it seems likely that the Holy Rose may have been introduced to Abyssinia from Phoenicia (Syria) by the Phoenician Apostle of Ethiopia, St Frumentius, in the fourth century A.D. This also may explain why the Rose was planted within the precincts of the Christian churches in his diocese, and thus preserved through the centuries.

---

[1] In view of the earlier and quite different R. *sancta* Andrews (1827), Rehder in 1922 amended R. *sancta* Richard (1848) to R. *Richardii*, and now both Richard's and Rehder's specific names become synonyms of × R. *damascena* Blackw.

The Rose of the Tombs

We next hear of the mysterious Holy Rose in the tombs of
Egypt. The tomb in which it was found was in the cemetery of
the town of Arsinoe of Fayoum in Upper Egypt, near to the
Labyrinth Pyramid, and judging by other remains found along-
side the Holy Rose it belonged to a period between the second
and the fifth centuries A.D. The remains of this Rose were twined
into garlands when found in the Egyptian tomb in 1888 by the
eminent English archaeologist, Sir Flinders Petrie, who sent them
to Kew Gardens for identification. Dr Oliver, having ascertained
that they were Roses, forwarded them to Professor Crépin,
Director of the Brussels Botanic Garden. Crépin reported that
the nine Roses composing the garland were all of the same variety
and were identical with *Rosa sancta* Richard, cultivated at the
present day in the courtyards of religious edifices in Abyssinia.
Crépin considered them to be a new form of R. *gallica* (R. *rubra*),
but he did not think that they had ever been indigenous in
Abyssinia or Egypt, but that they had been introduced from
Italy, Greece, or Asia Minor. There may be some connection
between the garlands of Abyssinian Holy Roses in the Egyptian
tomb and St Frumentius of Abyssinia, but until further evidence
is obtained it remains a mystery.

The Minoan Rose in Crete

Finally we arrive at the island of Crete, where Sir Arthur
Evans, in the course of his remarkable excavations, unearthed a
fresco-painting near the ancient palace of Cnossos that included
a lifelike representation of a Rose, which I saw in 1926 and which
seemed to me to bear a striking resemblance to the Holy Rose of
Abyssinia, Egypt, and Asia Minor. It is hoped that further
excavations will bring to light more of these Minoan Roses and
add to our present scanty knowledge of them.

The central date of the great historic Minoan civilization of
Crete may be put at about 2000 B.C. It apparently maintained close
contact with Egypt, Phoenicia, and Greece, and there is no doubt
that the beautiful Phoenician Roses would appeal to the high
artistic sense of the Minoans. The selection of a single-flowered

Rose by the Minoan artist for his fresco-painting does not necessarily mean that garden Roses were not cultivated by the Minoans; the double garden Roses of the time may have been too heavy for his artistic purpose.

So far as I have been able to trace, this Minoan fresco-painting is the earliest representation of a Rose in historical times.

(2) THE AUTUMN DAMASK ROSE (× R. *bifera* [Poiret]).

The Autumn Damask Roses are also very ancient and, like their parents *rubra* and *moschata*, have always been renowned for their fragrance and free-flowering qualities. We first hear of them in the island of Samos towards the tenth century B.C., where tney are said to have flowered twice a year and were freely used in the cult of Aphrodite (or Venus), which was later introduced to Greece and Rome, together with the Roses, which played a most important part in the ceremonies. There is little doubt that the Roses which Herodotus mentions as growing in Macedonia in the gardens of Midas, each with sixty petals and surpassing all other Roses in fragrance, were the Autumn Damask Roses × R. *bifera*, and not R. *centifolia*, as we used to believe. As we shall see later, R. *centifolia*, as we know it, and as the eighteenth and nineteenth centuries knew it, first arose in Holland in the eighteenth century of our era and was therefore unknown to the ancient Greeks and Romans. Their Roses with a hundred petals, which naturally they called *Rosa centifolia*, were not our *centifolia*, but evidently our *bifera* Damask Rose, which we know was cultivated by them at a later period at Paestum, Pompeii, and other places. It is possible that Midas, who was King of Phrygia, may have brought the Roses of Herodotus to Macedonia from his gardens in Asia Minor, and that afterwards they were distributed in Greece and Italy. Many Roses of the same kind were grown in Egypt for the Roman market, especially in the winter, as Martial tells us 'roses in winter bear the highest price'. In the first century B.C. Virgil, in his Georgics, sings of the Roses of Paestum and of their flowering twice a year, 'biferique Rosaria Paesti', which can only refer to our Autumn Damask Rose. Frescoes of this Rose were found in the ruins of Pompeii, which was destroyed in A.D. 79, and Pliny himself perished in the catastrophe through his eagerness to get a near view of the great eruption of Vesuvius. In the tenth century, according to the Arab physician Avicenna, the same Rose was cultivated on a large scale in Syria for making rose-water and for medicines. In the twelfth century it appears with the Arabs in Spain, and Ibn-el-Awam describes our Damask Rose with much detail, suggesting that it came from the East.

The Rose of Alexandria

In the sixteenth century, Nicolas Monardes, a Spanish physician, wrote a medical treatise on the Roses of Persia or Alexandria, which he said the Italians, Gauls, Germans, and others call Damascènae, because they believe them to have come from Damascus. His description agrees with the Autumn Damask Rose, although he says nothing of its flowering twice a year. There is, however, indirect evidence that these Spanish Damask Roses did flower twice a year, for M. Lachaume, writing to the *Journal des Roses* in 1879 from Havannah, Cuba, states that in almost every Spanish home in Cuba there is the antique Quatre-Saisons Rose, which in Cuba is universally known as the Alexandria Rose. This Rose and its name have evidently been handed down in Cuba from generation to generation from the time the Spanish colonists settled there in the sixteenth century. Other Spanish plants were also brought at the same time, and have survived with the Rose as souvenirs of their native homes in Spain. From M. Lachaume's detailed description of the Alexandria Rose, and his statement that it flowers twice a year, there can be no doubt that it is our Autumn Damask Rose, and it is most likely the same Rose as Monardes's Spanish Damascena of 1551, which he thought came from Persia or Alexandria, through the Arabs and the Moors.

In modern times the Autumn Damask Rose is still preferred to any other kind for the commercial production of rose-water and attar of Roses as in the old days, and there are vast plantations of this variety of Rose in Turkey, Bulgaria, Egypt, Persia, India, and Morocco. All the varieties of Damask Roses so far examined, except one, prove to be tetraploid with twenty-eight chromosomes in the body-cells and fourteen in the male and female germ-cells. The exception is a seedling Damask Rose in Kew Gardens which proves to be a pentaploid with thirty-five chromosomes in the body-cells, twenty-one in the female germ-cells, and fourteen in the male. This interesting Rose was raised at Kew from seeds of a hip gathered from the Rose growing on Omar's grave at Naishapur.

> When Omar died, the Rose did weep
> Its petals on his tomb;
> He would be laid, where North winds keep
> The Rose in freshest bloom.
>
> *Anna Hills*, 1884.

C. THE WHITE ROSE OF YORK (*Rosa alba* L.).

This familiar old garden Rose has persisted through the centuries, and has been in general cultivation from the times of the Greeks and Romans. In the thirteenth century it was rather neatly described by the Universal Doctor of the Schoolmen, Albertus Magnus, as 'the white garden rose which has often fifty or sixty petals, it is very bushy, and the branches are long and thin in a tree of which the trunk often attains the thickness of one's arm'. In 1307 Crescentius, the Italian agriculturist, recommends it for planting a hedge. The Italian painters of the fifteenth century were fond of this Rose, and portrayed the large 'Double White' and the 'Maiden's Blush' varieties (*alba maxima* and *alba regalis*), the flowers of which appear to be identical with those grown today.

In the Wars of the Roses the 'Double White' English Rose was traditionally adopted as a badge by the Yorkists. The old herbalists note and figure this Rose in the sixteenth century, and it usually appears first on their lists of Roses as 'most ancient and knowne Rose . . . King of all others' (Parkinson). In 1753 Linnaeus made it a species under the name of *R. alba*, and although it is obviously a garden plant most botanists have regarded it as a species until 1873, when Christ suggested that it was a hybrid between *gallica* (R. *rubra*) and *canina*, and Crépin, with others, have agreed with this interpretation.

An analysis of the characters of × R. *alba* L. shows the definite influence of R. *phoenicia* Boiss. in this hybrid, and I feel bound to conclude, therefore, that × R. *damascena*, rather than R. *rubra*, was one parent, and that a white-flowered, almost prickleless form of R. *canina* was the other. Further, from the chromosome number we can say definitely that *canina* was the female parent and not the male. × R. *alba* is a hexaploid with forty-two chromosomes; R. *canina* is a pentaploid with twenty-eight chromosomes in the female germ-cells and seven in the male; × R. *damascena* is a tetraploid with fourteen chromosomes in both male and female germ-cells. Consequently, if R. *canina* had been the male parent, × R. *alba* would have been a triploid with twenty-one chromosomes instead of a hexaploid with forty-two.

The only white-flowered *canina* with few prickles known to me is R. *c. Froebelii* Christ, which grows in Kurdistan, and possibly extends to the Crimea and the Caucasus. This is the form of Briar known in gardens as R. *laxa,* and formerly used as a stock for budding garden Roses. It has no connection whatever with the R. *laxa* of Retzius or of Lindley, nor, as Rehder suggests, with R. *coriifolia* Fries.

× R. *alba* has been reported as growing wild in the Crimea, and it may be that it originated there as a natural hybrid; it has also been reported from several places in Central Europe, but these may be garden escapes or otherwise of garden origin.

In the singles and semi-double forms of × R. *alba* which are fertile, the female germ-cells carry twenty-eight chromosomes, while the male germ-cells carry only fourteen. All the seedlings examined have forty-two chromosomes.

D. THE OLD CABBAGE ROSE (*Rosa centifolia* L.).

For many years most of us have believed that the Old Cabbage Rose of our great-grandmothers was the most ancient Rose in the world. We all followed the old herbalists who agreed that *Rosa centifolia,* the Queen of Roses and the Queen of Flowers, was cultivated by the Greeks and Romans, noted by Herodotus, and named by Theophrastus and Pliny. We took it all in, and it seemed to us the most natural thing in the world for the classic Roses with a hundred petals and the most fragrant of perfumes to be our *Rosa centifolia,* especially as Theophrastus and Pliny called them by that name. Modern research has changed all that, and will not be denied. It appears now that our R. *centifolia* did not actually arrive until the eighteenth century, and is therefore the youngest of all our old Roses.

Thanks to the initial spade-work of the late Edward Bunyard

we are now in a position to trace the origin, or rather the evolution, of the R. *centifolia* of Linnaeus, commonly known in England as the 'Provence' or 'Cabbage Rose'. Space will not allow full details here, and a brief summary must suffice.

Analysis shows that R. *centifolia* L. is not a wild species as many have supposed, nor is it a simple primary hybrid like the Damask Roses. It is a complex hybrid of four distinct wild species, R. *rubra*, R. *phoenicia*, R. *moschata*, and R. *canina*, and may therefore be presumed to have had a garden origin. Such a combination can, of course, be made in many different ways, and we have no knowledge of the actual steps taken. The quickest way to arrive at the combination is no doubt the direct cross between × R. *bifera* (*rubra* × *moschata*) and × R. *alba* (*canina* × *damascena*), which would give the whole combination. Experience of plant breeding, however, leads one to suppose that, working under the usual system of trial and error, many steps were taken, both backwards and forwards, before the object was attained.

Evidence from many varied sources in literature and art shows that R. *centifolia* L. was gradually and slowly evolved from the end of the sixteenth century to the beginning of the eighteenth century, when it apparently reached the perfection of a florist's flower. Definitely we owe this superb Rose to the genius and industry of the Dutch breeders who first took the matter in hand about 1580, and persevered until they attained perfection about 1710.

Soon after that date the old Moss Rose appeared in Holland as a bud-sport of the perfected type of × R. *centifolia*, which was, of course, completely sterile sexually, owing to the complete doubleness of the flowers. Afterwards at least sixty-two other bud-sports appeared, either from the original × R. *centifolia* or from its sports. These were much cultivated in the first half of the nineteenth century, and a few are still grown to this day. At Burbage I grew and studied about twenty of these bud mutations for many years, and during that time several of them reverted to the bud-parent × R. *centifolia* without any variation, so far as I could see, which suggests that these sports came from the stock of one seedling plant of × R. *centifolia*, existent about 1710. See also page 217.

The true type of × R. *centifolia*, i.e. the perfected form which

produced the Moss Rose, is tetraploid with twenty-eight chromosomes in the body-cells and fourteen in the male and female germ-
cells. Owing to doubleness the germ-cells do not mature and fail
to reach the final stage. Only once did I succeed in getting a seed,
and that failed to germinate.

Most of the bud-sports have the same number of chromosomes
as their parent, but a few, like the Rose of the Painters, are
triploid with twenty-one chromosomes in the body-cells and
irregular numbers in the germ-cells which fail to mature.

From the above notes it will be seen that the most important
of our ancient garden Roses have originated from four wild
species of Rosa, namely the Red Rose (R. *rubra* Blackw. 1757),[1]
the Phoenician Rose (R. *phoenicia* Boiss.), the Musk Rose (R.
moschata Miller), and the Dog Rose (R. *canina* L.). This completes
a brief survey of the ancient foundation Roses from which our
Garden Roses, ancient and modern, have sprung. There are a
few other ancient garden forms still in cultivation which have
not been noted, such as the Double Cinnamon Rose, the Double
Sweet Briar, the Double Sulphur Rose, and the Miniature forms,
such as the Burgundy Rose, the Rose de Meaux, and others of
that kind; these have not been noted because up to now they have
not been directly concerned in the evolution of our modern
Roses. They have had their day, but so far have not succeeded in
establishing a dynasty. Included in this category are the less
ancient forms of the eighteenth century, such as the Ayrshire
Roses from R. *arvensis* Huds., the Evergreen Roses from R.
sempervirens L., and the Burnet or Scots Roses from R. *spinoissima*
L., 1762 (*non* 1753). Finally, there are the important Yellow and
Copper Austrian Briars from R. *lutea* Miller which, though very
ancient, did not come into the direct line of modern Roses until
the dawn of the twentieth century. These will be noted in the next
article on the origin and evolution of our modern Roses since
A.D. 1800.

[1] Syn. R. *gallica* L., 1759 (*non* 1753).

II. MODERN GARDEN ROSES

1800–1940

Great events oft from little causes spring, and it is a remarkable fact that the most important improvement of our garden Roses in the last century was due to the introduction from China of a minute Mendelian gene, so small that it is quite invisible to the naked eye. The chromosome thread on which this tiny Rose gene is borne is plainly seen under a high-powered lens of an ordinary microscope, but an electron microscope would be required to make out the outline of the gene itself.

A pair of these genes, one from the father and one from the mother, is present in every growing cell of our best modern Roses, whether they be exquisite Teas, shapely Hybrid Teas, gay-coloured Pernets, dazzling Poulsens, or lowly Poly-Poms. In normal conditions of growth these genes cause a continuous pushing of shoots, with every shoot a flowering shoot, so that our modern Roses tend to flower all the year round, unlike the ancient Roses which for the most part flowered naturally only once a year.

In Rose breeding, except for certain complications met with in annual autumn-flowering species, this gene for perennial flowering behaves as a simple Mendelian recessive to the dominant wild gene for annual flowering. It is evidently a mutation which still appears from time to time in a state of nature among the wild Roses of China just as it did a thousand or more years ago when the Chinese gardeners first discovered it. This mutation seems to be peculiar to China and to the genus *Rosa*, although it is not limited to one species since I have found it in several Chinese species of *Rosa*.

China is a country rich in Roses, both wild and cultivated; indeed with its wealth of species it is considered by some botanists to be the original home and cradle of the genus. It was not, however, from these magnificent wild species that our modern garden Roses have sprung. That is reserved for future centuries. It was the humble dwarf China Rose that had been cultivated in Chinese gardens for more than a thousand years and bore the precious gene for continuous flowering which, transferred by hybridization to our Western garden Roses early in the nineteenth century, changed them as by a magic wand.

E. CHINA ROSES (Sect. *Indicae* Thory).

Since the introduction of the Poly-Poms. in 1875 China Roses have become rather old-fashioned, but they are still grown and cultivated by those who appreciate the loveliness of translucent colours.

The earliest records of the China Rose are found in the Chinese screen paintings of the tenth century on which are portrayed Blush China Roses which appear to be identical with the Blush Tea-scented China introduced to England in 1809. The earliest trace of the introduction of the China Rose to Europe that I have been able to find is in the National Gallery, London, where there is a painting by the Florentine artist, Angelo Bronzino, dating from about 1529, which shews a smiling cupid with his hands full of Pink China Roses in the act of throwing them over Folly, who is embracing Venus (Bronzino, No. 651). The small rose-pink flowers with translucent petals, incurved stamens, reflexed sepals, and small firm ovate shining leaflet are precisely those of the Pink China, and we may safely conclude that this Rose was cultivated in Italy early in the sixteenth century. It may have been this China Rose which Montaigne saw in flower at the Jesuit Monastery at Ferrara when he visited Italy in November 1678, and was told that the Rose flowered all the year round.

Among the early botanical specimens in the British Museum there is a quaint little remnant of a Crimson China Rose neatly arranged in a paper vase in the Herbarium of Gronovius (1690–1760). It is labelled 'Chineesche Eglantier Roosen', and dated 1733.[1] It was on this specimen of Gronovius that Jacquin founded his figure of the Crimson China in 1768 under the name of R. *chinensis*. In 1750 Peter Osbeck, a pupil of Linnaeus, and a collector of specimens for the Linnean Herbarium, set sail for China and the East Indies. On his return to Sweden in 1752 he published a brief account of his travels in which he describes his discovery of *Rosa indica* in the gardens of the Custom House at Canton on 29th October 1751.

---

[1] By some mischance the date of this specimen is given as 1704 by both Willmott (1911) and Bunyard (1936), and the latter refers to it as the Blush China, although it is definitely a Crimson China.

The China Roses of Linnaeus

The China Roses in the Herbarium of Linnaeus at the Linnean Society of London include three Crimson Chinas, one Pink China, one Blush Tea China, and one hybrid China, which is apparently a cross with R. *multiflora* Thunb. The most interesting and important specimen is the Blush Tea China (Sheet 38) which Linnaeus, in his own handwriting, indicates as his type specimen of R. *indica*. It is probable that this is the R. *indica* found by Peter Osbeck in 1751 in the Custom House garden at Canton.

The Pink China specimen (Sheet 37), according to Linnaeus, came from the Botanic Garden at Upsala, whither it had been brought from China, probably by Osbeck in 1752. It is the R. *sinica* of Murray in Linn. Syst. Veg. 1774, which according to the elder Aiton (1789) was cultivated by Philip Miller in 1759. This is an early date for the cultivation of the China Rose in England, but it seems hardly likely that Aiton was mistaken because in the early part of that year he was a pupil of Miller at Chelsea, and thus had an opportunity of knowing the plant at first hand. Miller was in close touch with Linnaeus at that time, and may well have received the Pink China direct from Upsala. In 1769 Sir John Hill, in his *Hortus Kewensis*, records the cultivation of R. *indica* L. in the gardens of the Princess Augusta at Kew House when Aiton was in charge.

In the younger Martyn's French edition of Miller's *Dictionary* of 1785, it is stated that a Deep Red China Rose was cultivated in England at that time, but I have been unable to trace its origin. French authors agree that the China Rose came to France through England, but they give a bewildering array of dates of their introduction from China and India to England, ranging between 1710 and 1780, and so far I have been unable to confirm these from English sources. In 1781 the Pink China was introduced to Holland by the Dutch East India Company, and in her *Memoirs* the Baroness D'Oberkirch relates that she saw this Chinese Rose in the gardens at Haarlem in 1782, and at once recognized the flower which was so often delineated on Chinese screens and fans. None of these early introductions of the China Rose to Italy, Sweden, Holland, and England, however, seems to have played any part in the development of our modern Roses. That role was apparently reserved for four special English introductions of 1792, 1793, 1809, and 1824, each of which had a definite and permanent influence on the evolution of our garden Roses.

THE FOUR STUD CHINAS: (1) SLATER'S CRIMSON CHINA, 1792 (*Rosa chinensis* Jacq.).

The first of the four stud Chinas was Slater's Crimson China, which was imported from China by Gilbert Slater of Knot's Green, Leytonstone, about 1792. The original plant was figured by Curtis in *Bot. Mag.* in 1794 under the name of *R. semper-florens*, and there is a specimen of it in the British Museum from Kew Gardens. Slater's Crimson China must have been introduced to France soon afterwards, for in 1798 Cels, the Paris nurseryman, Thory, the French botanist, and Redouté, the famous artist, commenced their breeding experiments with it in or about that year.

Slater's Crimson China reached Austria, Germany, and Italy before the close of the eighteenth century, and early in the nineteenth century in Italy it became the parent of the Portland Rose, and thus grandparent of the first Hybrid Perpetual 'Rose du Roi'. Slater's Crimson China is still in cultivation in old gardens, and there is an admirable modern figure of it in Willmott (1911) under the name of *R. chinensis semperflorens*. In its characters it is very near to Henry's Crimson China, collected in 1885 in the San-yu-tung Glen near Ichang in the Province of Hupeh, Central China, which is generally considered to be the wild species and original ancestor of the China Roses. Slater's Crimson China differs from the wild species in its dwarf habit, semi-double flowers, and perennial flowering, all of which are Mendelian characters, the genes for the first and last characters being closely linked in the same chromosome.

Like most of the cultivated Crimson Chinas Slater's form is a triploid with twenty-one chromosomes in the body-cells, fourteen in the female germ-cells, and seven in the male. Consequently the pollen is very defective, and on the average only one grain in seven is fertile. This 14 per cent fertility would no doubt be fatal to survival in a state of nature, but it is sufficient for the gardener and hybridist to raise new kinds of Roses. Some of the cultivated

Crimson Chinas are, however, diploid with fourteen chromosomes in the body-cells and seven in the male and female germ-cells, having retained their wild simplicity. I found one of these diploid Crimson Chinas in the Gravereaux collection at La Roseraie de l'Haÿ, near Paris. In spite of its air of culture it was a typical wild Crimson China with single cherry-red flowers, while in habit it was a graceful short climber. Its diploid chromosome behaviour was entirely regular and normal as in a species, with no signs of hybridity, consequently the pollen and embryo-sacs were regular and the plant was as fully fertile as a wild species.

(2) PARSONS'S PINK CHINA, 1793 (R. *chinensis* Jacq. × R. *gigantea* Collett).

Parsons's Pink China was first seen in his garden at Rickmansworth in 1793, according to Andrews (1805), and was said by the younger Aiton (1811) to have been introduced from China about 1789 by Sir Joseph Banks. In the Banksian Herbarium there are three specimens of the Pink China, two of which closely resemble Parsons's Pink China; one of these is marked 'China prope Canton, Lord Macartney', and the other 'Hort. Kew 1795 China'. Lindley, in 1820, based his R. *indica* on the Macartney specimen, crediting the collection of it to Sir George Staunton, who accompanied Lord Macartney's embassy to China in 1792. It is therefore possible that Parsons's Pink China was sent home by him to Sir Joseph Banks, who was at that time Director of Kew.

Soon after 1793 Colville secured a stock of Parsons's Pink China, and sent it out as the Pale China Rose, presumably to distinguish it from Slater's Crimson China of 1792. Parsons's Pink China soon arrived in France, for it was seen in the greenhouses of Dr Barbier in Paris in 1798, and Thory tells us that he and Redouté started to raise seedlings from it in that year.

About 1800 Parsons's Pink China appeared in North America, at Charleston in South Carolina, no doubt through the agency of the two brothers Louis and Philippe Noisette, who were nurserymen in Paris and Charleston respectively, and about 1802, in the hands of John Champneys of Charleston, Parsons's Pink China became a grandparent of the French Noisette Rose from which later on came our best Climbing Yellow Teas such as 'Maréchal Niel' and 'Gloire de Dijon'.

In 1805, at Colville's nursery in England, Parsons's Pink China gave rise to the Dwarf Pink China, a miniature Rose known in England as the Fairy Rose or R. *Lawranceana*. Louis Noisette imported this Rose to France and called it Bengale Pompon. It was largely planted at Lyon, and in 1868 became a grandparent of the first Poly-Poms. and ancestor of the Poulsen Roses.

About 1810 Parsons's Pink China appeared in the French island of Bourbon (Réunion), where the colonists used it to form hedges, and towards 1815, by natural crossing with the Autumn Damask Rose, also used as a hedge plant, it became a grandparent of the French Bourbon Rose, and thus an ancestor of the Teas, Hybrid Perpetuals, and Hybrid Teas.

Parsons's Pink China is still in cultivation in country gardens, and there is an excellent figure of it in Redouté (1817) under the name of R. *indica vulgaris*. Analyses of its characters show the influence of the Wild Crimson China (R. *chinensis*) in sixteen of these, while the remaining twelve characters show the influence of another species, the Wild Tea Rose (R. *gigantea*). Parsons's Pink China may therefore be regarded as a hybrid between *chinensis* and *gigantea*. It is not, of course, an ordinary primary hybrid produced directly [1] between the two species, but rather a derivative hybrid derived after generations of crossings in Chinese gardens. Parsons's Pink China is a diploid with fourteen chromosomes in the body-cells and seven in both male and female germ-cells. Although a diploid, its chromosomes are not regular in their behaviour and weak pairings in the germ-cell divisions lead to defective pollen and embryo-sacs and consequent sterility. In this respect the Pink Chinas behave as hybrids rather than pure species. Among the newer varieties of the Pink China I have found several triploid forms with twenty-one chromosomes, which have no doubt arisen by a duplication of the chromosomes in a pollen or egg-cell, as in the case of the triploid Crimson Chinas.

[1] Genetical confirmation of this is found in the appearance of true-breeding *gigantea* characters in the original crosses of Noisette and Bourbon with the Blush and Yellow Chinas, giving rise to the race of Tea Roses (R. *gigantea* Collett).

(3) HUME'S BLUSH TEA-SCENTED CHINA, 1809 (R. *chinensis* Jacq. ×
R. *gigantea* Collett).

Hume's Blush China is said to have been imported in 1809 by
Sir A. Hume, Bart., from the East Indies, at that time a comprehensive term which included China. It was figured by Andrews
in 1810 under the name of R. *indica odorata* from a plant flowering
in Colville's nursery. In the same year special arrangements were
made by both the British and French Admiralties for the safe
transit of plants of this new Tea-scented China to the Empress
Josephine at Malmaison in spite of the fierce war that was raging
between England and France at that time. In 1817 Redouté published a beautiful and accurate figure of the original plant under
the name of R. *indica fragrans*, which shows it to be a China considerably modified by the influence of the Wild Tea Rose (R.
gigantea), the bias in favour of that species being about 2 : 1. It
was not, however, a true Tea Rose as some have supposed,[1]
since it shows the influence of the Wild Crimson China (R.
chinensis) in eleven of its characters out of the thirty-one examined,
the remaining twenty characters showing the influence of the
Wild Tea Rose (R. *gigantea*). Hume's Blush China must therefore
be regarded as a derivative hybrid from *gigantea* and *chinensis*.
Crossed with the Bourbon, Noisette, and Yellow China towards
1830 Hume's Blush China gave rise to typical Tea Roses. Living
material of this Rose is no longer available, but like its ancestral
species it was most likely a diploid with fourteen chromosomes.
Material of its ancestral species the Wild Tea Rose (R. *gigantea*)
from both Cambridge and Burbage proved to be diploid.

(4) PARKS'S YELLOW TEA-SCENTED CHINA, 1824 (R. *chinensis* Jacq. ×
R. *gigantea* Collett).

The fourth and last of the Stud Chinas is Parks's Yellow China,
which was brought from China by Parks for the R.H.S. in 1824.
The following year it was imported to France by the enthusiastic
Rose breeder Hardy, of the Royal Luxembourg Gardens, where
its novel colour made it a general favourite. There is a good figure

---

[1] It was on this assumption that Rehder in 1915 reduced R. *gigantea* Collett to a
variety of R. *odorata* Sweet, a name given by Sweet in 1818 to Hume's Blush China.

of the original in the 1835 edition of Redouté under the name of
R. *indica sulphurea*, with a description by Pirolle. At first sight,
with its large yellow flowers, thick tea-scented petals, and bright
green leaves, Parks's Yellow China looks more like a Tea than a
China, and reminds one rather of the yellow variety of R. *gigantea*
discovered in Manipur by Sir George Watt in 1882. An analysis
of its characters, however, shows the influence of ten China
characters to twenty of the Wild Tea Rose, so that the plant must
be regarded as a hybrid. Parks's Yellow China was the ancestor
of many remarkable Roses; crossed with the Noisettes it produced
the typical Yellow Teas which, crossed with the Pink Teas
derived from Hume's Blush China and the Bourbon, gave rise to
those exquisite shades of refined colouring peculiar to Teas in
which the pink and yellow are indescribably mixed and blended.
Through the Teas, Parks's Yellow China was the ancestor of
many of the Hybrid Teas, Pernets, Poly-Poms., and Poulsen
Roses. No living material of Parks's Yellow China has been
available since 1882, but there is little doubt that it was a diploid
with fourteen chromosomes, since both ancestral species were
diploid, and crossed with the diploid Noisettes its descendants
proved to be diploid.

In concluding the account of the four Stud Chinas which have
had such a powerful influence in moulding our modern garden
Roses, it may be interesting to note that China Roses similar to
the four Stud Chinas are still cultivated in Chinese gardens. In
South-western China, in the province of Yunnan, some of them
are largely used for hedges. The Wild Tea Rose (R. *gigantea*) also
grows there naturally in ravines and on grassy hills, and in the
same locality at the same elevation garden forms of the Crimons
China (R. *chinensis*) are still cultivated there. The port of Yunnan
is Canton, from which the four Stud Chinas are presumed to have
come. It seems therefore fairly safe to conclude that the four Stud
Chinas which revolutionized our old garden Roses originated in
South-western China in the province of Yunnan, and probably
not far from Mengtsze.

1. The Great White Rose (*Rosa alba* 'Maxima'), gracefully luxuriating, without pruning, three years old.

2 Old Shrub Roses luxuriating, without pruning, when three years old in an Essex garden.

3. *Rosa damascena celsiana*, raised prior to 1750, in an Essex garden.

4.　I *Rosa gallica officinalis,* the Red Rose of Lancaster or Apothecary's Rose.
See pages 60, 148.

II *Rosa gallica versicolor,* or 'Rosa Mundi', the striped sport of R. *gallica
officinalis.* See pages 62, 151.

5. 'Camaieux', one of the most remarkable of the striped Gallica
varieties. The flowers are a medley of blush and old rose, fading to
white and lilac-grey.

6. I The Portland Rose, named after the Duchess of Portland in the first decade of the nineteenth century, and presumed to be a hybrid between a red China Rose and a hybrid of *Rosa gallica* and R. *damascena bifera*. It is the parent of the Hybrid Perpetuals. It flowers in summer and autumn and was consequently known as the 'Scarlet Four Seasons'. II 'Du Maître d'École', a Gallica rose of great size of soft deep rose, changing to lilac-pink with mauve and coppery shadings.

7. Hedges of 'Rosa Mundi' (R. *gallica versicolor*) in their midsummer splendour, at Kiftsgate Court, Chipping Camden. A very ancient rose of unrivalled garden value.

8. 'Tuscany Superb', a velvety, maroon-coloured Gallica of great garden value; the rich tone is greatly enhanced by the golden stamens. In cultivation before 1848.

F. THE NOISETTE ROSE

Miller's White Musk × *Parsons's Pink China*
Rosa *moschata* Miller × (R. *chinensis* Jacq. × R. *gigantea* Collett)

The honour of the first introduction of the Chinese gene for perennial flowering to our western Roses belongs to an American citizen, John Champneys, a wealthy rice planter of Charleston in South Caroiina, who was a great gardener. About 1802 he fertilized the old White Musk Rose of Miller with pollen of the new Pink China of Parsons, which he had recently received from France through the brothers Noisette of Charleston and Paris. The result was a handsome hybrid, which combined the climbing habit, large open clusters of flowers and odour of the Musk with the semi-double pink flowers of the China and the handsome foliage of both. Champneys called it R. *moschata hybrida*, but the Rose became such a great favourite in America that it came to be known as Champneys's Pink Cluster or the Champneys Rose. A few years afterwards Philippe Noisette, the French nurseryman at Charleston, sowed seeds of Champneys's hybrid and thus in the second generation raised the original French Noisette Rose, which he sent to his brother, Louis Noisette of Paris, in 1814, who distributed it in Europe in 1819. This Rose was figured by Redouté in 1821 under the name of R. *Noisettiana*, and quickly became a popular garden Rose. In the second generation Mendelian segregation took place, and the Noisette was less tall and more compact in growth than Champneys's Hybrid; the flowers were blush-white, borne in large dense clusters, equally fragrant, but above all they were produced continuously from June to the winter frosts.

Up to 1830 there was little variation in the Noisette race bred from seed except those with violet-crimson flowers which were hybridized with *multiflora* and *chinensis*, and those with lax flower clusters which were hybridized with R. *sempervirens* L. Among the latter was the old favourite 'Aimée Vibert', raised by Vibert in 1828, and still prominent in old gardens.

Towards 1830 attempts were made to create a Yellow Noisette by crossing the Blush Noisette with Parks's new Yellow China. This cross had far-reaching results since it gave rise not only to the Yellow Noisette, but also to the Yellow Tea Roses. In 1830

'Lamarque' and 'Jaune Desprez' appeared, and in 1833 Smith's Yellow, the last being a true dwarf Yellow Tea, although classed as a Noisette on account of its origin. The first two were yellowish Noisettes which, selfed, gave Yellow Climbing Teas: 'Celine Forestier' in 1842 and 'Cloth of Gold' (Chromatella) and 'Solfatare' in 1843. 'Cloth of Gold' was the parent of the famous 'Maréchal Niel'. Further breeding swamped the old Noisette characters, and transformed the Noisette into a Climbing Tea as seen in 'Gloire de Dijon' (1853), 'Maréchal Niel' (1864), 'Rêve d'Or' (1860), 'Bouquet d'Or' (1872), 'Caroline Kuester' (1872), 'William Allen Richardson' (1878), and 'Mme Alfred Carrière' (1879).

The original Blush Noisette proves to be a diploid with fourteen chromosomes, and all its early descendants, including the Yellow Teas, prove to be diploid except 'Gloire de Dijon', which is a tetraploid with twenty-eight chromosomes. Champneys's Hybrid must therefore have been a diploid as its parents were. Miller's Musk Rose is now very rare, but it is still in the Cambridge Botanic Garden where it was examined.

G. THE BOURBON ROSE

Pink Autumn Damask × *Parsons's Pink China*
(R. *rubra* Blackw. × R. *moschata* Miller) × (R. *chinensis* Jacq. × R. *gigantea* Collett)

The Bourbon Rose, like the Noisette and all other new races of Roses, appeared in the second generation of a cross in accordance with Mendel's Laws of Segregation and Fixity. The first generation of the Bourbon was a natural hybrid between the Pink Autumn Damask and Parsons's Pink China, found growing in a garden with its parents in the French island of Bourbon in 1817 by the Parisian botanist Bréon, who was in charge of the Botanic Garden at the time. It was a vigorous and decorative hybrid, intermediate in character between the Damask and China parents. Locally and in the adjacent island of Mauritius it was known as the 'Rose Edward'. In 1819 Bréon sent seeds of the new hybrid to his friend Jacques, the celebrated gardener of King Louis Philippe in Paris, and from these seeds Jacques raised

the first French Bourbon Rose and called it 'Rosier de l'île
Bourbon'. The new Rose was distributed in France about 1823
and in England about 1825. It was figured by Redouté in 1824
under the curious name of R. *canina Burboniana*. This Rose of the
second generation was a better garden Rose than its parent the
'Rose Edward', partly because of its more compact habit, but
mainly by its abundant autumn flowering. Mendelian segregation
had given it a double dose of the China gene for continuous
flowering, and it was a beautiful semi-double Rose with brilliant
rose-coloured flowers, and nearly evergreen foliage. From its
Damask grandparent it inherited a delicious fragrance which was
particularly marked in the late autumn months.

   During its reign of about half a century from 1820 to 1870 the
Bourbon Rose contributed much to the development of our
garden Roses. Crossed with Hume's Blush China it helped to
create our Pink Tea Roses, and it was the main source of the
typical Hybrid Perpetuals which, after all, were only the Bourbon
writ large. In 1825 the remarkable Bourbon 'Gloire des Rosomanes' appeared with its perennial scarlet-crimson flowers, and
vigorous habit of growth, and became the chief ancestor of the
scarlet and crimson Hybrid Perpetuals with their rich Damask
fragrance. Although from the first the Bourbon was a distinct
type of Rose with its stout prickly stems, vivid rose-coloured
flowers with rounded imbricated petals and broad leathery
leaves, various breaks occurred from time to time through
segregation as well as through hybridization. Between 1834 and
1841 the China reversion 'Hermosa' appeared independently with
four different breeders, and it is unlikely that all these were due
to a China back-cross. In 1831 the Bourbon-Noisette 'Mme
Desprez' appeared, adding purple to the rose colour which, in
1839, became a vivid crimson in 'Dr Rocques' (Crimson Globe).
'Mme Desprez' added to her laurels in 1842 by producing that
wonderful Bourbon Rose 'Souvenir de la Malmaison', which in
its turn produced the popular 'Gloire de Dijon'. In both cases
the other parent was a Tea Rose, and as in the case of the Noisette
repeated crossings with the Tea Roses towards the middle of
the nineteenth century completely changed the character of the
original Bourbon and improved it out of existence. Both the
original Bourbon and 'Souvenir de la Malmaison' are triploids

with twenty-one chromosomes, while 'Gloire de Dijon' is a tetraploid with twenty-eight.

H. THE TEA ROSE (*Rosa gigantea* Collett)
Hume's Blush and Parks's Yellow Chinas × Bourbons and Noisettes

The first typical Pink Tea Rose, appropriately enough, was
called 'Adam', and was raised by a florist of that name at Rheims
in 1833. Its characters are intermediate between those of Hume's
Blush China and the original Bourbon, and it is no doubt a hybrid
between them.

The first typical Yellow Tea Rose was raised in England in the
same year and was called Smith's Yellow; this was a cross made
between the Blush Noisette and Parks's Yellow China in an
attempt to raise a Yellow Noisette and was duly sent out as such.
Later, Foster of Devonport back-crossed the Yellow China with
Smith's Yellow, and raised in 1838 the beautiful Tea 'Devonien-
sis' with its thick creamy-white petals, pale straw-pink centre, and
sweet fragrance. In 1839 appeared the remarkable Tea Rose
'Safrano', with the outside petals bright rose and the inner petals
butter-yellow; it appears to have been raised from Parks's Yellow
China crossed with Noisette 'Desprez'. 'Safrano' became the
head of a special line of yellow and copper Teas, including 'Mme
Falcot' (1858), 'Perle des Jardins' (1874), and many others.
Various inter-crossings between the yellow Noisette-Teas and the
pink Bourbon-Teas gave rise between 1840 and 1890 to the most
exquisite Roses ever produced, but after that date they gradually
lost their typical qualities by crossings with the new Hybrid Teas
which they had helped to make, and today the typical Tea Rose
has disappeared from general cultivation. All the typical Teas
examined are diploid with fourteen chromosomes, except 'Gloire
de Dijon', which is tetraploid. The later Tea 'Lady Hillingdon'
(1910) is a triploid with twenty-one chromosomes, and is not a
true Tea.

It is to be hoped that the old Tea will be revived, if only for
crossing with the new Pernet and Poulsen Roses. We cannot
afford to lose its valuable breeding qualities of colour, form, and
fragrance.

J. HYBRID CHINAS
Chinas, Noisettes, and Bourbons × French, Provence, Damask, and other Summer Roses

Early in the nineteenth century the term Hybrid China was used in a special sense to cover all hybrids between the perennial and the summer-flowering groups. At that time nearly all the Roses grown in gardens were summer-flowering, and of these the so-called French Rose (R. *rubra* Blackw.[1]) held pride of place, with more than a thousand varieties in all the colours of the period. When the ever-blooming China came and was considered sufficiently hardy to plant outside about 1810, it was only natural that hybrids began to appear, and in 1815 the first two Hybrid Chinas came to light. The first was raised in England by Brown of Slough from Hume's Blush China fertilized by a French Rose, and was known as Brown's 'Superb Blush'. The second was one of Descemet's 10,000 seedlings rescued by Vibert, when the allied armies marched on Paris, and was known as 'Zulmé' or 'Bengale Descemet'. Up to 1830 about forty varieties of Hybrid Chinas appeared in France and two in England. Towards 1830 four superior varieties were produced which are particularly interesting to us, since they became the actual parents of the large Hybrid Perpetuals. One of these was 'Malton', a China-French hybrid, while the other three were 'Brennus', 'Athalin', and 'Général Allard', which were Bourbon-French hybrids. In flowers and foliage these varieties combined almost all that was beautiful in Roses but, like all the Hybrid Chinas without exception, they failed in one important character. They flowered only once a year owing to the Mendelian dominance of the gene for summer-flowering over the recessive gene for continuous flowering. These four Hybrid Chinas were all tetraploid with twenty-eight chromosomes, while the original Hybrid China was triploid with twenty-one.

K. HYBRID PERPETUALS
Hybrid Chinas × Portlands, Bourbons, and Noisettes

The first Hybrid Perpetual was the famous 'Rose du Roi', raised in 1816 by Souchet in the garden of the king at Sèvres,

[1] 1757. Syn. R. *gallica* L. 1759 (*non* 1753).

St Cloud, Paris, from the original Portland Rose whose history is chequered and somewhat obscure. It is known to have been in Dupont's nursery in Paris in 1809, and that Dupont obtained it from England and named it after the Duchess of Portland, who probably found it or obtained it from Italy early in the century. In England it was known as the *Rosa Paestana* or 'Scarlet Four Seasons', and was said to have been brought from Italy from the neighbourhood of the classic Paestum. The Portland Rose was a bright red verging on scarlet, and if treated well and pruned in a certain way it flowered twice a year, in summer and autumn. It was generally regarded as a cross between the French Rose and the Autumn Damask. Judging from Redouté's accurate figure of 1817 it is evidently a China-Damask-French hybrid which may well have originated in Italy, where, owing to the favourable climate, the China Roses had been largely cultivated in the open ever since their introduction about 1798. From the colour and dwarf habit of the Portland it may be presumed that the China parent concerned was Slater's Crimson China.

The 'Rose du Roi', with its charming crimson flowers, very double and very fragrant, and above all its continuous flowering throughout the season without special treatment and pruning, was certainly a great advance on its Portland parent, and it reigned supreme until the coming of the larger Hybrid Perpetuals in 1837, which displaced the smaller Portland and Bourbon Hybrid Perpetuals.

The fortunate raiser of these large-flowered Hybrid Perpetuals was Laffay, the well-known Rose breeder of Auteuil, who introduced the first typical Hybrid Perpetual 'Princesse Hélène' in 1837; he followed this up with 'Mme Laffay' and 'Duchess of Sutherland' in 1839, and finally crowned his successes in 1842 with that famous 'Rose de la Reine', with its large, strangely cupped flowers of a beautiful lilac-rose and fragrant as a Cabbage Rose. From 1837 to 1843 Laffay produced eighteen Hybrid Perpetuals of merit, and it is understood that all these were raised from seeds of the Hybrid Chinas (mostly Bourbon-French) selfed, and crossed with Portlands and Bourbons. In this way pairs of the recessive genes for continuous flowering were brought together and the Hybrid Perpetuals created. This also explains why many of the earlier and some of the later Hybrid Perpetuals sent out were not truly perpetual. From 1840 other breeders joined in, and in 1851 a new type appeared in 'Victor Verdier' from a Bourbon-Tea cross. In 1852 'Jules Margottin' and the famous 'Général Jacqueminot' arrived, the former a Brennus perpetual (Hybrid China selfed) and the latter a descendant of the Bourbon 'Gloire des Rosomanes'. 'The General', with its brilliant scarlet-crimson flowers and damask fragrance was a fertile tetraploid, and left a host of descendants of a similar type. From 1840 to 1890 the Hybrid Perpetual completely dominated the outside Rose garden until it was gradually replaced by the Hybrid Tea, which it helped to make. All the Hybrid Perpetuals examined are regular tetraploids with twenty-eight chromosomes, show traces of hybridity in their weak pairings, and are sterile to some degree.

L. HYBRID TEAS
Hybrid Perpetuals × Teas

The first Hybrid Tea was the favourite Rose 'La France', which was raised by Guillot in 1867 out of the Hybrid Perpetual 'Mme Victor Verdier' by the Tea 'Mme Bravy'. It was a worthy representative of its class with its silvery lilac-pink flowers of excellent shape and delicious fragrance. It combined the free-flowering habit, fine shape, and delicate colouring of the Tea with the hardiness and vigorous growth of the Hybrid Perpetual. In 1873 'Cheshunt Hybrid' and 'Captain Christy' appeared, but it was not until 1884 that the Hybrid Tea was recognized as a new group distinct from the Hybrid Perpetuals. Up to 1895, when 'Mme Abel Chatenay' and 'Mrs W. J. Grant' appeared, Hybrid Teas were mostly bred on the original lines, but afterwards they were not only bred *inter se*, but also back-crossed to the Hybrid Perpetual, giving 'Liberty', 'Richmond', and other red bedding and decorative Roses.

In 1905 the Hybrid Teas began to change their original characters owing to their hybridization with the new Pernet Rose which appeared in 1900. At first the influence of the Pernet Roses on the Hybrid Teas was slight, but gradually year by year the Pernet characters permeated the Hybrid Teas in geometrical progression, so that at the present time it is rare to see an original Hybrid Tea among the new Roses without a trace of the Pernet influence.

These Roses are still called Hybrid Teas, but they have lost their original characters. The cause of this revolution is that for the first time in a century a new species, R. *lutea* Miller, has been incorporated with our garden Roses.

All the Hybrid Teas examined prove to be tetraploid with twenty-eight chromosomes.

M. THE PERNET ROSE [1]

Hybrid Perpetual × *Austrian Briar* (R. *lutea* Miller) [2]

The twentieth century, like the nineteenth, opened with the introduction of a new species to the garden Roses of the period. Last century it was R. *chinensis* from China, with its habit of continuous flowering, this century it is R. *lutea* from Persia, with its brilliant yellow flowers. Both species have revolutionized our garden Roses as no other species have done during the two centuries. R. *lutea* Miller is an ancient cultivated species grown by the Saracens in Syria, Tripoli, Tunis, and Egypt in the twelfth century, and in the same period cultivated by the Arabs and Moors in Spain, who had a tradition that it was brought from Persia in the seventh century. It is no doubt an oriental species, and has been reported in a wild state from the Crimea through Asia Minor and Persia to Turkestan, and even in the Punjab, Afghanistan, and Tibet. Some of these, however, may be garden escapes, since it has been found in several places in Europe growing apparently wild. It was figured by Gesner in 1542, Lobel in 1581, Dodonaeus in 1583, and exactly described by Dalechamps in 1587. Clusius found it in Austria towards 1583 and introduced it to the Netherlands and England, where it has been known ever since as the Austrian Briar. There were two forms of this, the Austrian Yellow and the Austrian Copper, both well-known garden plants. The Yellow is the ordinary R. *lutea*, while the Copper is a bicolor form with the petals of two distinct colours, brilliant nasturtium-red on the upper inner surface and shaded yellow on the lower outer surface, the general effect being a coppery-red. Cornuti in 1635 and Miller in 1768 gave this form

---

[1] The rules of nomenclature prevent the use of 'Pernetiana'.

[2] Since there is a doubt about Herrmann's older name R. *foetida* of 1762 I am using the next oldest name, which is Miller's R. *lutea* of 1768.

specific rank under the name of R. *punicea*, and Jacquin in 1770 as R. *bicolor*. We now know that the Copper is simply a bud-sport of the Yellow, and that often the two colours may be found on the same bush. This explains why so many of our dazzling Pernet Roses, bred from the yellow, present this fantastic bicolor effect. The Pernet Roses originally came from the Persian Yellow Rose, which appears to be only a double form of R. *lutea*. It was brought from Persia by Sir Henry Willock in 1838.

After a thousand years of cultivation in gardens R. *lutea* had become notoriously sterile in both seeds and pollen, and it was no easy matter to incorporate the species with the partially sterile garden Roses. All the more credit is therefore due to the persistent and untiring efforts of that great Rose breeder Pernet-Ducher of Lyon, which were ultimately crowned with success. From 1883 to 1888 he patiently and persistently crossed thousands of Hybrid Perpetuals with pollen of Persian Yellow, following a fixed idea of his own. All these crosses failed except one with 'Antoine Ducher', which gave him a few seeds in 1888. 'Antoine Ducher', the grandmother of the Pernet Rose, was just an ordinary Hybrid Perpetual raised by Ducher in 1866 with large, full, shining rose-red flowers and a strong old rose fragrance.

Two hybrids were reared and the first flowered in 1891. This was interesting in its preponderance of the paternal *lutea* characters, but being completely sterile it took no part in the creation of the Pernet race, and was sent out as a Pillar Rose under the name of 'Rhodophile Gravereaux'. The other plant first flowered in 1893, but it was not until 1894 that it showed itself in its true colours. On the whole it was more like the mother Hybrid Perpetual in its habit of growth, large globular full flowers shaded with rose, and in its delicious old rose fragrance. On the other hand, it resembled the father *lutea* in its red-brown wood, prickles, rounded leaflets, solitary flowers with bicolor petals which were orange-red within and golden-yellow without, and in its summer-flowering. This unnamed seedling was retained by Pernet as a breeder, and when mated with Hybrid Teas produced in the second generation the first Pernet Rose, 'Soleil d'Or', and many which followed it. As in the cases of the Noisette and the Bourbon the second generation was necessary to fix the continuous flowering in the race, in accordance with Mendel's Laws. 'Soleil d'Or' was first exhibited at Lyon in 1898, and was sent out in 1900 as a forerunner of the Pernet Roses of the twentieth century. After forty years' breeding the Pernet Roses have become thoroughly incorporated with the Hybrid Teas, and have revolutionized their colours and colour patterns. One of the chief contributions made by the Pernet Rose is the production of deep yellow Roses, much deeper and richer, but perhaps not so refined as the paler yellow of the Tea Rose. That was Pernet-Ducher's original aim in bringing in *lutea*, and his object has been achieved. No one, however, could have foreseen the myriads of new shades, tones, and patterns of colours which have been created in our garden Roses by the simple introduction of a yellow species. The peculiar glistening foliage and the numerous exaggerated prickles of the Pernet Roses are also rather unexpected in the product, constituting as they do new types of foliage and prickles which in a wild species we should probably regard as specific. Early in the century there was another side to the picture. Side by side with the good qualities of *lutea* introduced by the Pernets there were naturally some bad ones, such as bad constitution and winter die-back, liability to Black Spot, and consequent early loss of leaves, flat-topped and quartered flowers, lack of fragrance or presence of disagreeable odours, and complete sterility of seeds and pollen. Fortunately by careful breeding with the best Hybrid Teas and rigid selection these faults have largely disappeared in the latest Pernet-Hybrid Teas that are now being bred for the dual purpose of garden decoration and exhibition.

Since both R. *lutea* Persian Yellow and the Hybrid Perpetual 'Antoine Ducher' are tetraploids with twenty-eight chromosomes it follows that Pernet-Ducher's two hybrids of the first generation are also tetraploid. 'Soleil d'Or' and the 'Lyon-Rose' have been examined and both found to be tetraploid with fourteen pairs. The chromosomes of both varieties show signs of hybridity, and the pollen is defective. The same may be said of R. *lutea* Austrian Yellow and its bud-sport Austrian Copper, in which I found only about 5 per cent of fertile pollen.

N. THE POLY-POMPON ROSE[1]

Japanese Multiflora × *Dwarf Pink China*

R. *multiflora* Thunb. × (R. *chinensis* Jacq. × R. *gigantea* Collett)

About 1860 Jean Sisley of Lyon received from his son in Japan seeds of the wild R. *multiflora* of Thunberg, a strong climbing Rose with single white flowers, which was quite different from the Chinese Multiflora of gardens, which had pink or crimson double flowers. Guillot, the famous Rose breeder of Lyon, planted some of these Japanese Multifloras in his nursery, and in 1868 saved seeds from them. The result was a medley of forms in the flowers, large and small; single, semi-double, and full; white, rose, and cream; but all were climbers and summer-flowering like the mother parent, and all closely resembled the Noisette Rose in their wood and foliage. One of these had large, tinged white flowers with two rows of petals and produced good seeds, which were sown in 1872, and thus produced in the second generation the first two Poly-Poms., 'Paquerette' and 'Mignonette'. Both varieties were dwarf Pompons a few inches high, while their fellows in the same batch of seedlings were tall climbers several feet high like their mother parent. Both were continuous in their flowering right through the season from May to December from their first year, while their tall fellows were summer-flowering in their second year. 'Paquerette' was a pure white, while 'Mignonette' was rosy-pink and white; both combined the characters of *multiflora* and the Dwarf Pink China, and it is evident that in 1868 the original Japanese Multifloras were naturally fertilized with Dwarf Pink Chinas, which at that time were commonly grown in the Lyon nurseries as specimens.

This Dwarf Pink China was known in the Lyon nurseries as Bengale Pompon, and was raised in England in 1805, where it was known as R. *Lawranceana* or the Fairy Rose. The first Poly-Pom., 'Paquerette', was exhibited at Lyon in 1873 and distributed in 1875. 'Mignonette' was not sent out until 1881, but it became the chief ancestor of most of our modern varieties through its remarkable offspring 'Gloire de Polyantha' (1887), and its line of 'Mme Norbert Levavasseur' (1903), 'Orleans Rose' (1909), 'Edith Cavell' (1917), and 'Coral Cluster' (1921).

[1] The rules of nomenclature prevent the use of 'Polyantha' or 'Floribunda'.

In 1880 'Cécile Brunner' and 1883 'Perle d'Or' introduced the characters of the Tea Rose.[1] In 1903 the well-known Crimson Rambler became an ancestor of the Poly-Poms., and in 1911 'Dorothy Perkins' entered the list. In 1920 the Pernet Rose was introduced by 'Rayon d'Or', giving the Poly-Pom. 'Evaline'. One of the most popular Poly-Poms. of today is 'Éblouissant' (1918), which is a pure China descended from a dwarf Crimson China, and is about the smallest of the Poly-poms. 'Yvonne Rabier' (1910), derived from the Japanese species R. *wichuraiana* with its pure white flowers and handsome glossy foliage, is still a popular variety. Most of the modern varieties, however, while retaining their dwarf habit and continuous flowering, produce their flowers in tight bunches of rosettes of the Crimson Rambler type.

All the Poly-Poms. examined prove to be diploid with fourteen chromosomes. The original 'Paquerette' and its ancestral species R. *chinensis*, R. *gigantea*, and R. *multiflora* are all diploid.

The Pernet and *lutea* Poly-Poms. have not been examined, but they may be expected to be triploids with twenty-one chromosomes.

O. THE POULSEN ROSE.[2]

Poly-Pom. × Hybrid Tea

In 1924 a new and distinct group of garden Roses appeared from Denmark, and caused quite a sensation in British and American Rose circles. They were originated by the Danish Rose breeder Poulsen by crossing the Poly-Pom. with a Hybrid Tea. He crossed the Poly-Pom. 'Orleans Rose' with pollen of the Hybrid Tea 'Red Star' and raised therefrom two seedlings of similar type and habit of growth, but with very different flowers. Both were vigorous growers, producing large open clusters of flowers on long stems, which in 'Else Poulsen' were amaranth-pink with carmine reverse and semi-double, while those of 'Kirsten Poulsen' were bright cherry-scarlet and single.

---

[1] These varieties are now classed with the Poulsen Roses owing to their taller habit of growth.

[2] The rules of nomenclature prevent the use of 'Polyantha' or 'Floribunda'. ('Floribunda' is now accepted as a group name for these large-flowered 'polyanthas'. G.S.T.)

In 1928 'Greta Poulsen' appeared with rich crimson-pink flowers, while in 1930 'D. T. Poulsen', with deep blood-red flowers which are not very lasting, proved rather a disappointment. In 1932 this was amply made up by the appearance of the remarkable 'Karen Poulsen' with dazzling scarlet single flowers which defy description. This Rose was raised by Poulsen out of 'Kirsten Poulsen' by pollen of 'Vesuvius'. In 1935 in 'Anne Poulsen' there came a development towards the Hybrid Tea which seems to be a move away from the typical Poulsen Rose. Its flowers are a lovely velvety crimson with a delightful fragrance, but the blooms are large and full, produced in small clusters, and the general habit is not so vigorous. A similar type appeared in 1939 in 'Poulsen's Copper' with flowers rosy-cerise on a copper base, large and double in small clusters, but the growth is vigorous. The latest Poulsen Roses to appear are 'Poulsen's Pink' and 'Poulsen's Yellow', which seem to be a similar type. The future will show if these are to displace the original type, and other breeders are now taking a hand on somewhat different lines. The chromosomes of the Poulsens have not been examined, but most should be triploids with twenty-one.

GENERAL

Space will not allow me to deal with the evolution and development of various minor groups of garden Roses, in which so many different species have been concerned in the nineteenth and twentieth centuries. Ayrshire Roses from R. *arvensis* Huds., Evergreen Roses from R. *sempervirens* L., Sweet Briars from R. *Eglanteria* Mill., Scotch Roses from R. *spinosissima* L., Banksian Roses from R. *Banksiae* Ait., Prairie Roses from R. *setigera* Michx., Musk Roses from R. *moschata* Miller, Rugosa Roses from R. *rugosa* Thunb., Macartney Roses from R. *bracteata* Wendl., Cherokee Roses from R. *laevigata* Michx., Microphylla Roses from R. *microphylla* Roxb., Multiflora Climbers from R. *multiflora* Thunb., **Wichuraiana Climbers from R. *wichuraiana* Crép., and the old** cultivated Roses of American species which, crossed with the China Rose, gave us the Old Boursault Roses which for more than a century have passed as hybrids of R. *alpina* L. All these interesting garden Roses must be left for future articles.

In conclusion, we find that the major groups of our garden Roses are descended from seven main species, namely: R. *rubra* Blackw., R. *phoenicea* Boiss., R. *moschata* Miller, R. *canina* L., R. *chinensis* Jacq., R. *gigantea* Collett, and R. *lutea* Miller. The specific characters of these species can still be traced in our garden Roses, and it is the happy combinations of these various characters that have given us the manifold beauties of the Rose.

FIRST STAGES IN THE EVOLUTION
OF GARDEN ROSES IN EUROPE

PRE–1800

by Gordon D. Rowley after Hurst, 1941 and MSS.

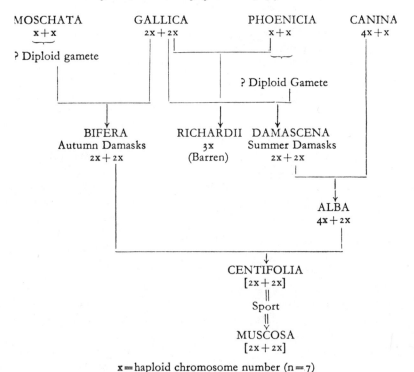

x = haploid chromosome number (n = 7)

FIG. 1

Note on Fig. 1

The earliest stages in the evolution of garden roses have long excited speculation, which until recently had no more foundation than the fancied resemblances of long-cultivated garden roses to certain of the wild species. It was not until 1920, when cytology, the study of chromosomes, was first applied to the Rose, that these speculations could be tried and tested. Great credit is due to Dr C. C. Hurst (and no less to his widow, Mrs R. Hurst) for realizing the value of chromosome studies, and using them to supplement his great morphological and historical survey of Rose history. The article reprinted on pages 59–94 gives an outline of his findings, but it is only a summary of a much greater work which he unfortunately never lived to publish. However, further chromosome studies of garden roses by Miss A. P. Wylie, of Manchester University, will doubtless fill in many of the missing details.

Hurst's work forms the basis of the two family trees shown in Figs. 1 and 2. The former epitomizes his solution of the difficult problem of the early stages. It is but one of many possible solutions, and as such must still be regarded as pure speculation, but at least it is feasible in the light of existing knowledge of rose chronology and breeding behaviour.

All that it lacks is experimental proof—the re-synthesis of the ancestral hybrids from their wild parent species. To make and rear sufficient crosses to attempt this recapitulation of Rose history is an ambitious and lengthy, but not impossible, task. It is, in fact, one of the aims of the National Rose Species Collection at Bayfordbury, in Hertfordshire, where likely combinations of wild species are being made and raised under carefully controlled conditions.

G. D. R.

Note on Fig. 2 (overleaf)

From chromosome counts taken since this figure was drawn, Mr Rowley tells me that the Boursault roses are unlikely to have been derived from *R. pendulina*, but most probably from *R. blanda*.

G. S. T. 1978

SIMPLIFIED GENEALOGY OF THE MAIN GROUPS
OF GARDEN ROSES
by Gordon D. Rowley after Hurst, 1941

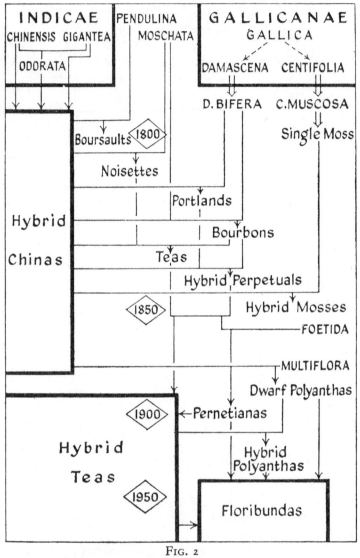

Fig. 2

A single line indicates hybridization.
A double line indicates sporting.
A dotted line indicates possible relationship.

SIMPLIFIED GENEALOGY

MAIN GROUPS OF GARDEN ROSES

Note on Fig. 2

Any attempt at a two-dimensional family tree of garden roses (Fig. 2) is bound to be an over-simplification of the facts. The impression it gives of new groups springing into being by the union of old, whilst true in a broad sense, requires a word of explanation. The first members of a new group, like the earliest Hybrid Teas, are usually very distinct from anything that has gone before, and were in fact selected by their raisers for combining the best features of widely dissimilar parents. Later introductions, however, include backcrosses and hybrids combining characters of three and more groups, so that even where their pedigrees are known their grouping under one name or another is barely possible.

True, the dominant groups in favour at any time over the past one hundred and fifty years show genetic continuity, from the Portlands and Hybrid Perpetuals, through the Hybrid Teas, to the modern Hybrid Polyanthas and Floribundas. But concurrently with these ran many smaller alliances, sometimes centering round other species such as R. *rugosa*, R. *spinosissima*, or R. *rubiginosa*.

The tendency in recent years has been to interbreed both major and minor groups, and blur the outlines of the older recognized types. Hence the modern dilemma over Floribundas, and the growing awareness that distinctions based on ancestry will largely have to be forsaken in favour of simple, artificial classifications based on habit, flower size and grouping, and so on.

The concept of a family 'tree' does not, therefore, give an ideal picture of rose evolution in the garden and nursery. Rather we should visualize a delicate sponge—a network in which the branches diverge and reunite, sometimes coming to a dead end (through sterility or just neglect), sometimes picking up a new strand (as when a new species makes its debut).

Nor can our genealogy ever near completion while so many roses are of unrecorded parentage. Truly it has been said that 'the fascination of pedigree-hunting no doubt lies in its inscrutable conundrums'.

G. D. R.

NOTES ON THE ORIGIN OF THE MOSS ROSE

by C. C. HURST, SC.D., PH.D. (CANTAB.), F.L.S., *and*
MABEL S. G. BREEZE, B.SC.

IN 1908 experiments were undertaken at Burbage to investigate the genetics of certain variable species and garden hybrids of *Rosa* (Hurst, 1911).[1] These experiments were continued until the outbreak of war in 1914, when more urgent affairs demanded priority, and it was not until 1919 that it was possible to resume the experiments and to prepare a report on what had been done. Among the many interesting problems in the genetics of *Rosa*, the question of the Moss Rose presented itself as one of outstanding interest from many points of view. But before attacking the problem genetically it seemed necessary to trace as far as possible the history of the original Moss Rose, its direct descendants, and its parent species. The following notes represent the more important results of these researches.

Characters peculiar to the Moss Rose

The original Moss Rose, R. *muscosa* of Miller (1768), appears to be identical in all its external characters with the old Cabbage Rose, R. *centifolia* (Linnaeus, 1753), except that it possesses the following additional characters: The stems, branches, petioles, stipules, pedicels, peduncles, and calyx-tubes are densely covered with irregular aciculi and glandular branched bristles, while the sepals are copiously compound and covered on the back and edges with multitudinous branched gland-edged mossy processes, which give off a resinous or balsamic odour when bruised. In other words, the Moss Rose differs from the Cabbage Rose in its multiplicity of glandular organs. It is important, however, to note that the difference is not simply that of presence or absence of glands, for the Cabbage Rose is glandular in parts, e.g. petioles, stipules, peduncles, and sepals. Nor is it a difference merely of many or few glands, nor even of more extended or less extended glandular areas. It is also a difference of compound or simple

---

[1] Names and dates in brackets refer to the bibliography at the end of this paper.

glands, and these are multitudinous partly on account of the extension and increased density of the glandular areas, but mainly through the multiplicate branching of the gland-bearing organs (cf. Blondel, 1889).

Whether the presence of these additional characters in the Moss Rose entitles it to specific rank, or whether it should be regarded as a variety of R. *centifolia* L. is a question concerning which systematists are divided. Miller, who appears to have been the first to describe the Moss Rose fully (1760), gives it specific rank under the name of R. *muscosa* (1768), which is accepted by the following: Du Roi (1772), Retzius (1779), Curtis (1793), Willldenow (1799), Aiton (1789) (1811), Lawrance (1799), Rössig (1802), Andrews (1805), Persoon (1807), Deleuze and Desfontaines (1809), Thory and Redouté (1817), and Prévost (1829); on the other hand, the following authorities regard the Moss Rose as a variety of R. *centifolia* L. (or its synonym R. *provincialis* Mill.): Linnaeus (1762), Dumont de Courset (1805), Smith (1815), Seringe (1818), Lindley (1820), Guimpel (1825), Rössig (1826), Crépin (1892), and Willmott (1912).

Some modern authors, e.g. Regel (1877), Dippel (1893), Köhne (1893), Bois (1896), Rehder (1902), and Schneider (1906), place both the Moss Rose and R. *centifolia* L. under R. *gallica* L.

Characters common to the Moss Rose and the Cabbage Rose

Whatever the systematic status of the Moss Rose may be, one thing is certain, all authorities agree that the old Moss Rose and the old Cabbage Rose are closely allied. Anyone who has seen the two growing side by side, and has carefully examined them, must acknowledge that they have many characters in common, which are quite distinct from any other species or sub-species. For example, both have very double globular flowers, which are red in the bud and rose-pink when open. Both have about a hundred short and broad petals, which are closely incurved and rolled inwards towards the centre, which is frequently quartered like a crown. Both yield the same distinctive fragrance from the petals, which is peculiar to R. *centifolia* L. and distinct from the fragrance of R. *gallica* L. (The resinous and balsamic odour from the mossy glands of the Moss Rose is naturally much more powerful than the odour from the same area in the Cabbage Rose, which is but faint.) Both have cernuous or nodding flowers, usually solitary or up to three only, unlike those of R. *damascena* Mill., which are usually erect and many, in corymbs or clusters. Both have the sepals spreading and persistent, not reflexed and deciduous as in R. *damascena* Mill. and R. *gallica* L. Both have a medium habit of growth, not so tall and prickly as R. *damascena* Mill., nor so dwarf and bushy as R. *gallica* L. Both have leaves softer to the touch than the more rigid and coriaceous leaves of R. *gallica* L. and the allied forms. Last, but not least in importance, both the old Moss Rose and the old Cabbage Rose are sterile, inasmuch as neither develops perfect fruits (which all the allied species do as a rule), and neither has been known to produce fertile seeds so far as we can ascertain. So far, all attempts to obtain seed from the old Moss Rose and the old Cabbage Rose at Burbage have failed, both outside and under glass, though miniature fruits were sometimes obtained containing no seeds.[1] In view of the fact that some apparently good pollen was found and that some of the styles appeared to be normal and not petaloid, the result is so far unexpected. From the genetic point of view the sterility of the old Moss Rose is a serious disadvantage, but this difficulty is not insuperable, as will be seen later. A full discussion of this important question of sterility must be deferred for a time, and for the present we simply record the fact.

History of the old Cabbage Rose (R. *centifolia* L.) [2]

The old Cabbage Rose has been freely cultivated in European fields and gardens for more than two thousand years. About 450 B.C. Herodotus observes that the Roses growing in Macedonia, near the gardens of Midas, have sixty petals, and are the most fragrant in the world. This is a very neat description of the Cabbage Rose, and at the same time a critical one, because it is difficult to conceive how such a description can be applied to any other known species of *Rosa*. A century later Theophrastus, the first historian of the Rose, mentions the Roses with a hundred petals, and calls them *Centifolia*. In the first century Pliny, who

---

[1] In 1921 a few fruits matured under glass, and one contained a seed, the germination of which has not yet been tested.

[2] Readers will realize, on reading Dr Hurst's notes on page 70, that he subsequently revised some of these opinions on the origin of the old Cabbage Rose.

devotes a whole chapter to Roses, repeats the observations of Theophrastus, and adds that the *Rosa Centifolia* grows at Campania in Italy, and near Philippi, a city in Greece (Macedonia). He also states that these Centifolia Roses grow naturally on Mount Panfaeus close by, with a hundred leaves but small, and when transplanted into richer soil do thrive mightily, and prove to be much fairer than those growing on the mountain; all of which seems quite natural. From other classic authors we learn that vast numbers of Rose petals were used by the Greeks and Romans for their decorations and festivities, and it is reasonable to suppose that the Cabbage Rose with its hundred petals and delicious fragrance was cultivated for this purpose in the fields of Italy, Greece, and Macedonia. In these circumstances it does not necessarily follow that the Cabbage Rose is a true native of the south of Europe, as many of the early authorities conclude (Smith, 1815); on the other hand, it appears more probable, as Lindley (1820) believed, that the Cabbage Rose was introduced into Europe from Asia at a remote period. As a matter of fact, early in the nineteenth century Bieberstein (1808) found the Cabbage Rose growing apparently wild on the eastern side of the Caucasus, on the borders of Armenia and Persia. Rau (1816) states that it is a native of northern Persia, and Boissier (1872) gives the habitat as eastern Caucasus, while according to Loureiro (1790) it is a native of China.

Notwithstanding these records we are inclined to believe that the Cabbage Rose has been cultivated in the fields and gardens of Asia from time immemorial, and that its native country can only be surmised. The fact of its sterility suggests an origin under cultivation, and it is worthy of note that R. *centifolia* L. does not 'stool' so freely as R. *gallica* L., nor does it root so well from cuttings and layers as R. *damascena* Mill., so that its chances of survival and increase in a wild state would be very small. The fact that the habitats given are on the borders of or in Persia is also significant, for Persia is a country which has been famous for its fragrant Roses from the earliest times. Flückiger (1862) refers to a Persian document in the National Library in Paris which states that in the year 810 the province of Farsistan was required to pay an annual tribute of 30,000 bottles of Rose-water to the Treasury of Baghdad. The most important cultivations of Roses for distilling Rose-water were near Shiraz, and are 'even to this day'

(Flückiger, 1883). Lindley (1820) in commenting on the celebrated Roses of Shiraz, praised so enthusiastically by Kaempfer (1712), suggests that the Rose of Shiraz may be the Cabbage Rose (R. *centifolia* L.) or possibly R. *damascena* Mill. It was at Shiraz that one of the manuscripts of the *Rubáiyát* of Omar Khayyám was transcribed in 1460. The immortal Persian poet and philosopher, who flourished in the eleventh and twelfth centuries, was a passionate lover of the Rose—as well of the Vine—and red, white, yellow, and flesh-coloured Roses are referred to in the Rubaiyát.

It is related by FitzGerald (1859) that one day in a garden Omar Khayyám said to one of his pupils, Khwajah Nizami of Samarcand, 'My tomb shall be in a spot where the North wind may scatter Roses over it', and it was so, for on his grave at Naishapur a Rose-tree was planted. In Willmott (1914) the late Dr J. G. Baker (whose botanical knowledge of Roses was unrivalled) relates how a hip of this Rose was brought home by Mr Simpson, the artist of the *Illustrated London News*, and sent to Kew by the late Mr Bernard Quaritch, from which seedlings were raised which proved to be R. *damascena* Mill., a species, as we have seen, that is allied to the Cabbage Rose, R. *centifolia* L., but distinct from it. All of which goes to confirm Lindley's conjecture, that the celebrated Rose of Shiraz may have been one of these species. The date of the introduction of the Cabbage Rose to England is unknown; it may have come during the Roman occupation of Britain with the 'English' Elm, or it may have come later through the monastery and convent gardens, in which, according to Amherst (1895), Roses were cultivated as far back as the eleventh century, in the reign of William Rufus. On the authority of Anselm it is related that the Red King, in order to see the twelve-year-old Matilda at the convent of Romsey, entered the convent on the pretext of looking at the roses in the garden.

The late Canon Ellacombe (1905) believed that the Cabbage Rose was certainly in cultivation in England in the fifteenth century and probably earlier. He identifies it with the 'Rose of Rone' of Chaucer, and with the 'Provincial Rose' of Shakespeare, and adds that the name of this Rose would be more properly written 'Provence or Provins'. It is a curious fact that at Burbage the old Cabbage Rose for eighty years at least has been more commonly called and known as the 'Red Province', which is the old name used by the English Herbalists, Gerard (1596), Parkin-son (1629), and Salmon (1710). Apparently Miller (1733) was the first to change 'Province' to 'Provence', though he still retained *provincialis* for the Latin name. It may be that the old name for the Cabbage Rose, 'Red Province', has lingered on in remote country districts for centuries, like that archaic word of Chaucer, 'glede', which is still in common use at Burbage to signify the glowing embers in the fire. Baker in Willmott (1914) states that the first botanical figure of the Cabbage Rose (R. *centifolia* L.) is that of L'Obel (1581), who describes it under the name of R. *damascena maxima*. Gerard (1596) includes it in his catalogue of plants under the name of 'R. *damascena flore multiplici*, the Great Holland Rose, commonly called the Province Rose'. In his Herbal of 1597, how-ever, he describes and figures it under the name of 'R. *Hollandica sive Batava*, the Great Holland Rose or Great Province'. Clusius (1601) describes it under the name of R. *centifolia batavica*. Parkin-son (1629) describes fully and figures what is undoubtedly the Cabbage Rose under the name of 'R. *provincialis sive Hollandica Damascena*, the Great Double Damaske Province or Holland Rose, that some call *Centifolia Batavica incarnata*'.

Ellacombe (1905) suggested that Parkinson's (1629) 'R. *Anglica rubra*, the English Red Rose', is the Cabbage Rose, but the description 'abideth low and shooteth forth many branches from the roote . . . with a greene barke thinner set with prickles . . . red or deepe crimson colour . . . with many more yellow threds in the middle, the sent . . . is not comparable to the excellencie of the damaske Rose, yet this Rose being well dryed and well kept, will hold both colour and sent longer than the damaske, bee it never so well kept', seems to correspond precisely with the characters of R. *gallica* L., the old French Rose, and not at all with R. *centi-folia* L., the old Cabbage Rose.[1]

Ferrarius (1633), in Italy, describes the Cabbage Rose under the

[1] It is interesting to compare Parkinson's remarks above, concerning the drying properties of the 'English Red Rose', with the statement of a modern practical chemist, Sawer (1894), who states that 'the flowers of R. *gallica* (which are used officinally) are but feebly odoriferous when freshly gathered; their perfume develops gradually in the process of desiccation, while that of the Damask Rose is almost destroyed by drying'. From this it appears that there is a real physiological and chemical difference between R. *gallica* L. and R. *damascena* Mill., apart from their morphological differences which to some modern systematists appear to be negligible.

PLATE IV

TOP LEFT. More mystery has reigned over the white Moss Roses than over any others, and I am glad to record here the sporting in 1954 of the 'Perpetual White Damask Moss' back to a pink Autumn Damask, thus proving its identity. The true Moss Roses belong to *Rosa centifolia*, not to the Damasks. Recorded by Carrière in 1865. Cf. Pl. 19. (See page 161.)

TOP RIGHT. *Rosa gallica officinalis*, the Red Rose of Lancaster and its sport R. g. *versicolor* or 'Rosa Mundi'. See also Pls. 6 and 7. Two of the most spectacular and floriferous of all flowering shrubs, in cultivation for hundreds of years. (See page 148.)

BOTTOM LEFT. These flowers of 'York and Lancaster' were cut from one plant (R. *damascena versicolor*), showing the normal variations. First named in 1551. (See page 161.)

BOTTOM RIGHT. 'Léda' or the 'Painted Damask'. The top flower shews an excellent button eye. The red colouring of the buds remains on the edges of the expanded flowers, giving it the popular name. Early nineteenth century. (See page 158.)

name of R. *Batava centifolia*. Chabraeus (1677), in Switzerland, describes and figures it under the name of R. *centifolia rubella plena*. In her monograph of the genus *Rosa* (1914), Miss Ellen Willmott draws attention to the interesting fact that the Cabbage Rose was a favourite subject with the old Dutch painters, especially Van Huysum (1682–1749), who excelled in portraying it. Liger (1708), in France, mentions it under the name of 'La Rose d'Hollande a cent feuilles, avec odeur'. Salmon (1710) describes and figures it as 'The Great Double Damask Province, or Holland Rose'. Finally, Linnaeus (1753) describes the Cabbage Rose under its accepted name of R. *centifolia*. Miller (1768), owing to a misunderstanding of Linnaeus's diagnoses of 1753 and 1762 (which it must be admitted were not very clear) describes the Cabbage Rose under the name of R. *provincialis*, the Provence Rose, and others followed him. Fortunately Lindley (1820) cleared the matter up, and since then the Cabbage Rose has been known correctly under the original name of Linnaeus, R. *centifolia*. In conclusion it may be useful to mention that the most accurate and lifelike coloured drawing of the old Cabbage Rose is to be found in Redouté (1817). Miss Willmott (1912) considers this to be the most beautiful of all his wonderful drawings of Roses, and we agree.

History of the Old Moss Rose

The Old Moss Rose is of recent origin compared with the Cabbage Rose. Its mossy flower-buds and stalks, and bristly stems and branches, together form such a striking variation that its appearance could hardly fail to be noticed by even the most casual observer. So far as we can trace, no mention of it is made by any of the ancient authors who were familiar with the Cabbage Rose, nor do any of the old herbalists appear to have noted it. If it had been in existence in their day, the balsamic odour of its mossy glands would surely have attracted them in their search for medicinal virtues and specifics. Gerard (1596) does not mention the Moss Rose in his Catalogue of Plants, but Dr Daydon Jackson (1876), in his edition of Gerard's Catalogue, suggests that Gerard's R. *holosericea*, the Velvet Rose, may be the Moss Rose (R. *muscosa* Mill.). This plant is described and figured by Gerard (1597), and the flowers and fruits are described as 'double with some yellow thrums in the midst of a deepe and black red colour resembling red crimson velvet . . . when the flowers be faded there followe red berries full of hard seeds'. This description does not appear to correspond at all with the old Moss Rose which has pink flowers when expanded, and is so double that the stamens and styles are seldom exposed, and finally being sterile rarely, if ever, sets either fruits or seeds. The figure (which is identical with that of L'Obel, 1581) shows no trace of the familiar and striking mossiness, while the flowers are 'semi-single' (two rows of petals), with stamens and styles fully exposed, and it is bearing rounded fruits. Parkinson (1629) also gives figures of both the single and the double Velvet Rose. In his description he states that they have 'very few or no thorns at all upon them . . . very often seven flowers on a stalk . . . yet for all the double rowe of leaves these roses stand but like single flowers . . . all of them of a smaller sent than the ordinary red Rose'. Salmon (1710), after repeating Parkinson's description of the Single and Double Velvet Rose, states that 'there is another Velvet Rose much more double than the last, consisting oftentimes of sixteen leaves or more in a Rose, and most of them of an equal bigness, of the colour of the first single Velvet Rose or something brisker, but all of them of a weaker smell than the Common Red Rose'. Lawrance (1799) and Andrews (1805) figure both the Single and Double Velvet Rose under the name of R. *centifolia*, but both appear to be forms of R. *gallica* L., the old French Rose. Thory (1817) refers R. *holosericea* to R. *gallica* L., quoting L'Obel's figure which is the same as Gerard's. Finally Lindley (1820) refers R. *holosericea* to R. *gallica* L.

In any case, judging by the descriptions quoted above, it seems clear that whatever Gerard's Velvet Rose (R. *holosericea*) may have been, it was not the Moss Rose (R. *muscosa* Mill.),[1] and we can find no evidence that the Moss Rose was known in England in 1596, to support the repeated statements in the books on garden Roses from Rivers (1840) to Pemberton (1920), that it was introduced in that year from Holland.

So far as we know, there is no mention of the Moss Rose in Chaucer, Shakespeare, or in any literature of that period. Parkinson (1629) describes in detail twenty-eight forms of Roses, but none corresponds in any way to the Moss Rose. Ferrarius (1633)

[1] Dr Jackson, to whom I submitted this opinion, concurs.

in Italy, Chabraeus (1677) in Switzerland, Liger (1708) in France, and Salmon (1710) in England, give long lists, descriptions, and figures of various kinds of Roses, but there is no trace of the Moss Rose in any of them. There is, however, in Ducastel (1746), quoted by Paquet (1845) and Jamain and Forney (1873), a circumstantial account of the existence of the Moss Rose in the south of France, at Carcassonne, as far back as 1696, and this appears to be the earliest date mentioned for the existence of the Moss Rose. The account is that the Hundred-leaved Moss Rose was in cultivation in Cotentin, Messin, and La Manche in 1746, and that it was brought there by Fréard Ducastel, who had found it at Carcassonne, where it had been known for half a century.

The first botanical reference to the Moss Rose is apparently that of Boerhaave (1720) in his Index of Plants cultivated in the Physic Garden at Leyden under the name *Rosa rubra plena spinosissima, pedunculo muscosa*. In 1724 the Moss Rose is said to have been in cultivation in London, for Miller (1724) states that it is included in Robert Furber's Catalogue of Plants cultivated for sale at Kensington. Miller (1760) tells us that he first saw the Moss Rose 'in the year 1727, in the garden of Dr Boerhaave near Leyden, who was so good as to give me one of the plants'. On the whole we consider it safer to accept Miller's 1727 date.

Martyn (1807) refers to what is apparently the first figure of the Moss Rose in *Hort.-Angl.*, a *Catalogue of Trees, Shrubs, Plants, and Flowers cultivated for sale in the Gardens near London*, 1730 (folio) (66 n. 14, t. 18), in which it is called *Rosa provincialis spinosissima pedunculo muscoso*, and under the same name it appears in Miller (1733) who adds 'or the Moss Province Rose'.

The second illustration of the Moss Rose that we can trace is in that exquisite little book, *The Flower Garden Display'd* by Furber (1732) under the name of 'Moss Provence Rose'. The coloured drawing, though rather fantastic, is unmistakable. In the letterpress it is called the 'Moss Province Rose', and it is said to be 'like the Province Rose, and bears blossoms almost as double as that, only somewhat redder; and all the stalks are covered with a green Down, like Moss, which gives it its name'. The drawing is said to have been 'coloured from the life'. Willmott (1912) mentions that there is a specimen of the Moss Rose in the British Museum from the Chelsea Physic Gardens (Miller's) with the date

1735. About the year 1735 is the period which Shailer (1852), quoted by Darwin (1893), gives as the first introduction of the old Red Moss Rose into England. He states: 'It was sent over with some orange trees from the Italian States to Mr Wrench of the Broomhouse Nurseries, Fulham, in or about the year 1735. It remained in that family twenty years without being much noticed and circulated, until a nurseryman of the name of Grey of Fulham brought it into note.' In 1746, as we have already noted, the Moss Rose was in cultivation in France in four districts of the south and west. Linnaeus (1753) does not mention the Moss Rose. Miller (1760) published a coloured drawing of the Moss Rose, with an interesting description of the plant, and following Boerhaave (1720) describes it as '*Rosa rubra plena, spinosissima, pedunculo muscosa*. The most prickly double red Rose with a mossy footstalk, commonly called the Moss Provence Rose. . . . This sort sends out but few stalks from the root. These are covered with a dark brown bark, and closely armed with sharp thorns, the leaves are composed of five oblong oval lobes, which are hairy and sawed on their edges; the footstalks of the flowers are strong, standing erect, and are covered with a dark-green moss, as is also the Empalement of the Flowers. The flowers are the same shape and colour as the common Provence Rose, and have the like agreeable odour. It flowers in June or July, but is not succeeded by fruits.'

Linnaeus (1762) adds R. *rubra plena spinosissima pedunculo muscoso* of Miller (1760) to R. *centifolia* as probably belonging to it. Martyn (1807) quotes Retzius's (1779) description of the Moss Rose, which is worth requoting for its originality and acute observation: 'Stem very prickly and hispid: peduncles long, beset with curled strigae terminated by a resinous globule, as are also the whole calyxes: these strigae are often branched. Petioles less hispid and unarmed. Leaflets very large 3 or 5, smooth. The colour and smell of the clammy resinous glands are very much the same as in the Flowering Raspberry, or *Rubus odoratus*.' (It is, of course, the fragrant foliage of the *Rubus* to which Retzius refers and not the flowers.) De Grace (1784) mentions the Moss Rose in France.

It is said (Wright, 1911) that in 1785 the Moss Rose was sent from Caen Wood, Highgate, by Lord Mansfield to Mme de Genlis in France as a new introduction to that country. (Cf. Vibert's reference page 110.) We have already seen that it was in cultivation in four districts in France in 1746, and at Carcassonne in the south of France as far back as about 1696.

Rössig (1802) gives under the name of R. *muscosa* the figure of a pink Moss Rose, less mossy than usual, and states that it is found on the Alps.

Brotero (1804) includes R. *muscosa* in his *Flora of Portugal*, while Rivers (1840) alludes to a traveller's report that the Moss Rose grew wild in the neighbourhood of Cintra, but considers that most likely the plants were of garden origin.

Andrews (1805) states of the Moss Rose (R. *muscosa provincialis*): 'There can be little, if any doubt, that this beautiful variety is the spontaneous effusion of Nature in this country, of which we ever shall regard it as indigenous, since we have never heard of any importations of this species, but frequent exportations.'

Thory (1817) appears to have taken this 'effusion' of Andrews quite seriously, and replies as follows: 'A cet égard, independamment de ce qu'une conclusion de cette espèce est inadmissible en histoire naturelle, nous ferons observer qu'il n'est pas rare de voir les Iconographes anglais considérer beaucoup de plantes comme indigènes au sol de leur pays, toutes les fois que le lieu dans lequel elles végètent naturellement leur est inconnu, circonstance qui doit faire rejeter toutes les assertions de ce genre.'

Apparently Thory had not seen Ducastel.

Origin of the Moss Rose

We have reviewed the history of the Old Moss Rose and have traced it back to about the year 1696, when it was apparently in cultivation at Carcassonne, in the south of France, until it was found there by Ducastel, and introduced by him to the gardens of three districts in the north-west of France. We have seen that it was in cultivation in Holland in 1720, in England in 1727, and in Italy in 1735. Andrews (1805) states that '. . . the origin of this beautiful Rose has ever been considered as enveloped in obscurity, but we have no hesitation in assigning it to the Province, to which it assimilates in every particular—with the addition of a rich luxuriant Moss, that gives it a decided superiority, and at the same time a specific distinction. . . . There can be little if any doubt that this beautiful variety is the spontaneous effusion of Nature in this country.'

Rivers (1840) states: 'The Moss Rose or Mossy Provence Rose is most probably an accidental sport or seminal variety of the Common Provence Rose.'

Vibert (1844) of Angers, France, states, curiously enough, that the first Moss Rose, the Common Moss, was discovered in England. He quotes the statement of Mme de Genlis in her *Botanique Historique* that she brought the first plant of the Moss Rose to Paris from England a few years before the Revolution of 1789, but he seems sceptical about her further statement that in Germany, round Berlin, the Moss Rose grew as high as cherry-trees! Vibert proceeds to say that the Moss Rose is evidently a sport of Nature, a happy accident that Art has fixed, and that the date of introduction has not been preserved in a positive manner. He remarks that in France in 1810 only the Common Moss was known, and that the species R. *centifolia* has produced more sports or side-steps ('jeux ou écarts') than all the other species of *Rosa* put together.

Loiseleur-Deslongchamps (1844) also states that the Moss Rose originated in England, and that Miller is supposed to have been the first cultivator of it in 1724.

Paul (1848) states: 'The history of the Moss Rose is wrapped in obscurity. It was first introduced to England from Holland [in the 1888 edition he adds 'in 1596'] and it is generally believed that it was a sport from the Provence Rose: that it was not originated by seed, as most new varieties are, but by a branch of the Provence Rose sporting . . . flowers enveloped in Moss.

'Some tribes of plants are more disposed to sport than others; and the Provence and Moss Roses possess this peculiar property to a remarkable degree.'

Finally Darwin (1893), who devoted considerable attention to the question of the origin of the Moss Rose, states: 'Its origin is unknown, but from analogy it probably arose from the Provence Rose (R. *centifolia*) by bud-variation.' After a careful survey of the facts available to him in 1868, Darwin concludes: 'That the original Moss Rose was the product of bud-variation is probable.' Many facts have come to light since the time of Darwin, which more fully confirm this conclusion.

Records show that on three distinct occasions the Moss Rose mutation has appeared among the Cabbage Roses. First, about 1696, the Old Moss Rose appeared, as we have seen, in the south of France. Second, in 1801, the Moss de Meaux appeared in the west of England as a bud-mutation on the Rose de Meaux (Hare, 1818). Third, about 1843, the Unique Moss appeared in France, as a bud-mutation on the Rose Unique (Vibert, 1844; Paul, 1848).

Both the mother parents probably originated as bud-variations of the Old Cabbage Rose, the Rose de Meaux about 1637 in France (Willmott, 1912), and the Rose Unique in 1775 in the east of England (Shailer, 1852).

A confirmation of this view is found in the fact that both the Rose de Meaux and the Rose Unique reverted by bud-variation to the Old Cabbage Rose (Andrews, 1810; Rivers, 1840).

Origin of the Rose Unique

The Rose Unique, or White Provence, is a white Cabbage Rose, which differs from the Old Pink Cabbage Rose in colour only. As a matter of fact it is not a true albino, but a tinged white with pink buds.

Usually the flower is pure white when expanded, but the five outer petals are tinged with colour, and occasionally the centre of the flower too. There is an excellent coloured drawing of this Rose in Redouté (1817) under the name of R. *centifolia mutabilis*, or Rosier Unique. Andrews (1805) also figures it under the name of R. *provincialis alba*, White Provence or Rose Unique. This Rose was apparently found in a garden in the eastern counties in 1775. Andrews (1805) states that 'its introduction in 1777 was entirely accidental, through the medium of the late Mr Greenwood, Nurseryman, a great admirer and collector of Roses, who, in an excursion which he usually made every summer, in passing the front garden of Mr Richmond, a baker near Needham in Suffolk, there perceived the present charming plant, where it had been placed by a carpenter who found it near a hedge on the contiguous premises of a Dutch merchant, whose old mansion he was repairing. Mr Greenwood, requesting a little cutting of it, received from Mr Richmond the whole plant; when Mr Greenwood, in return for a plant so valuable, presented him with an elegant silver cup with the Rose engraved upon it; and which in com-memoration has furnished food for many a convivial hour. It is of dwarf growth, and remains in flower nearly six weeks longer than the other Province Roses, which renders it still the more estimable.

'We wish it had been in our power to have accounted for its having been till so lately a stranger to us, and whence indigenous; but at present our information is entirely confined to the know-ledge of its casual introduction, and until some further light is thrown upon the subject to elucidate its genealogy, we shall regard it as a native!' Another account is that of Rivers (1840), who states: 'The Unique Provence is a genuine English Rose, which, I believe, was found by Mr Greenwood, then of the Ken-sington Nursery, in some cottage garden, grcwing among plants of the Common Cabbage Rose. This variety was at first much esteemed, and plants of it were sold at very high prices. Most probably this was not a seedling from the Old Cabbage Rose, as that is too double to bear seed in this country, but what is called by florists a sporting branch or sucker.' A final account is that given by Shailer (1852), and referred to by Darwin (1893). Shailer states: 'The Rose Blanche Unique, or White Provins, was discovered by Mr Daniel Greenwood of Little Chelsea, Nursery-man. He was on a journey of business in the County of Norfolk in the month of July 1775, when, riding very leisurely along the road, he perceived a rose of great whiteness in the Mill; he alighted and on close inspection he discovered it to be a Provins Rose; he then sought an interview with the inmate of the Mill, who was an elderly female; he begged a flower, which was instantly given him; in return he gave her a guinea.

'In cutting off the flower he cut three buds; he went to the first Inn, packed it up, and sent it direct to my father, at his Nursery, Little Chelsea, who was then his foreman, requesting him to bud it, which he did, and two of the buds grew: in the following autumn he went down to the same place, where for five guineas he brought the whole stock away; he then made an arrangement with my father to propagate it, allowing him 5s. per plant for three years; at the expiration of that time he sold it out at 21s. per plant, my father's share amounting to upwards of £300.

'Mr Greenwood sent the old lady at the Mill a superb silver Tankard, etc., to the amount of £60.'

Darwin (1893), referring to Shailer's version above, states: 'Many other instances could be added of Roses varying by buds. The White Provence Rose apparently originated in this way,' with which we agree. The statement that Greenwood paid a guinea for one flower and three workable buds distinctly suggests that only one small shoot of this new White Rose was available at the time, and that it was a bud-variation growing on a Common Pink Cabbage Rose as Rivers suggests. The 'stock' that Greenwood bought for five guineas in the autumn was no doubt the original plant from which he cut the sport (cf. Andrew's account), because from his two budded plants and the old 'stock' plant Shailer would, with ordinary good fortune, get his 1,200 plants in the three years stated.[1]

Origin of the Rose de Meaux

The Rose de Meaux is a miniature Cabbage Rose which differs from the Old Cabbage Rose only in the smaller size of all its parts. There is a good coloured drawing of this Rose in Redouté (1817) under the name of *Rosa Pomponia* or Rosier Pompon. This Rose is an old inhabitant of French gardens, but its precise origin is not known. Miss Willmott (1912) suggests with good reason that it may have come from the garden of Doménique Séguier, Bishop of Meaux (1637), who was a great cultivator of Roses in his day. In any case, wherever it arose, there can be little doubt that it originated from the Old Cabbage Rose and probably as a bud-variation.

Aiton (1789) mentions two 'Rose de Meaux' as varieties of *R. provincialis* Mill. (i.e. *R. centifolia* L.), viz. 'the Great Dwarf Rose', which is no doubt the Spong Rose (*R. provincialis hybrida*) of Andrews (1805), a half-dwarf; and the 'Small Dwarf Rose', which is clearly the 'Rose de Meaux'. Both these forms are figured by Miss Lawrance (1799) under tt. 31 and 50 respectively.

During a period of more than two thousand years only three Moss Roses have been recorded that were not derived from Moss Roses. Two of the three are definitely recorded as bud-variations of Cabbage Roses, viz. Moss de Meaux (1801) in England and Unique Moss (1843) in France. The third is the Old Moss Rose, whose origin is in question. Each of the two is identical with the

[1] It is probable that in the above five paragraphs 'Greenwood' is given in error for Grimwood' (Grimwood & Hudson). Mr J. N. Harvey kindly sent me this correction. G. S. T.

particular form which produced it, except in the 'Moss' character, which is additional. Further, the 'Moss' character is apparently identical in the three Moss Roses. None has been recorded as a seed-variation, and all are sterile, like the forms which produced them.

Further, on at least seven occasions between 1805 and 1873 the Old Moss Rose has reproduced the Old Cabbage Rose by bud-variation or 'bud-reversion' (Andrews, 1805; Hare, 1818; Lindley, 1820; Shailer, 1822; Piper, 1842; Jamain, 1873; Darwin, 1893).

The conclusion, therefore, is irresistible that the original Moss Rose mutation arose as a bud-variation of the Old Cabbage Rose (R. *centifolia* L.).

We conclude, therefore, that the original Moss Rose first appeared at Carcassonne, in the south of France, about the year 1696, as a bud-mutation of the Old Cabbage Rose (R. *centifolia* L.).

The second 'Moss' mutation was the 'Moss de Meaux', which appeared in the west of England in 1801 as a bud-mutation of Rose de Meaux.

The third and last 'Moss' mutation was the 'Unique Moss', which appeared in France about 1843 as a bud-mutation of Rose Unique.

All other Moss Roses have been derived directly or indirectly from one of the three original mutations. As a matter of fact, between 1788 and 1832 no less than seventeen distinct Moss Roses appeared as bud-variations of the Old Moss Rose in England and France. One of these had single and fertile flowers (Shailer, 1852), and became the ancestor of many hybrid Moss Roses raised in England and France between 1824 and 1860.

Further confirmation of the origin of the Moss Rose may be found in the interesting fact that twelve of the distinct bud-variations of the Old Moss Rose which appeared between 1788 and 1832 have precise parallels in twelve bud-variations of the Old Cabbage Rose which appeared between 1637 and 1813, the only difference between them being the presence and absence of 'Moss' respectively. This can only be due to their like factorial composition in all respects except in the presence or absence of the 'Moss' factor.

Presumably this implies a common origin, and here we seem to get a glimpse of the true nature of related species and varieties, for these twelve bud-variations are indistinguishable in kind from the seed-variations that normally arise among seedlings of related species and varieties of *Rosa*.

Another noteworthy fact has become prominent in the course of this inquiry, and that is the comparatively few bud-variations recorded in the fertile R. *gallica* L. and R. *damascena* Mill. compared with the large numbers found in the sterile R. *centifolia* L.

Is it possible that there is a definite connection between sterility and bud-variation? Are we to regard bud-variation as an alternative mode of expression of variation in the presence of sterility?

The facts in *Rosa* certainly point in that direction. It is interesting to note that no other species of *Rosa* presents the 'Moss' mutation but R. *centifolia* L. No trace of it is ever seen in the closely allied species or sub-species R. *damascena* Mill. or R. *gallica* L. The nearest analogues to the mossiness of R. *centifolia* L. are the extreme hairy and glandular forms of R. *rubiginosa* L. (Sweet Briar) and R. *moschata Brunonii* (Musk Rose), which, however, are quite distinct from R. *centifolia muscosa* Seringe, both in their structure and their glandular secretions.

Genetic Significance

In concluding this inquiry it may be of interest to add a few genetic notes on the probable nature and significance of the three definite appearances of this 'specific' bud-mutation, after more than two thousand years of intensive cultivation and vegetative propagation.

That the 'Moss' character in *Rosa* is a genuine bud-mutation, and not a fluctuating variation or bud-variant, is evident from its somatic persistence through many bud-generations, and its germinal persistence through various seed-generations.

Rivers (1840) states that 'plants produced by the seed of the Moss Rose do not always show Moss; perhaps not more than two plants out of three will be mossy, as I have often proved'.

Again, Darwin (1893) states that 'Mr Rivers informs me that his seedlings from the old Single Moss Rose almost always produce Moss Roses'.

We do not yet know definitely whether the 'Moss' character in *Rosa* is to be identified with a single Mendelian factor or not, though all the evidence so far is in favour of its being a simple dominant. If it is, and Rivers's matings of the Single Moss Rose were, on the average, one-half selfings and one-half crossings with other Roses, as they probably were, judging by his methods, the Mendelian expectation, on the average, would be the actual ratio he obtained, viz. 2 Moss; 1 Plain. It is evident that 'Moss' is a dominant character, for if it were recessive no hybrid Moss Roses would have the 'Moss' character, and we know that some have. It is also clear that the Single Moss, a bud-variation from the Old Moss Rose, is a heterozygous dominant, for according to Rivers (1840) and Darwin (1893) it throws 'plain' as well as 'Moss' Roses from seed in the proportion of about one in three.

We have already seen that the Old Moss Rose produced 'plain' (i.e. 'unmossed') Cabbage Roses. So that it is probable that the first mutation of the Moss Rose was itself a heterozygous dominant for 'Moss'.

In view of the important results recently reported by Morgan (1919) and his colleagues, in their experiments with *Drosophila*, which have led them to formulate the chromosome theory of heredity, it seems on this hypothesis that if the first mutation of the Moss Rose was a heterozygous dominant, the mutational change would take place in one of the chromosomes in a single locus. In accordance with the 'presence and absence' method, this mutational change in a single locus from m to M involves the presence of an additional factor M, which is dominant to the normal allelomorph m from which the factor M is absent.

This conception, however, does not necessarily imply the actual presence or absence of a structural gene as Morgan seems to infer, and in the present state of knowledge it seems safer and sounder to continue the use of the non-committal term 'factor' with its 'presence and absence', which need not necessarily involve any assumption as to the nature or constitution of either the factor or its allelomorph, though it does provide an indispensable symbolic method of denoting the difference between them.

On the other hand, the reversionary change by which the Moss Rose reproduced the Cabbage Rose by bud-variation involves the absence of the factor M in a single locus of one of the chromosomes, either by somatic segregation with a reduction division, or by a reverse mutational change in the locus concerned. In any case it is evident that in view of Morgan's discoveries bud-mutations take on a new importance, and the case of the Moss Rose is clearly one of considerable genetic significance; for in a simple way it seems to narrow down to a fine point the difficult and usually complex problem of the origin of a definite mutation, and may bring us within measurable distance of the possibility of tracing the origin to a certain cause.

For the present, however, we must be content to work and wait patiently for the genetic and cytological facts, which alone can offer even an approximate solution.

List of Authors Cited

AITON, W. T. 1789. *Hortus Kewensis*, ed. 1, ii, p. 207.

——. 1811. *Hortus Kewensis*, ed. 2, iii, p. 264.

AMHERST, The Hon. Alicia. 1895. *A History of Gardening in England*, pp. 6 and 7.

ANDREWS, H. C. 1805–10. *Roses: a Monograph of the Genus Rosa*, with coloured figures (unnumbered).

BAKER, J. G. 1914. In Willmott, Ellen, *The Genus Rosa*, xxv (Hist. Intro., x and xi).

'BANBURY'. 1845. In *Gard. Chron.*, p. 564 (16 Aug.). (Cor. 'Sports'.)

BATESON, W., and SAUNDERS, E. R. 1902. *Rep. Evol. Com. Roy. Soc.*, i, pp. 159 and 160.

BIEBERSTEIN, F. G., Marschall von. 1808. *Flora Taurico-Caucasica*, i, p. 397.

BLONDEL, Dr. 1889. *Les Produits odorants des Rosiers*. Paris, 1889 (also in *Bull. Soc. Bot. de France*, Feb. 1889).

BOERHAAVE, Hermann. 1720. *Index Plantarum Hort. Acad. Lugd. Bot.*, ii, p. 252.

BOIS, A. G. J. M. 1896. *Atl. Pl. Jard.*, t. 86.

BOISSIER, E. P. 1872. *Flora orientalis*, ii, p. 676.

BROTERO, F. De A. 1804. *Flora Lusitanica*, p. 345.

CASPARY, Prof. 1865. *Schrift. Phys. Oek. Ges. König* (3 Feb.) (also *Trans. Hort. Congress, Amsterdam*, 1865).

CHABRAEUS, D. 1677. *Omn. Stirp. Sci. Icon.*, p. 106 with fig.

CLUSIUS, C. 1601. *Rariorum Plantarum Historia*, iii, p. 113.

CRÉPIN, F. 1892. *Bull. Soc. Bot. Belg.*, xxxi, pt. 2, p. 73.

CURTIS, W. 1793. *Bot. Mag.*, i, t. 69.

DARWIN, C. 1893. *Var. Animals and Plants Dom.*, ed. 2, i, pp. 404–6.

DELEUZE. 1809. In Desfontaines, R. L., *Hist. arb. Desf.*, Paris. *La Monographie du genre Rosa*.

DIPPEL, L. 1893. *Hand. Laubholz*, iii, p. 566.

DUCASTEL, F. 1746. *L'École du Jardinier Fleuriste*.

DUMONT DE COURSET, G. L. M. 1805. *Le Botaniste Cultivateur*, v, p. 478.

Du Roi, J. P. 1772. *Harbk. Baum.*, ii, p. 368.

Ellacombe, Canon H. N. 1905. 'Roses' in *Cornhill Magazine* (July), p. 27 (see also Hill, 1919).

Ferrarius, J. B. 1633. *De Florum Cultura*, lib. iv, p. 203.

Fitzgerald, E. 1859. *The Rubáiyát of Omar Khayyám.* (Intro. to 1904 ed. Methuen.)

Flückiger. 1862. *Notices et extraits des manuscrits de la Bibliothèque Impériale,* xix, p. 364.

——. 1883. *Pharmacognosie des Pflanzenreichs*, p. 159.

Furber, R. 1724. *Catalogue of Plants* in Miller, 1724.

——. 1730. In *Hort. Angl.* Catalogue of Plants, 66, n. 14, t. 18.

——. 1732. In *The Flower Garden Display'd* (June), pp. 49, 53.

Gerard, J. 1596–9. (Reprint 1876 by B. Daydon Jackson.) *Catalogue of Cultivated Plants.*

——. 1597. *Herball*, Roses, chap. i, f. 6; chap. ii, p. 1085, f. 3.

——. 1633 (and Johnson, T.), *Herball*, lib. 3, p. 1262, fig. 6; p. 1266, fig. 4.

Grâce, De. 1784. *Le bon Jardinier.*

Guimpel, F., Otto, F., and Hayne, F. G. 1825. *Abbild. Deutsch. Holzart,* i, p. 47, t. 39.

Hare, T. 1818. *Trans. Hort. Soc. Lond.*, ii, p. 242. (Read 3 Sept. 1816.)

Herodotus (*circa* 450 B.C.). *Hist.*, lib. viii, chap. 138.

Hill, A. W. 1919. 'Henry Nicholson Ellacombe: a Memoir.' *Roses*, pp. 292–308.

Hurst, C. C. 1911. *Rep. IVᵉ Conf. Int. Gen.* Paris, 1911.

Jackson, B. Daydon. 1876. Reprinted. Of *Gerard's Cat. Plants Cult.* 1596–1599.

Jamain, H., and Forney, E. 1873. *Les Roses* (Paris), p. 57.

Kaempfer, E. 1712. *Amoenitatum exoticarum.*

Köhne, E. 1893. *Deutsche Dendrol*, p. 282.

Lawrance, Mary. 1799. *A Collection of Roses from Nature*, tt. 2, 14, 51.

Liger, L. 1704. Ed. 1. *Le Jardinier Fleuriste.*

——. 1708. New ed. *Le Jardinier Fleuriste*, II, chap. vii, pp. 515–600.

Lindley, J. 1815. *Bot. Reg.*, p. 53 (see Smith, 1815).

——. 1820. *Rosarum Monographia*, pp. 64–7.

Linnaeus, C. 1753. *Species Plantarum*, Rosa, ed. 1, i, p. 491.

——. 1762. *Species Plantarum*, Rosa, ed. 2, i, p. 704.

L'Obel, M. De. 1581. *Kurydtboeck*, ii, p. 240 with fig. and p. 241.

Loiseleur-Deslongchamps, J. L. A. 1844. *La Rose* (Paris), pp. 263–6.

Loureiro, J. De. 1790. *Flora Cochinchinensis.*

Martyn, T. 1807. New ed., *Miller's Dictionary*, iii, Rosa, 14 and 22.

Miller, P. 1724, 1731, 1733. *Gardener's Dictionary*, Rosa.

——. 1760. *Icones*, Rosa, ii, p. 148, pl. ccxxi, fig. 1.

——. 1768. *Gardener's Dictionary*, ed. VIII, ii, Rosa, 22.

—— and Martyn, T. 1807. *Gardener's Dictionary*, iii, Rosa, 14 and 22.

Morgan, T. H. 1919. *The Physical Basis of Heredity.*

Paquet, V. 1845. In *Choix des Plus Belles Roses*, sub. t. 1.

Parkinson, J. 1629. *Paradisi in Sole, Paradisus Terrestris* (1904 reprint), pp. 412–14, 415, fig. 2; 416, 419, ff. 3 and 4.

Paul, W. 1848. *The Rose Garden*, ed. 1, p. 32.

——. 1888. *The Rose Garden*, ed. 9, p. 2.

Pemberton, Rev. J. H. 1920. *Roses*, p. 62.

Persoon, C. H. 1807. *Synopsis Plantarum*, ii, p. 49.

PIPER. 1842. *Report Roy. Hort. Soc. Lond.* in *Gard. Chron.*, p. 422 (25 June).
PLINY, C. (*circa* A.D. 50). *Hist. Nat.*, lib. xxi, cap. 4.
PRÉVOST, J. 1829. *Catalogue des Rosiers*, p. 64.
RAU, A. 1816. *Enum. Ros. Wirceburgum*, p. 109.
REDOUTÉ, P. J., and THORY, C. A. 1817. Ed. 1, *Les Roses*, i, with tt. (folio).
——. 1821. Ed. 1, *Les Roses*, ii, with tt. (folio).
——. 1824. Ed. 1, *Les Roses*, iii, with tt. (folio).
——. 1835. Ed. 1, *Les Roses*, i, ii, iii, with tt. (8vo.) (and Pirolle, M.).
REGEL, E. A. 1877. (*Tent. Ros. Monogr.*, p. 70) in *Act, Hort. Petrop.* v, pt. 2, p. 354.
REHDER, A. 1902. In Bailey, L. H., *Cycl. Amer. Hort.*, iv, p. 1552.
RETZIUS, A. J. 1779. *Obs. Bot.*, i, p. 20, No. 58.
RIVERS, T. 1840. *The Rose Amateur's Guide*, ed. 2, pp. 1–19.
RÖSSIG, C. G. 1802–20. *Die Rosen*, No. 6.
SALMON, W. 1710. *The English Herbal*, pp. 952 and 953.
SAWER, J. C. 1894. *Rhodologia*, p. 13.
SCHNEIDER, C. K. 1906. *Ill. Handbuch Laubholz*, i. p. 547.
SERINGE, N. C. 1818. *Mus. Helv.*, ii, p. 19.
——. 1825. In De Candolle, *Prodromus*, ii, p. 619.
SHAILER, H. (sen.). 1822. *Trans. Hort. Soc.*, Lond., iv, p. 137 (Exh., 15 June 1819).
—— (jun.). 1852. *Gard. Chron.*, p. 759 (27 Nov.).
SMITH, Sir James Edward. 1915. In Rees's *Encyclopaedia* (see *Bot. Reg.*, 1815, p. 53).
THEOPHRASTUS, E. (*circa* 350 B.C.). *Hist. Plant.*, lib. vi, cap. 6.
THORY, C. A., and REDOUTÉ, P. J. 1817. Ed. i, *Les Roses*, i, with tt. (folio).
——. 1821. Ed. 1, *Les Roses*, ii, with tt. (folio).
——. 1824. Ed. 1, *Les Roses*, iii, with tt. (folio).
——. 1835. Ed. 3, *Les Roses*, i, ii, iii, with tt. (8vo.) (and Pirolle, M.).
VIBERT, J. P. 1844. In Loiseleur-Deslongchamps, *La Rose*, pp. 266–72.
WILLDENOW, C. L. 1799. *Species Plantarum*, ii, p. 1074.
WILLMOTT, ELLEN. 1912. *The Genus Rosa*, xviii, pp. 341 and 345, tt.
—— and BAKER, J. G. 1914. *The Genus Rosa* (Hist. Intro.), xxv.
WRIGHT, W. P. 1911–14. *Roses and Rose Gardens*, p. 37.

BUD-VARIATIONS OF THE OLD CABBAGE ROSE (*Rosa centifolia* L.)

C. C. HURST

The chart of the Cabbage and Moss Roses by C. C. Hurst places on record all the written evidence that he was able to discover of the periodic 'sporting' of *Rosa centifolia*. It will be seen that several mutations occurred again and again, and reversions were also frequent. Several such occurrences have been observed in my collection.

NOTE. B_1, B_2, ... B_6 Successive generations by sporting (mutation).
F_1, F_2 Successive generations by seeding (sexual reproduction).

B_1	B_2	B_3	B_4	B_5	B_6
Rose de Meaux, 1637 (Willmott, 1912)	Moss de Meaux, 1801 (Hare, 1818)	Rose de Meaux, 1810 (Andrews, 1810)			
	Spong Rose, 1805 (Andrews, 1805)	Cabbage Rose, 1810 (Andrews, 1810)			
	White Moss, 1788 (Shailer, 1852)	Blush Moss, 1789 (Shailer, 1852)	Shailer's White Moss, 1790 (Shailer, 1852)	Striped Moss, 1845 (Banbury, 1845)	
				Cabbage Rose, 1865 (Caspary, 1865)	
				Striped Moss, 1865 (Caspary, 1865)	
	Striped Moss, 1790 (Shailer, 1852)	Old Moss, 1792 (Shailer, 1852)			
		Striped Cabbage, 1843 (Rivers, 1843)			
	Cabbage Rose, 1805 (Andrews, 1805)				

F₁ → **ENGLISH HYBRID MOSS ROSES,** 1835–60

F₁ → FRENCH HYBRID MOSS ROSES, 1824–60

Cabbage Rose

—Old Moss Rose, 1696 (Ducastel, 1746)

—Single Red Moss, 1807 (Shailer, 1852)

—Scarlet Moss, 1808 (Shailer, 1852)

—White Bath Moss, 1810 (Andrews, 1823)

—Sage-leaf Moss, 1813 (Shailer, 1852)

—Single Moss, 1814 (Vibert, 1844)

—Cabbage Rose, 1816 (Hare, 1818)

—Minor Moss, 1818 (Vibert, 1844)

—Semi-double Moss, 1819 (Shailer, 1822)

—Cabbage Rose, 1819 (Shailer, 1822)

—Mottled Rose, 1819 (Shailer, 1822)

—Cabbage Rose, 1820 (Lindley, 1820)

—Tinwell Crimson Moss, 1820 (Rivers, 1843)

—Scarlet Cabbage, 1836 (Rivers, 1843)

B₂

—Old Moss, 1848 (Paul, 1848)

—Striped Moss, 1848 (Paul, 1848)

—Semi-single Moss, 1817 (Redouté, 1817)

—Semi-double Red Moss, 1819 (Shailer, 1822)

Cabbage Rose

B₁   B₂   B₃   B₄   B₅

Deep Rose Moss,
1820
(Vibert, 1844)
Flesh Moss, 1822
(Vibert, 1844)
Striped Semi-double
Moss, 1824
(Vibert, 1844)
Striped Double
Moss, 1826
(Vibert, 1844)
Proliferous Moss,
1828
(Vibert, 1844)
Zoe Moss, 1830
(Vibert, 1844)
Carnation Moss,
1832
(Vibert, 1844)
Cabbage Rose, 1842
(Piper, 1842)
Cabbage Rose, 1868
(Darwin, 1893)
Cabbage Rose, 1873
(Jamain, 1873)

Old Moss Rose, 1696
(Ducastel, 1746)

Unique Moss, 1843   **Rose Unique, 1843**
(Vibert, 1844)   (Rivers, 1843)

Rose Unique, 1775 —— **Striped Unique,**
(Shailer, 1852)   **1843**
                          (Rivers, 1843)   **Cabbage Rose, 1843**
Blandford Rose,   **Perpetual Unique,**   (Rivers, 1843)
1791   **1920**
(Andrews, 1805)

F$_2$

F$_1$

—Semi-double Cabbage, 1794 ——→ Single Cabbage Rose, 1796 ——→ FRENCH PROVENCE AND HYBRID PROVENCE ROSES, 1820–50

—Carnation Rose, 1800 (Redouté, 1817)
—Flesh Cabbage Rose, 1801 (Redouté, 1817)
—Lettuce Rose, 1801 (Redouté, 1817)
—Proliferous Rose, 1801 (Redouté, 1824)
—Semi-double Provence, 1804 (Andrews, 1805)
—Single Provence, 1805 (Andrews, 1805)
—Celery Rose, 1805 (Redouté, 1835)
—Blush Provence, 1805 (Andrews, 1805)
—Leafy Rose, 1809 (Redouté, 1821)
—Minor Cabbage, 1813 (Redouté, 1835)
—Anemone Rose, 1815 (Redouté, 1835)
—Crested Moss, 1826 (Jamain, 1873) —— Cabbage Rose, 1843 (Rivers, 1843)

PLATE V

TOP LEFT. One of the most free-flowering of the Bourbons, 'Commandant Beaurepaire' (1874), produces leafy sprays well set with loose, cupped blooms, amazingly striped in a variety of colours. Extremely fragrant. (See page 195.)

TOP RIGHT. Beautiful 'button eyes' are shewn in this display of Gallica 'Belle de Crécy', dating from the time of Mme de Pompadour, who lived at the château of that name. Extremely fragrant. (See page 142.)

BOTTOM LEFT. 'Alain Blanchard' (1839) is one of the most effective of the old spotted roses, and has the added attraction of yellow stamens. (See page 140.)

BOTTOM RIGHT. No other Moss Rose has such beautiful growth as 'James Mitchell' (1861), with miniature blooms appearing from very mossy buds, along sturdy arching branches, early in the season. (See page 187.)

Chapter X

. . . .

Old Roses in Paris

They are not long, the days of wine and roses.
Ernest Dowson

I NEED HARDLY repeat that the home of our old roses is in France. With very few exceptions the names are in French, and a visit to the gardens around Paris provides one with much food for thought.

In England the old roses are being planted again because they fit in with the modern trend of shrub gardening. They are barely represented in our parks and national gardens, but enthusiasm is growing for them in the gardens of amateurs. In Paris exactly the opposite obtains. The amateurs have no interest in them whatever, but in two of the public gardens really large collections are to be seen.

A visit to one of the great gardens of Paris such as Bagatelle or the Roseraie de l'Haÿ is a step back in history. The visitor is carried back at least fifty years by comparison with our own gardening. The very roses that are now being grown in England because they are free-growing flowering shrubs, are, in Paris, carefully pruned down to be kept as very dwarf bushes. A dozen flowers to each plant is the result, instead of fifty or a hundred.

The rose gardens of both the Roseraie de l'Haÿ and at Bagatelle are laid out in geometrical designs with a scope and exactitude such as we do not dream of over here. As a general rule the paths are of carefully raked shingle, bordered by grass or box edging. The lines are impeccably correct, the edgings perfect, and the grading of the plants most carefully effected by pruning and training.

The beds inside the grass edges are inevitably of carefully tended soil, but the beds surrounded by box edging contain, surprisingly often, grass, which is mown by scythe or sickle; these grass beds may be 3 or 4 feet wide, and along the centre small earth beds are cut about 1 foot wide, each containing one little rose bush, pruned to 2 feet in height or less. A series of these little beds will be broken by a pillar rose or a standard—again with impeccable straightness of stem, and at frequent intervals arches span the paths.

At the Roseraie de l'Haÿ by far the most extensive collection of roses is to be found. The centre piece, midway between the offices and museum, is a small geometrical pond, surrounded by long beds of decorative shape, containing fine modern roses and also such old Hybrid Perpetuals as 'Frau Karl Druschki' and 'Ulrich Brunner'. As a background there is the great pergola and central arbour, all of which is completely covered with the Wichuraiana variety 'Alexandre Girault'. This perfectly trained tableau of rich glossy green bespangled all over with the warm, rosy-red flowers is a demonstration of what these old Wichuraiana Roses will do. It is strange how they became neglected owing to the rise of the *Rosa multiflora* × *wichuraiana* Ramblers such as ' Excelsa ' and 'Dorothy Perkins'. 'Albéric Barbier' remains a great favourite, with 'François Juranville' a good second; 'Auguste Gervais', 'May Queen', 'Gerbe Rose', 'La Perle', 'Léontine Gervais', 'Paul Transon', are all worthy varieties with typical glossy leaves and sweetly scented flowers of good size and charm.

From this central focal point paths radiate at every angle, with arched alleys in some directions, crossed and sub-divided at every point by less important vistas, which frequently meet at an orna-mental architectural feature, such as a temple, an urn, or a seat. And on every side above and below the eye are roses—roses short in little bushes; roses swinging on ropes between pillars; standard roses of all heights with solid bushy heads, or weeping from a perfect umbrella top; roses over arches square or rounded. Everywhere are blossoms and scent, giving just so much beauty as the careful treatment and severe training will allow.

There are Hybrid Teas and Hybrid Perpetuals, Dwarf Polyan-thas and Floribundas; Chinas and Teas, Noisettes and Bourbons; Wichuraiana and Multiflora Ramblers, Climbers and species, Rugosas and Sweet Briars, and many an obscure hybrid and form which do not fit in anywhere particularly, such as, for instance, the *Rosa roxburghii* hybrids, 'Jardin de la Croix' and 'Domaine de Chapuis'.

Very modern varieties are planted in some of the beds, but generally speaking it is a panorama of rose history. A new planting of Rose species is to be seen on the large lawn away from the rose garden, and many large established bushes of species and near hybrids are in the borders surrounding the rose garden proper.

One of the triangular plots formed by the arrangement of the paths has beds filled entirely with the old roses. The outer beds contain large alphabetical collections of Gallica, Moss, Provence, and Damask Roses, with large central beds given to displays of one variety. Many old favourites are grown and also a number of varieties unknown over here. Particularly does this refer to the collection of twelve Portland Roses, to which I refer on page 155.

During the war these gardens obviously became gravely neglected, and many labels were misplaced or lost, but it is wonderful what peace and work will do, and I fully believe it will not be long before the Roseraie de l'Haÿ will once more be a great centre of rose culture. The collection is unique, and in addition to the plants themselves and the nineteenth-century design, there is the Rose Museum, and also the Malmaison border. In this as many as possible of the roses grown by the Empress Josephine are growing, and one can walk along seeing plate after plate of Redouté's immortal drawings in reality.

For at the Château of Malmaison there are few roses. 'Souvenir de la Malmaison' itself is growing in several beds and a few rambling roses are on the garden walls. None of the former horticultural splendour is to be found around this beautiful grey building, enhanced by its avenue of clipped limes and its small undulating park.

At Bagatelle the French hold their trials of new roses. Unlike the garden at L'Haÿ les Roses, this is a large public park with orangery, lake, and many fine specimen trees; a tunnel of box; a long wall thickly planted with climbing roses and clematis, and a charming small formal iris garden. Here again, as at l'Haÿ, the main rose garden is laid out in severe geometrical lines, offset by an occasional statue or a yew, clipped to a perfect cone. The gravel paths are mostly bordered by box edging, and the beds are nearly all sown with grass. The green setting for the little rose beds in these areas is very appealing, but the work entailed must be unending. Apart from certain beds being given over to the new plants on trial, a fairly representative collection of older roses is also grown, arranged botanically, and with the various beds attractively ornamented by half standards and tall weeping standards. Some fine old Bourbons like 'Duhamel Dumonceau' and 'Giuletta' are grown, and many Gallicas and Mosses. All are, however, pruned down to small bushes.

Around the geometrical beds are some species and some rare shrubby roses such as the *Rosa macrophylla* hybrid 'August Roussel'; towards the north the ground rises to a Japanese temple set among trees.

My visit to these gardens was well worth while. The superintendents were most helpful and abounding in courtesy. The nomenclature was at the time of my visit (early June 1953) rather disappointing, and only here and there did I find correct names for some of my own foundlings. The difficulties in getting these old roses named correctly are very great, but not insurmountable. Comparing living specimens of my own with the German collection from Sangerhausen, and then seeing them all over again in France, has enabled me to sift many of the names thoroughly. The test comes when all the old books agree on the colour of a variety, which may be just the opposite of the plant we grow!

We realize then that we are wrong, and the search begins again, starting from a totally different angle. By degrees, through comparison and elimination, order is being restored, and the numerous examples I have been able to give of coloured plates of the older varieties prove how many are definitely and correctly named.

It is to be hoped that the French collections will be combed thoroughly and nomenclature restored to its pre-war level. The authorities have up to the present scarcely had time to do more than restore the actual gardens and rejuvenate the plants. This in itself is a triumph, and the presentation of beautifully kept period gardens shews us one way of growing our roses.

Chapter XI

. . . .

Old Roses in Pictures

Rose amiable et chérie
Tu charme notre vie.

THE ROSE APPEARS in design and in pictures throughout the ages, both as the principal and also the incidental motif. In many instances the general feeling of a specific type of rose is portrayed in the old religious pictures, but otherwise it is not often that any definite species can be recognized until we come to the age when the beauty of flowers was considered individually, and especially in the great upsurge of flower painting that occurred in the seventeenth and eighteenth centuries in the Low Countries.

The Dutch at this time were very much in the ascendant. With the defeat of the Armada in 1588, and the revolt of the Dutch under the Spanish yoke, the power of Spain was on the wane; England and Holland were competing for mastery of the seas. At home a strong national feeling was afoot and it is small wonder that the arts spread under the benefit of the Dutch freedom. The tulip boom is an indication of the enthusiasm of the Dutch for flowers at that time, and their paintings include many old favourite flowers. Tulips in fantastic stripes, roses, the double hyacinth, double opium poppy, peony, ranunculus, lily, hibiscus, crown imperial, hollyhock, together with fruits, insects, and birds' nests, were brought in to give variety and reality to the most magnificent pictures of their kind ever produced.

Hundreds of these old flower pieces are found all over the continent in museums, private collections, and in the hands of dealers, and there are no doubt many here and there in this country. Several were in the Dutch and Flemish exhibitions at the Royal Academy in 1952, 1953, and 1954; the pictures exhibited were mainly painted in the seventeenth century, but in addition to these I have been privileged to see the splendid collection* belonging to Major the Hon. Henry R. Broughton, in which several

TOSR - 5   * now in the Fitzwilliam Museum, Cambridge.

eighteenth- and nineteenth-century works are included. It is obvious, however, that the seventeenth century saw the climax of this wonderful period of art.

In Holland Jan van Huysum (1682–1749) stands out as the creator of the most elaborate flower pieces. The transparency of the petals is exquisite to say the least, while a more extravagant statement is that trite but very true remark, 'the flowers look so real that you feel as if you could pick·them off the canvas'. His work may be regarded as the highest achievement in a century of flower painting during which many famous names occur, among them being Jan Brueghel (1568–1625), who must be considered the earliest expert of this kind; Balthazar van der Ast (1590–1656); Ambrosius Bosschaert II (1612–45), Jan de Heem (1606–84), Jacob Marell (1614–81), Simon Verelst (1644–1721), noted for his wonderful lighting effects and subdued colourings, Rachel Ruysch (1664–1750), Jacob van Walscapelle, who was producing pictures from 1667 to 1716, and Jan van Os (1744–1808).

In Flanders further great names are found, although national freedom was not attained until later; the widespread growth of the Renaissance, however, had obviously made itself felt. Roelandt Savery (1576–1639), Daniel Seghers (1590–1661), Jacob Jordaens (1593–1678), and Nicolaes Verendael (1640–91) are some of the names which are nearly as famous as the Dutch.

In his absorbing and exhaustive book, *The Art of Botanical Illustration*, Wilfrid Blunt tells us how, after van Huysum's death, Gerard van Spaendonck and others carried on the tradition, but never surpassed the great man's work, although the spark was rekindled in Spaendonck's pupil, Redouté.

No such other outpouring of floral art has ever recurred, although we have isolated artists producing exceptional work such as Fantin-Latour (1805–1904). This celebrated Frenchman loved the rather squat arrangement of flowers in a bowl, the blooms closely pressed together, with a very natural softness pervading the whole. His was a soft and very sympathetic touch, and the early forms of Teas and Noisettes can be recognized in his roses, although I do not feel competent to name varieties. I am tempted to add that some of his flat, double, pale pink roses might well be 'Souvenir de la Malmaison' or even the rose we call 'Fantin-Latour' itself.

Apart from the exhibitions, there are some fine examples of Dutch and Flemish art at the National Gallery, also of Fantin-Latour; and for a summary or introduction the freely illustrated volume by Ralph Warner, *Dutch and Flemish Fruit and Flower Painters of the Seventeenth and Eighteenth Centuries*, may be recommended. I have also seen the illustrated volume *Flower Painting through the Centuries* by Colonel Maurice H. Grant. This is a delightful book, published in a limited edition, to record many pictures in Major Broughton's collection. The Ashmolean Museum at Oxford also has a splendid volume of illustrations of the pictures there: *A Catalogue of Dutch and Flemish Still-life Pictures in the Ashmolean Museum, Oxford.* There are without doubt other books to be seen, but during the limited time at my disposal I found the above the most helpful of those I have handled. While it is pleasant to see form and design in photogravure, one does, of course, need the original colour to enable one to appreciate the pictures to the full.

To return to the artists of the Low Countries, it seems to have been an accepted thing in those days only to paint certain types of flowers. There are, of course, many pictures with something unusual in them, but in general the same flowers recur again and again, and this applies also to roses.

Rosa centifolia is the favourite rose with them all, and there are many superlatively beautiful paintings of it; Verelst and Verendael among others have given their half-open blooms a living quality, while Van der Aelst has alone, among the pictures I have seen, shewn the quartering of the fully open bloom. Bearing in mind the nodding grace of the half-open blooms which provides the receding centres with an added richness, it is not surprising that it was the first favourite among roses.[1] In fact it is not only prominent in the old flower paintings, but often is the only flower to decorate a group of fruits, where it competes for pride of place with the amazingly transparent grapes and cherries which are depicted in an almost too lifelike freshness. Its leaves, too, are broad and broadly toothed, which gives further scope to the painter.

Van Huysum, Walscapelle, and others have included frequently

[1] It is not surprising that they wished to immortalize it whenever possible if it was their own production (see page 103, The Great Holland Rose).

a large white rose, which from its similarity in shape and foliage I would consider to be R. *centifolia* 'Unique Blanche', but according to all records this rose was not mentioned until 1778, and this must be a wrong supposition. I have seen, however, what is undoubtedly an authentic portrait of this rose by Arnoldus Bloemers, a celebrated Dutch painter of 1792–1844, and another is a picture by J. C. Roedig (1751–1802). The flowers shew very clearly the red tips of the petals, which are so often evident in sunny weather. There may have been another 'White Provence' rose earlier, but this is unlikely as it would almost certainly have been included in Redouté's portraits had it still been in cultivation. These Centifolia sports were, however, short-lived in those days when they were not widely spread in cultivation.

We have therefore to suppose that all the double white roses in these old pictures are none other than the 'Great Double White Rose', *Rosa alba maxima*. In many instances the creamy colouring found in the centre of freshly opened blooms is carefully shewn, while in others the flat, fully open flower is discarded for a shape nearer to R. *centifolia*.

I have only seen one rose in a flower group that might be *Rosa gallica*, and that was in a painting belonging to Major Broughton by Marcellus, and it would appear to be an accurate portrayal of the form we know as R. *gallica officinalis*.

On the other hand R. *gallica versicolor* is obviously intended by some French artists in Major Broughton's collection, namely, Baptiste, Denysz, and Hardime, all, I believe, seventeenth-century painters, and also in a picture by Verelst.

An occasional *Rosa foetida* and its variety *bicolor* are found, unmistakable in their single flowers of intense colouring, but the most usual yellow rose is a fully double kind. This must inevitably be *Rosa hemisphaerica*, as the only other double yellow old rose, *Rosa foetida persiana* ('Persian Yellow'), was not introduced until 1837. A really good flower of this capricious variety can well have inspired the painters; it has a fine globular shape and intense sulphur yellow colouring. Here and there its shape has been made more globular still, thus representing a yellow 'Provence Rose' of the painter's imagination. Van Huysum has some fine examples.

The double white 'Musk Rose' (*Rosa moschata*) occurs in a few pictures; I remember pretty sprays of it by Van Huysum and

Verendael, and a portrait of 'de Meaux' is almost certain in a work of Jean François Bony (1760–1825) in the collection of Major Broughton.

A hundred years later, in the day of Redouté, a much wider selection of roses was portrayed; but we must remember that Redouté was deliberately figuring a collection of roses. At the same time it is remarkable that, spurred on by the beauty of the 'Provence Rose', artists did not search farther for beauty from the rose. The rich tones of 'Tuscany' and other purplish varieties were available, but possibly this colouring was not in fashion. Generally speaking the flower groups painted by Van Huysum and others verge towards the brilliant, red and yellow being favourites. In the rise of the arts and the success of men in those days perhaps something more positive than the subdued tones of the Gallicas, for instance, was needed.

Looking again at a collection of these pictures, one is impressed by the rather artificial arrangement of many of the flowers. From the mixtures of spring and summer blooms in the same container it is obvious that the artists did not paint the arrangement as a whole; indeed the life of the flowers, could they even flower at one time together, would not permit such painstaking and time-absorbing work. Apart from this, many of the flowers have an appearance of individuality, as if they had been arranged on the canvas, having been copied separately from studies, and there is no doubt that this is the solution to the galaxies of blooms depicted. In this way I feel the flowers lived in the artists' minds as beautiful apotheoses of the originals, and we must therefore forgive them for including so few of our old favourite roses, and for confusing the issue here and there by exaggerating the shape or using the wrong foliage. They are after all 'Flower Pieces', not botanical studies, and their beauty will at all times enthrall the beholder.

At the Royal Horticultural Society's Sesquicentenary Exhibition, the florally decorated Royal Signatures in the Society's possession were shewn, and I was interested to trace the favours bestowed on the rose through several reigns.

The single flowered *Rosa foetida* and *spinosissima* are clearly depicted on that of H.R.H. the Grand Duke of Saxe-Weimar, 1817, while two years later an equally beautiful chaplet of double roses was chosen for the signature of the Prince of Wales, later to become George IV. The Moss Rose and the 'Maiden's Blush' are most beautifully drawn; on accession to the throne, however, even roses were discarded, and fruits of all kinds took their place in the sovereign's signature, the date of which would be 1820 or 1821.

The 'Maiden's Blush' occurs again in 1820 (H.R.H. Augustus Frederic, Duke of Sussex), and large double white roses on the Prince Consort's signature in 1840. A red and a white double rose were chosen by Edward VII when Prince of Wales in 1861, while Queen Mary's choice lay in an assortment of Hybrid Teas; with them my old friend E. A. Bowles included what seems to me to be the old double Musk of Shakespeare which grew on the west side of Myddleton House.

The present Patron of the Society, H.M. Queen Elizabeth the Queen Mother, has chosen lilac, magnolia, and roses, and the latter are clearly *Rosa webbiana*, one of the most exquisite of the Western Himalayan species.

PART II

Old Roses in Cultivation Today

The roses make the world so sweet,
   The bees, the birds have such a tune,
There's such a light and such a heat
   And such a joy in June.

George LL. D. Macdonald

Chapter XII

. . . .

The Rose of Provins

Rosa gallica (R. *rubra*)

'Prick not your finger as you pluck it off,
Lest, bleeding, you do paint the white rose red,
And fall on my side so, against your will.'

Shakespeare, King Henry VI

THESE ARE AT ONCE the most ancient, the most famous, and the best garden plants among the old roses. They are also the ancestors in part of most other old roses, and their delicious fragrance is carried down through all their descendants.

Several characters are noticeable not only in the oldest garden forms like *Rosa gallica officinalis* and 'Tuscany', but also in some of the most sumptuous of the nineteenth-century productions. Firstly their almost thornless stems; just a few prickles are present which rub off at a touch of the finger, and abundant harmless tiny bristles; secondly their leaves are rough, neat, dark green, and often poised upwards, unlike the large drooping leaves of the Provence Roses, and the Damask's and White Rose's grey tones. The buds are round and blunt, and the calyx does not as a rule project far. The most important character from a garden point of view is the poise of the flower. Almost without exception they form compact bushes with the flowers well disposed and held aloft, erect, on firm stalks. They lose the charm of the nodding flower thereby, but gain immeasurably in general value. Their colours embrace all the pinks and mauves, purples and maroons imaginable, but I have found no white variety. This is rather surprising. I believe all the purplish varieties listed under *Rosa centifolia* probably owe their intense colouring to this species. Striped sports are numerous.

In addition, they are extremely prone to suckering. I have seen groups of Gallicas which have run over several yards of ground and the result is a floral sight of very high order. They thrive with the absolute minimum of attention and are not so dependent on good soils as the Damask, Provence, and Moss Roses, thriving in poor, gravelly, sandy, chalky, or shaley soils, and annually giving a display that cannot but meet with satisfaction. Their performance on good soils is correspondingly and infinitely better.

As low hedging plants many varieties can be annually clipped with shears at the end of January. The result of this clipping is the formation of hundreds of fairly uniform flowering shoots, each bearing from 1 to 4 flowers upturned to the sky. (Fuller details are on page 51.)

Without any pruning at all they can go on year after year flowering well, as their new shoots replace the old from the base. Dead wood can be cut away in the spring. Alternatively, by a little careful removal of flowering wood in July, after the flowering is over, an encouragement is given to produce better new growths, and they richly deserve and benefit from this treatment.

The group as a whole is well represented in gardens and nomenclature is less confused than in other groups. On the other hand, a surprising lack of dates accompanies entries in the old books. A glance through a collection of varieties leaves no doubt in one's mind, however, that in *Rosa gallica officinalis, versicolor, conditorum,* and 'Tuscany' we are looking at unsophisticated early cultivated forms. The breeders' later perfection is probably found in 'Belle de Crécy', 'Gloire de France', 'du Maître d'École', and 'Duc de Guiche', while the influence of other roses than Gallica is found in 'Agathe Incarnata', 'Cardinal Richelieu', 'Hippolyte', and *violacea*.

THE FRANKFORT ROSE

I was for years puzzled over the identity of a pair of roses which I grew as 'Empress Josephine' and 'Pope Pius IX', and it was not until I was once again turning over the pages of Redouté's wonderful paintings in the Lindley Library, that I suddenly realized I was looking at these two roses under different names. In Vol. 1, Plate 127, was *Rosa turbinata*, 'Rosier de Francfort', surely my 'Empress Josephine'. Rehder lists this as *Rosa francofurtana*; it is also figured in Lawrance, Plate 69, and Roessig, Plate 11; Clusius in 1583 records it. It is an interesting hybrid, probably between *Rosa cinnamomea* and *Rosa gallica*, which has occurred from time to time on the Continent, and was named in the first instance from a specimen found in Saxony. Its garden forms include the variety 'Agatha', which appears to be identical with my 'Pope Pius IX'. There is an old specimen of this on the outside of the west wall of the University Botanic Garden at Oxford. See also page 207.

It is a strange fact that my plants of the 'Empress Joséphine', which came to me originally from the Hon. Robert James of Richmond, Yorks, bore the simple designation 'Miss Willmott's rose'. Although *Rosa francofurtana* is given a short description in her *The Genus Rosa*, Miss Willmott did not have a portrait made of it. I suspect, therefore, that she may not have connected this rose with her description.

It is easily recognized by being practically thornless, with smooth grey-green twigs; by the very large stipules as much as half an inch wide; by the smooth, thin, greyish leaves noticeably corrugated by the veins, like those of an elm or hornbeam, and by the great turbinate hip. This is most clearly seen in its early state under the bud, and is broader and bigger than that of any other old rose at that time. The flowers have a papery quality, of rich Tyrian rose, flushed with lilac and purple, and veined exquisitely all over with a deeper tone. Fragrance is rather lacking in 'Empress Joséphine', but in the form 'Agatha' it is as delicious and strong as any; the flowers of this form are, however, smaller, less shapely, and of more purple tone. 'Agatha' is a vigorous grower up to 6 feet, while the type hybrid is a lowly bush slowly making an effective plant up to 3 or 4 feet.

GALLICA ROSES

ROSA GALLICA (the 'French Rose' or 'Rose of Provins'). The title Provins is also found in the old name, *Rosa provincialis*, but must not be confused with the Provence Rose, *Rosa centifolia*. The wild type is a sprawling shrub up to 3 feet or so, with abundant suckers in light soils. There are few prickles of any size. The leaves are smaller and more rounded and of a lighter green than the 'Red Rose of Lancaster' (*Rosa gallica officinalis*), and the flowers are simple, of true wild rose beauty, daintily shaped, and clear pink in colour. The colour is less intense around the circlet of yellow stamens, and the scent from this wildling, though sweet, is far less strong than that of many of the doubles. For colonizing poor soils this rose has its value, and the heps are quite ornamental in early autumn, but otherwise it cannot be classed for garden value with its more effective and richly coloured forms.

Redouté, Vol. 2. Plate 63. *Rosa gallica pumila*; 'Rosier d'Amour'. This plate appears to portray exactly the only wild form in my collection, received from the Hon. Robert James of Richmond, Yorkshire. See also page 207.

AGATHE INCARNATA. An ancient variety probably hybridized with a Damask Rose. It bears considerable affinity with *Rosa damascena* 'Petite Lisette' and 'Omar Khayyám'. The grey-green downy leaves point to the Damask group, as also the thorny shoots up to 4 feet in height. It is a compact plant and extremely free flowering. The bunches of buds open quickly to flat round flowers, composed of quartered, quilled petals, with distinct button eyes. Pale pink of even tone. I found this rose in the garden of Mr W. B. Hopkins at Hapton, Norwich, and also in that of Major Roger Hog at Kirkliston, East Lothian.

There were many 'Agatha' varieties of *Rosa gallica*, and they had usually fully double small flowers. Prior to 1815.

Redouté, Vol. 3. Plate 77.

ALAIN BLANCHARD, 1839. An open thorny bush, which thereby indicates its possible Centifolia parentage, with mid-green, rather unattractive foliage. In spite of the date given I suspect that this is probably a very old type; it has cupped, nearly single flowers, rich in crimson tone, effectively lit by the golden stamens in the centre. Very soon after opening the petals develop maroon shading in a mottled pattern; lastly they become purple with a mottling of light crimson. This and 'La Plus Belle des Ponctuées' are the two most attractive spotted varieties I have come across; 'Royale Marbrée' is an unpleasant little double flower of unimpressive shape and colour. 5 feet. (Pl. V.)

ALAIN BLANCHARD PANACHÉE. I received this beautiful and unique rose from the late Mrs Riall of Dublin, and it would appear to be a definite sport or the original of 'Alain Blanchard', being identical in every particular except the pattern of its colour. Instead of being spotted, its purple tones are striped and pencilled on the rich magenta crimson ground. On cool days both varieties are full of an indescribable richness greatly enhanced by their golden centres.

ANAÏS SÉGALES, 1837. In the old French books this rose is generally described as a crimson variety of *Rosa centifolia*. The colour we need not take too seriously, as true crimson was non-existent among roses of this type. The thorny stems do, however, denote parentage other than true *Rosa gallica*, but otherwise I think it fits best here. It forms a pleasingly branched small bush up to 3 feet or so, and the leaves are to scale, neat and light green. It may well be described as one of the most beautifully shaped among the Gallicas; every petal is held in place, and neatly rolled back, displaying a flat, well-filled bloom with a green eye. The colour at first is a rich mauve crimson, fading to pale lilac pink at the edges in maturity. Very free flowering.

ANTONIA D'ORMOIS. Fresh green growths appear with the flowers, and the plant shews a diversity of shoots and foliage. The flowers are late, and their warm blush colour and shape resemble the exquisite Alba variety 'Maiden's Blush'; at first cupped and later reflexing and fading to blush white at the edges. Has not proved very free flowering. 5–6 feet.

ASSEMBLAGE DE BEAUTÉS (' Rouge Éblouissante '), 1790. A compact bush with very few real thorns, and rich green leaves which make a hard contrast to the startling, extremely vivid blooms. At first they are of intense cerise crimson, later becoming flushed with purple, and the multitudes of small petals reflex into a ball, revealing a small green point in the middle of a hard button eye. It creates an amazing picture in flower, and makes an excellent contrast to some of the softer tones, such as 'Anaïs Ségales', and intensifies the purple and maroon tones of 'Tuscany' and others of that tint. This is the rose one finds labelled 'Ponceau' in some collections. 'Poppy coloured' is a slight exaggeration, but it is certainly a vivid piece of colour. 4 feet.

BELLE DE CRÉCY. One of my favourites among the Gallicas, in fact I consider it supreme for its soft parma violet colourings—supreme among all old roses—and for fragrance it is hard to beat. Unfortunately it is not of very erect habit, but with a little support among other bushes it is admirable and will then attain 4 feet, and is only slightly armed. The leaves tone well in their dull leaden green with the colours of the flowers, and are neat and well poised. On first opening the flowers give little indication of their ultimate colour, being of intense cerise pink freckled and veined with mauve. On exposure, and particularly in hot weather, they quickly begin to turn to softest violet, eventually being almost entirely lavender grey with purple and cerise tints here and there. A perfect flower, of which there are many, opens wide, with reflexing and flat petals, leaving a pronounced button eye. With white roses such as 'Madame Hardy' the contrast is exquisite. Prior to 1848. (Pl. V.)

BELLE DES JARDINS. A striped Gallica rose which I have not yet come across. Purple roses have been given this name of recent years.

BELLE ISIS. One of the shorter Gallicas, seldom attaining 4 feet. Neat little light-green leaves, coarsely toothed; this character and the thorny stems denote possible Centifolia parentage, together with the winged and elegant calyx, but the flowers and flower stalks are pure Gallica. It is the only Gallica I have found in which an almost flesh pink colouring is found; this tint remains in the centre of the slightly reflexing full flowers after their edges have turned nearly white. Fat round buds. A pretty little rose bringing a distinct tint to the group. About 1845.

CAMAIEUX. One of the most remarkable of all striped roses, but unfortunately not a very strong grower. It makes quite a healthy bush up to 4 feet or so, with somewhat arching growth and few thorns, and fairly typical sage-green leaves. The changes of colour in the petals are arresting and fascinating. The flowers are only semi-double when compared with some varieties, and have loosely arranged petals, which gently recurve. At first the blush white of the petals is heavily striped and splashed with light crimson, which quickly flushes with violet purple. Later the purple fades to magenta and eventually, just before falling on the third or fourth day, one can enjoy the delicacy of pale lilac-grey stripes on a white ground. The perfect complement at that stage to 'Belle de Crécy' and 'Mme Hardy'. (Pl. 5) 1830.

CARDINAL DE RICHELIEU, 1840. One of the most famous varieties which has qualities all to itself. It makes one of the best bushes up to 4 or 5 feet, with shiny green wood and very few thorns, and smooth, dark green leaves. The fat round buds are almost pink on first unfolding, and a partly open bloom shews a dome of balled petals of coppery rosy-lilac surrounded by the opening reflexing petals of indescribably rich velvety-purple, paling to almost white at the base. Later, when practically all the petals have reflexed, with conspicuously rolled edges, the whole ball-like flower is of a rich dark purple quality with the sumptuous bloom of a dark grape. This is a rose which well repays the best cultivation, and its most admirable companions are found in 'Céleste' and 'Maiden's Blush'. Not much fragrance.

CHARLES DE MILLS. A compact shrub which makes one of the best displays every year. It is nearly thornless and the leaves are neat and fairly typical. The shape of the flowers is unique. They are extremely full-petalled, and when partly open they appear to have been sliced off in the bud, so flat and regular is the cupped formation. Later the petals open out, eventually resembling an African Marigold!—but with much more quality. When fully expanded into this ball-like shape it is noticed that in the centre there is a pale green cavity; one can see right into the receptacle, there being no button eye. As for colour, anything from richest crimson-purple through maroon to dark lilac and wine shades may be found on any bloom at any time. This is rather a coarse bloom, but is really splendid when planted with strong pink varieties. 5 feet. Not much fragrance.

COMPLICATA. I have been unable to find this name in any book, but it is widely known on the Continent. It is perhaps a *Rosa canina* or *macrantha* hybrid, with strong arching branches reaching to 5 feet in height and as much across, well clothed in large, pointed, clear green leaves. The large blooms, as much as 5 inches wide, are single, of pure brilliant pink, paling to white around the circle of golden stamens. This is without doubt one of the most strikingly beautiful of single pink roses, and is a good hearty plant. I like it mixed up with yellows such as 'Lawrence Johnston', the two being strong in colour and able to vie with one another. When established among other shrubs it will ramble into trees to the height of 10 feet. (Pl. 1.)

CONDITORUM. My plant came from the University Botanic Garden at Oxford. The rose used in Hungary for attar and preserving. Recorded in 1900, but it is undoubtedly a very old form, rather than the result of late selection, for it approximates *Rosa gallica officinalis* and 'Tuscany' in many ways. It forms a bushy plant with loose tousled flowers, semi-double, of rich, magenta-crimson tone, slightly flushed and veined with purple in hot weather, and shewing yellow stamens. 3–4 feet.

COSIMO RIDOLFI. A compact little bush; a true Gallica with neat soft green leaves and upstanding flowers, each a model of perfection. The fat reddish buds open to circular cupped little flowers of a sombre old rose, rapidly becoming flushed with parma violet, shewing cerise veins and a button eye. One of the most exquisitely fashioned of old roses. Synonym 'Casimo Ridolphi'. 3 feet. 1842.

CRAMOISI PICOTÉ, 1834. An erect grower up to 4 feet or so, with daintily poised, neat, small dark-green leaves, and a charming companion for small striped varieties such as 'Georges Vibert', 'Pompon Panachée', to which it is obviously closely related. The small compact blooms are very double, mere pompons, crimson in the bud, opening to a softer tone, and retaining a picotee edge of crimson. A pretty little flower, giving a vivid effect.

D'AGUESSEAU. The most brilliant red I have found among the Gallicas. A vigorous plant up to 4 or 5 feet with big foliage of typical Gallica form. The flowers are very full, and open quickly to flat, quartered blooms sometimes with button eyes; the outer petals reflex and develop a vivid cerise-pink, leaving the intense cerise-scarlet in the centre. 1823.
Paul, Plate 3. A rather faded portrait.

DUC DE GUICHE. This is undoubtedly a more recent variety with a sophisticated beauty and perfect petal formation, and comparable with 'Madame Hardy' and 'Belle de Crécy'. Extra

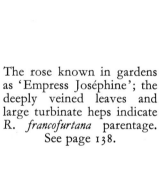

PLATE I
The most valuable of the Portland Roses, 'Comte de Chambord', which produces an excellent autumn crop of blooms, in true Gallica persuasion. See page 210.

The rose known in gardens as 'Empress Joséphine'; the deeply veined leaves and large turbinate heps indicate R. *francofurtana* parentage. See page 138.

PLATE II

ABOVE. 'Koenigin von Danemarck', one of the most striking varieties of *Rosa alba*, dating from early in the nineteenth century; the partly opened bloom already shews the flat expanded form and beautiful quartering. Extremely fragrant. See page 168.

BELOW. The coarsely toothed leaves indicate the Provence Rose, of which the 'Crested Moss' or 'Chapeau de Napoléon' is a sport. First recorded in 1820. Description under R. *centifolia cristata*. See page 174.

PLATE III

ABOVE. 'Maiden's Blush' or 'Cuisse de Nymphe' was known before the fifteenth century, and may be found in many gardens owing to its vigour and delicious fragrance. It is one of the best known varieties of R. *alba*, and the photography shews the characteristic muddled centres. See page 169.

BELOW. The three pale blooms shew 'Mme Pierre Oger', a sport from the darker 'Reine Victoria'. These two varieties and 'Louise Odier' have the most exquisite shape among the Bourbon varieties. See page 198.

PLATE IV

PLATE V

PLATE VI

The strong contrast of silky undersides and velvety upper surfaces of the petals, incurved round the button eye, is well shown in this Moss Rose 'Capitaine John Ingram' (1856). See page 185

PLATE VII

ABOVE. 'Robert le Diable', probably a hybrid between a Provence and a Gallica Rose, has everything to recommend it except a sturdy habit. It produces quantities of flowers of excellent shape and unrivalled for their sombre mixed colourings. Very fragrant. See page 177.

BELOW. A foretaste of the future. The new hybrid Gallica Rose, 'Scarlet Fire' ('Scharlachglut') from Herr Wilhelm Kordes of Holstein. Its dazzling sheen is unsurpassed by any rose, old or new. See page 153.

PLATE VIII

A Bourbon with muddled centres and expanded form, 'Prince Charles'. The veining and crinkled petals are characteristic of this nearly thornless variety. See page 198.

well-filled flowers, opening cupped and reflexing into a ball, with a handsome moment when the outer petals are reflexed, leaving the centre cupped. The colour is intense crimson-magenta, minutely yet densely veined with purple in hot weather. It has a green eye, and is often quartered. 4-5 feet. See also page 207.

DUCHESSE D'ANGOULÊME (the 'Wax Rose'). *À pétales minces et transparents*, as Max Singer so aptly puts it. This has indeed a delicacy which one does not expect among Gallicas; possibly *Rosa centifolia* has again been the refining influence, although the smooth, light green leaves, green smooth wood, and few thorns do not indicate this. It will grow to about 3 feet, but its growth is always arching and nodding—the flowers nod very much, and it is thus admirable as a standard. The shell-like transparent petals are pale blush-pink, tipped with crimson from the well-stained bud, giving a globular, exquisitely formed flower of very soft colouring. 1836.

DUCHESSE DE BUCCLEUGH. A robust shrub, almost thornless, with rich, green, luxuriant foliage, nearly as handsome as that of 'La Ville de Bruxelles'. It is one of the last to come into flower, and the first blooms are sometimes badly shaped. The flowers are exceptionally large, cupped, but opening quite flat, quartered, and with a button eye and tiny green centre. The intense magenta-pink, with crimson tones, fades slightly at the edges. 5-6 feet. 1846.

DUCHESSE DE MONTEBELLO. This is a charmer and cannot be omitted, although it does not appear to qualify for this name by which it is so well known. One can cut sprays a yard long from the lax bushes of free growth, and the neat greyish leaves provide just the right greenery for the sweet little blooms of clear blush-pink. It flowers early in the season, and makes a delightful picture when its sprays grow through one of the large purple flowered varieties. 5 feet.

DU MAÎTRE D'ÉCOLE. Although there is a French village called La Maître École, where Messrs Pajotin-Chédane used to grow a wonderful collection of the older roses, I like to think of this as the schoolmaster's favourite. Messrs Pajotin disclaim any connection with this rose. It is a practically thornless bush up to

3 or 4 feet, with good foliage. The growths are stout, but arch under the weight of the exceptionally large blooms, up to 5 inches across, and very double; from round reddish buds with long calyx lobes they open flat, later reflexing, often quartered, and with pronounced button eyes. A small green point is in the centre. The colouring is very soft, deep old rose, giving way to lilac pink, with delicate mauve and coppery shadings. One of the great flowers of old days.

EMPRESS JOSEPHINE. See *Rosa francofurtana*, page 138.

FORNARINA. An unusual rose of erect and bushy growth, few thorns, and mid-green leaves. The flowers are particularly well and freely presented. The reddish buds open to muddled blooms with petals reflexed at the edges. There is a strong, rich, Tyrian pink in the centre of the flower, but pale tints develop around the circumference, the whole being mottled and spotted with blush. A poor bloom, but an effective bushy plant. 4 feet. Synonym 'Belle Flore'. 1826.

GEORGES VIBERT, 1853. An erect-growing small bush up to 3 or 4 feet, with numerous small leaves, neatly poised, in dark green, on somewhat thorny shoots. The flowers are not large, although their narrow petals, opening flat and showing a green centre point, have a carnation-like charm in their neatly striped array. The blush-pink and dark crimson-pink stripes fade to paler tones. It is pretty quilled and quartered.

GLOIRE DE FRANCE. I had grown this beautiful form for many years before being sent it under the name of 'Fanny Bias' by Mr Will Tillotson of Watsonville, California. The old French descriptions of either name would apply. It is a low-growing variety, covered with wonderfully double flowers, so filled with neat reflexing petals as to make a large pompon. The colour is a warm lilac-rose, the centre retaining its tone, while the circumference rapidly fades to lilac-white. A pretty shrub up to 4 feet, and full of charm. 1828.

HENRI FOUCQUIER. This was received, like 'Fornarina', 'Nestor', and 'Marie Louise', from Mr Will Tillotson of Watsonville, California. It has a rather procumbent habit, and is almost thornless; the flowers are large, very rounded, composed of many small petals, of rich uniform pink, reflexing and fading to lilac-pink. Button eye. 4 feet. 1811. 'Cocard Majestueuse'.

HIPPOLYTE. A vigorous shrub, practically thornless, with neat small leaves, reaching some 5 or 6 feet. The long sprays bear beautiful flat little flowers, like rosettes, smooth-petalled, reflexing almost to a ball with button eyes. An occasional cerise petal, or one of dove-grey, light the many others, which are generally of soft violet. Not a typical Gallica.

IPSILANTÉ. William Paul speaks very highly of this rose, and it certainly produces some most handsome blooms. It is a vigorous plant up to 4 or 5 feet, with good foliage and wide flat blooms, quartered and quilled, of palest lilac-pink. 1821.

JENNY DUVAL. One of the tragedies of my quest for these old roses has been the complete failure to find the correct name for this unique variety, which came from Messrs Bobbink and Atkins of New Jersey. It is a fairly strong bush up to 4 feet, bearing normal leaves. The buds are specially shapely, and when partly opened on a cool morning they are of an exquisite uniform lilac-grey. On hot mornings they are frequently of startling magenta-cerise. A fully open bloom can contain cerise, magenta, parma violet or lilac, grey, soft brown, and lilac-white. 'Président de Sèze' has some of these colours, but 'Jenny Duval' certainly holds pride of place among Gallica roses for the most spectacular colouring, and is at all times exquisite.

LA PLUS BELLE DES PONCTUÉES. It cannot be claimed that a spotting of pale pink on a rich pink ground can create a flower of any special beauty, although it may be interesting to examine. But this variety is fortunately blessed with a very vigorous constitution, and makes a fine shrub of luxuriant greenery, amid which the pink flowers shine in contrast. They are loose-petalled with muddled centres. Essentially a plant for garden effect. 6 feet.

MARCEL BOURGOUIN, 1899. An old type of Gallica, nearly allied to *conditorum* and 'Tuscany' with loose semi-double flowers of dark purple velvet; the muddled centres shew the lighter pink-toned reverses of the petals. Unfortunately in some seasons the flowers do not develop their full colour, and remain a flat magenta, but when at their best on good soils they are astonishingly sumptuous and richly coloured. 3-foot bushes of small growth, with dark green leaves. I have grown this variety under many names, including 'Belle des Jardins' and 'Le Jacobin'.

NANETTE. Few thorns grow on the upright stems reaching to 3 feet or so, otherwise it is a typical Gallica with good, small leaves, somewhat shiny. All the flowers are borne on stout stalks; they are small but of intense colouring. The vivid crimson petals are veined and streaked heavily, especially towards the centre of each, with purple, presenting a very rich effect when fully expanded. The colour becomes lighter on fading, but at all times the striping is evident. 3-4 feet.

NESTOR. Fresh green foliage. The half-open blooms are cupped and the lilac-pink petals guard a heart of intense rosy-magenta. The quartering is very beautiful later, when mauve and grey shadows predominate. Few thorns. An extremely handsome rose. 4 feet. Prior to 1846.

OFFICINALIS (R. *gallica maxima*). Sometimes also called 'splendens', this renowned rose is also known by the confusing name 'Red Damask', although it is obviously of pure Gallica development, and has given us the sport 'Rosa Mundi'. It is the Apothecary's Rose, and is also probably the 'Red Rose of Lancaster'. A much-branched bush, of strong suckering proclivities when on its own roots, bearing abundant dark green, well-poised, acute foliage. Few thorns. The flowers do not open until the season is well advanced, and then create a most arresting display for some weeks, being held well aloft, over the bushes. They are semi-double, of light crimson, lit with yellow stamens. It is referred to in Prince's *Manual of Roses* (New York, 1846—a book closely following Rivers) as being much cultivated in Surrey for the druggists. It is probably the oldest cultivated form of *Rosa gallica*, and is right in the forefront of good garden shrubs, and very telling in the landscape. For a full explanation of the confusion over the name 'Red Damask', see page 61. 4 feet. (Pls. IV, 6.) See also page 207.

Kingsley, facing page 40. Described as *Rosa gallica*, 'Red Damask' (the 'Apothecary's Rose').

Bunyard, Plate 25. Bunyard elsewhere refers erroneously to this, the Apothecary's Rose, being fully double.

Redouté, Vol 1, Plate 73. 'Le Rosier de Provins ordinaire.'

Roessig, Plate 17. *Rosa gallica duplex*, 'Le Rosier de France semi-double.'

PERLE DES PANACHÉES, 1845 ('Cottage Maid'). Another of the 'Georges Vibert' family; this has light green leaves, small growth, with coppery foliage on the young shoots. The flowers are only semi-double, of rather loose shape, almost white with scattered pencillings of crimson, sometimes accompanied by a larger flake of colour. 3 feet. Plate 16.

PETITE ORLÉANNAISE. A vigorous bush up to 5 feet, bearing many neat flat pink blooms with button centres. Rather too large a bush for the size of its flowers, which are individually perfect.

POMPON PANACHÉE. I have been able to find no authority for this name, but it is so apt that I feel it warrants inclusion; it describes so exactly this charming miniature variety. The very small leaves on wiry erect branches recall 'Georges Vibert' in their shape, poise, and colour. Every short side-shoot bears one or two small double blooms striped with dark pink on a *cream* ground. It is the only striped variety that I have seen with this cream colouring on opening; it fades later to pale pink and white. An admirable companion for 'Cramoisi Picoté' or a contrast to some strong-coloured large flower like the Bourbon 'Prince Charles'. 4 feet. May be synonymous with 'Pompon', raised in 1856. Synonym 'Variegata Marmorata'.

PRÉSIDENT DE SÈZE. One of the most remarkable of the two-toned, fully double Gallica roses. A bloom just fully open presents a combination of intense dark magenta-crimson in the centre and lilac-white around the circumference. The sudden change from the one to the other in the confines of the one flower is very striking. Even a fully open flower with its beautifully rolled petals still retains rich colouring in the centre, which is muddled and slightly quartered. The buds are soft pink and very beautiful. Altogether one of the 'great' Gallicas, and a good sturdy bush with broad foliage. 4–5 feet. Prior to 1836. 'Mme Hébert'.

ROYALE MARBRÉE. Erect vigorous shrub up to 4 or 5 feet. Shapely buds, opening cupped, later quite flat, quartered, and reflexing to a ball with rolled petals. Violet-crimson at first, later intense crimson-pink spotted with pink. Not of great garden value, and a poor flower.

SISSINGHURST CASTLE. Ancient Gallica found by The Hon. V. Sackville-West at Sissinghurst, where it had held its own for many years away among the brambles and nettles. It now grows, freely suckering, in a long bed, reaching 2 or 3 feet in height, and shewing its semi-double flowers well above the plentiful, neat, pointed leaves. Few thorns. The rich plum-coloured petals have light magenta-crimson edges and are flecked with a similar tint, while their reverses are soft magenta-pink, and very telling in the half-open flowers. Golden stamens. I have been unable to find the suggested name 'Rose des Maures' in any old French book. 3–4 feet.

SURPASSE TOUT. Vigorous, with distinct Gallica foliage, this variety bids fair to be a good grower. The fat buds open slightly cupped, revealing a brilliant rosy crimson, passing to a vivid cerise-pink colouring. The petals reflex around a large button centre, and are delicately veined with a darker shade. A handsome rose of promise. 4–5 feet.

TRICOLORE ('Reine Marguerite') The stems bear some mixed prickles while the foliage is good, of Gallica type. The flowers are borne in small clusters or singly, cupped at first and later reflexed, vivid, rich magenta-crimson, quickly flushing with purple at the edges. A small white stripe is noticeable in the centre of each petal, thereby earning its name. 4 feet. c. 1840.

TRICOLORE DE FLANDRES, 1846. Closely resembles 'Camaieux' at first glance, but it is proving a little more vigorous, with rather smoother leaves; the flowers have more petals and they are more distinctly reflexed and rolled. The striping is heavier and narrower, and the colour is a definite magenta-purple, with less of the rosy tint. A very desirable variety. Delightful as a contrast to the rich purples of 'Hippolyte' or 'Tuscany'. Mr Trelawney Dayrell Reed has given me a sport from this rose, in which the colouring has reverted presumably to the original dark tone without the white stripes. 3-4 feet. See also page 207. Komlosy. A good portrait.

TUSCANY (the 'Old Velvet' Rose). One of the very best garden plants among the Gallicas, extremely effective in the colour and presentation of the flowers, but not quite so intensely fragrant as some. It will reach 4½ feet in good conditions, but is usually 3-4 feet. The small dark green leaves are well folded and curved, and the flowers are semi-double with rather flat petals, of intense dark maroon-crimson, assuming maroon-violet tints, and offset in their richness by the yellow stamens. I should say this is one of the older types of Gallicas, and bids fair to remain a favourite as long as any, being of such stalwart and bushy growth and thrifty on its own roots, when it will sucker freely. *Botanical Register*, Vol. VI, page 448.
Andrews, Plate 43. *Centifolia subnigra*.

TUSCANY SUPERB. Described by Paul in 1848. Of equally good growth to the original 'Tuscany', this has broader leaves and much larger flowers. They are extremely handsome, flat, and well filled, and make a better garden effect than 'Tuscany', but the doubling of the blooms results in fewer stamens, and in consequence some of the contrast of colour is lost. (Pl. 8.) 4 feet.

VERSICOLOR ('Rosa Mundi', *Rosa gallica variegata*). Recorded in the early seventeenth century. This, most popular of the old roses, and found with 'Maiden's Blush' in many an old garden, is the most vivid of the striped roses, and cannot fail to arrest attention wherever it is planted. It is capable of making as brilliant a display as any other flowering shrub. It is a sport from *Rosa gallica officinalis*, and has the same admirable growth, few thorns, and good foliage; the same excellent presentation of its flowers, held well aloft, of light crimson splashed and striped with palest pink. The few petals are lit with yellow stamens and the astonishing display lasts well. Of first-class garden value. This rose has been frequently confused with the pink-and-white 'York and Lancaster', whose growth, leaves, and floral shape and colouring are completely distinct.

I think it can be said without reserve that this rose and its parent, *Rosa gallica officinalis*, are two of the most valuable hardy flowering shrubs for brilliant effect that are available for general planting today. Their floral shape is happily insufficiently formal to preclude them from association with species shrubs, but just sufficiently double to give them ease of entry into more sophisticated plantings. 4 feet. (Frontispiece, Pls. IV, 7.) See also page 208.

Bunyard, Plate 23.

Lawrance, Plate 13.

Roessig, Plate 14. 'Rosier d'Yorck et de Lancastre', *Rosa versicolor*. The colouring of the flower shews that *Rosa gallica versicolor* was depicted, not *R. damascena versicolor*.

Andrews, Plate 46. *Rosa gallica variegata*.

Redouté, Vol. 1. Plate 135.

VIOLACEA ('La Belle Sultane', 'Gallica Maheka', 'Cumberland'). A difficult rose to place, both in a book and in a garden. It has undoubtedly many Gallica characters, but its vigorous arching growth up to 6 feet presents a problem. The stems are nearly smooth, and the leaves neatly rounded and drooping, suggesting a Damask inheritance; it has an early though rather short flowering season, but when in full flower presents a glorious burst of colour, from its almost single blooms. At first they are rich deep crimson, rapidly assuming violet flushes, but the bases of the petals remain nearly white around the golden stamens. It would seem to be an old type of rose with some of the characters found in 'Alain Blanchard'. The winged calyx suggests Centifolia influence. It is best grouped behind some such variety as *Rosa gallica complicata* over which it can sprawl and create a mixed colour effect.

Keays, facing page 36.

Redouté, Vol. 3. Plate 78.

Willmott, Plate facing page 359. Described as *Rosa provincialis* and synonymous with *Rosa gallica officinalis* of Redouté! Two entirely distinct roses. This plate agrees with Redouté's.

Roessig, Plate 16. 'Le rosier semi-double velouté', *Rosa holosericea duplex*. This seems to have rather more petals than my specimen.

VIVID (sometimes called *Rosa gallica phoenicea*, 'Rose de Normandie'). A hybrid rose of great vigour, with thorny stems reaching to 6 feet, and shining leaves; probably related to the

Centifolias. The flowers are very double, opening from dark crimson buds, to vivid magenta-crimson, with a hint of cerise. Very well filled with petals, reflexing to a flat circle, and becoming flushed with magenta in hot weather. Rather upsetting among the Gallicas, and best with such companions as 'Zigeuner Knabe' and 'Adam Messerich', two newer Bourbon Roses. I have never felt that this rose was a real Gallica and the late M. Jean Muraour of Mougins informed me that it was classed as a Hybrid Bourdon; raised by Paul in 1853.

YPSILANTÉ, see IPSILANTÉ.

'Scarlet Fire' ('Scharlachglut'), a rose raised by Mr Wilhelm Kordes of Holstein, Germany, is a spectacular hybrid of *Rosa gallica*, crossed with the Hybrid Tea 'Poinsettia'. A healthy arching bush, with attractive stems and foliage. The flowers are the most sumptuously velvety that I have seen, of an intense and glorious scarlet-crimson, large, single, and of beautiful shape, borne all along the branches. This is a valuable garden plant. Fully described in *Shrub Roses of Today*, page 192. (Pl. VII.)

Chapter XIII

· ·

The Damask Roses

(*Rosa damascena*)

And here I prophesy,—this brawl today
Grown to this faction, in the Temple garden,
Shall send, between the red rose and the white,
A thousand souls to death and deadly night.

Shakespeare, King Henry VI

THE DAMASK ROSES have proved the most elusive and most diverse of all these old types. There were fewer Damasks to be found in old gardens and their nomenclature has been, and still is, the most puzzling. This is partly because they have so many different types, which is not very remarkable when we consider their probable parentage, so fascinatingly indicated by Dr Hurst. It always strikes me as strange that some hybrids inclining more towards *Rosa moschata* have not been found. In view of their mixed parentage it is very difficult to fix on a particular rose as a type of the group; some of them are open and thorny like the Centifolias, while others incline to the Gallicas. *Rosa phoenicea*, one of the parents of the Summer Damasks, is not a very imposing plant; it is sprawling, with thorny wood and small single white flowers. Its characters are scarcely noticeable in its hybrids at first sight. The more compact Damasks shew obvious Gallica affinity, but all of the distinct Damasks do have a soft pubescence on the upper surface of their leaves; this is specially evident in 'Léda', 'Omar Khayyám', 'Petite Lisette', 'Quatre Saisons', and *versicolor*.

It is safe, therefore, to think of the Damasks as having downy grey foliage, with rather thorny wood, and, in many instances, rather weak flower stalks. This is a character of the 'York and Lancaster' Rose. In addition the receptacle or hip is usually attenuated, and by no means globose as in *Rosa gallica*, and the flowers are frequently borne in long bunches. Especially may this be noted in *Rosa damascena versicolor*, 'Ispahan', and *Celsiana*.

'Ispahan' has possibly the longest flowering period of the Summer Damasks.

The Autumn Damasks were to me unknown until suddenly the rather poor 'Perpetual White Moss' sported to a pink moss-less rose. This gave me the clue and I realized I had had R. *damascena bifera*, or the 'Quatre Saisons' Rose for some years without knowing what it was. From that moment the White Mosses also fell into their places in my mind. (Pls. IV, 19.)

Dr Hurst's notes regarding the 'Scarlet Four Seasons' are of great use here, for they point to the probable origin of the race of Portland Roses. These are bushy roses, probably not exceeding 4 feet in height, and have one character which is very peculiar. In my own mind I always think of it as 'high shouldered'. The blooms have very short stalks or 'necks', and sit tightly upon a rosette or 'shoulder' of leaves. They are mostly compact, quartered flowers, full-petalled, and keep on pushing up fresh flowering shoots through the season. The following varieties are still in cultivation:

Arthur de Sansal, 1855. Crimson-purple.

Blanc de Vibert, 1847. White, narrow pale green leaves.

Céline Dubois. White.

Comte de Chambord. 1860. Pink.

Jacques Cartier, 1868. Light pink, a vigorous variety, light-green leaves. Pronounced button eye.

Madame Knorr, 1855. Large, brilliant rose, reverse pale. Loose flower, semi-double.

Panachée de Lyon, 1895. A striking variety of bright pink striped with dark Tyrian rose and purple. Bushy.

Pergolèse, 1860. Rich magenta-purple and Tyrian rose.

For fuller descriptions please refer to page 209.

Once seen, these roses are unmistakable, and bear a remarkable resemblance to the Perpetual Moss Rose 'Mousseline'. In fact, this resemblance, and the finding of two similar Mosses at the Roseraie de l'Haÿ ('Marie Leczinska' and 'Mélanie Valdor', both raised in 1865) quite forcibly prove that the Autumn Damask Rose has played some part in the formation of the Mosses. The hard almost woody moss of 'Quatre Saisons Blanc Mousseux' is undoubtedly encountered again in 'Mousseline' and 'Comtesse de Murinais'. The soft moss of *Rosa centifolia muscosa* is very different to the touch.

In cultivation the Summer Damasks need the same good attention as the Provence Roses; the same good soil and pruning. Their twiggy pieces should be removed early after flowering, and the long, strong shoots shortened by one-third in the winter. The Autumn Damasks, Perpetual Mosses, and the Portland Roses will only produce a really good succession of flowers provided they are pruned rather like Hybrid Tea Roses in December or January.

The 'Kazanlik' rose had been a mystery to me for many years. I had received no less than three distinct roses under this name; one was a *gallica,* one turned out to be 'Ispahan' and a third was identical with another rose I had been given labelled 'Professeur Émile Perrot'. This proved to be the real rose from Kazanlik, R. *damascena trigintipetala,* the rose grown in greater quantity than any other in Bulgaria for the production of 'attar' or 'otto'. It is a similar type to 'York and Lancaster', R. *damascena versicolor,* with spindly growth up to 6 feet or so, soft light green leaves, and rather small flowers, loosely double, of soft pink. In spite of its name this rose, over here at least, seldom has as many as thirty petals.

Through the kindness of Mr V. M. Staicov of the Bulgarian State Agricultural Institute for the Investigation of Medical and Aromatic Plants, who kindly sent me both herbarium specimens and, later, living material of the roses grown at Kazanlik, I have been able to elucidate the matter. The varieties are:

R. *damascena.* This appears to be almost if not quite identical with my R. *damascena trigintipetala.*

R. *alba,* with various numbers of petals. One is liable to get variation of this kind when raising R. *alba semi-plena* from seed.

'Stambulska' and 'Trendaphil', which I have so far been unable to identify with anything in this country.

R. *rugosa* 'Roseraie de l'Haÿ'. This variety is only on trial at Kazanlik and has not been used for industrial purposes.

Much further information about the rose fields and industry in Bulgaria will be found in the sequel to this book, *Shrub Roses of Today* (1962), Chapter 16.

Miss Willmott's plate of R. *damascena* is, to me, unrecognizable.

Two roses introduced by Miss Lindsay probably fit into the Damask group. They are her No. 849 ('Rose de Resht'), which is a highly desirable compact shrub (? an Autumn Damask or near hybrid), producing neat rosette flowers in dark crimson-pink through the summer; and No. 1409 ('Rose d'Hivers'), a twiggy little bush that may be a hybrid with *Rosa alba*. The flowers are dainty and of perfect shape, the larger outer petals, nearly white, guarding the flesh-pink central petals, which remain in bud formation for some days.

DAMASK ROSES

BLUSH DAMASK. Frequently labelled 'Blush Gallica'. I have a suspicion it may be a hybrid with a Scots Briar; it is certainly not a typical Damask. It forms a large, very twiggy bush, in time as much as 6 feet high and wide, bearing neat dark leaves, and is well covered in June with multitudes of nodding blooms. They are dark lilac-pink when half open, reflexing into a ball, lilac-white at the edges. Short flowering season.
Bunyard, Plate 30.

CELSIANA. Prior to 1750. A very beautiful rose, and it was a great pleasure to find it figured in Redouté after having grown it for years under the erroneous and misleading name 'Incarnata Maxima', which is only another way of saying 'Great Maiden's Blush'. With this rose it has, of course, no connection. *Celsiana* is a graceful shrub with attractive light green leaves, smooth and greyish. The flowers are borne in typical clusters, and are wide and open, semi-double, revealing bright yellow stamens in the centre. When first open they are of a warm, light pink, fading later to blush. They are at all times extremely beautiful, in a loose informal way, with silky and folded petals. 4-5 feet.
Redouté, Vol. 2. Plate 53.

CORALIE. A fine arching shrub with somewhat thorny stems growing to about 4 feet, bearing small greyish leaves. The cupped blooms are of soft, warm pink, with rolled petals fading at the edges to blush. An attractive colour scheme.

GLOIRE DE GUILAN, 1949. A most attractive sprawling shrub up to 3 or 4 feet, with very fresh green leaves and small curved thorns. The cupped blooms soon open flat, being quartered, and with some petals remaining folded, in a particularly clear and beautiful pink. In the Caspian provinces of Persia this rose is used for making Attar of Roses, whence it was brought and named by Miss Nancy Lindsay.

ISPAHAN ('Rose d'Isfahan'). Also known as 'Pompon des Princes'. This is one of the first old roses to open and one of the last to finish, and creates a brilliant display for the whole period. It is a fine bushy upright shrub, up to 5 feet or so, and extremely free flowering in clusters, although its small rather shiny leaves suggest other parentage than pure Damask. Neat buds, and exquisite half-open blooms, reflexing loosely later, and at all times a clear and 'pretty' pink.

LA VILLE DE BRUXELLES, 1849. A fine luxuriant shrub, with notably long and large leaves, well shaped and poised, and of clear light green. The flowers are among the largest of old roses, and when fully open reflex at the edges, from a large convex centre massed with short petals, with a button eye. The clear rich pink is constant. The individual flowering spray is of high quality, but the weight of the blooms tends to send the flowers downwards among the leaves—its only fault. 5 feet.

LÉDA (the 'Painted Damask'). Originated in England. This rose has certain qualities all of its own, particularly its luxuriant *dark* green rounded foliage and red-brown buds, which look bruised and battered, shewing the colour of the petals long before they open. When the flower opens to an iridescent milky white just suffused with blush, the external red tones develop to carmine, remaining on the extremities of the outer petals, and giving the reason for its popular name. Most flowers have a pronounced button eye, and are well filled with petals, which reflex into almost a ball. 3 feet. (Pl. IV.)
Smith, *The Florist's Museum*, page 113. Poor.

LÉDA, PINK FORM. There is little doubt that this is a sport from the above variety, or it may be that the 'Painted Damask' arose from this pink type. They are identical apart from colour; in this form the colour is a soft uniform rosy-pink, darker in the bud and again very fragrant. This form was apparently better known on the Continent, while the 'Painted Damask' was more grown over here.

MADAME HARDY, 1832. This rose, one of the most superlatively beautiful of the old white varieties, and having few peers among the coloured varieties, is not a pure Damask, but

probably owes some of its beauty and vigour to *Rosa centifolia.*
The bush is sturdy, up to 5 or 6 feet on good soils, with a
variety of thorns and broad mid-green leaves shewing little
connection with the Damask Roses. The clusters of flowers do,
however, shew this affinity, while the perfect shape of the
blooms is found again only in some of the Gallica Roses.
There is just a suspicion of flesh pink in the half-open buds,
emerging from their long calyces, and the flowers open cupped,
rapidly becoming flat, the outer petals reflexing in a most
beautiful manner, leaving the centre almost concave, of pure
white, with a small green eye. A bunch of these roses with some
'Belle de Crécy' among them give to me the most satisfying
complement imaginable. Both have exquisite form, and are
sumptuous and ravishing. Paul mentions in 1848 that this one
variety would suffice to make M. Hardy's name famous.
What true words! This variety is still unsurpassed by any rose.
(Pl. 9.) See also page 208.

Bunyard, Plate 14. *Rosa centifolia alba.*
Bunyard in *New Flora and Silva,* Vol. 2. Fig. 1. *Rosa centifolia alba.*
Journal des Roses, Août 1880. Rather gross.
Komlosy. The plate obviously refers to the rose 'Mme Plantier'.

MME ZÖETMANS. The flowers are very much like the *gallica*
'Duchesse de Montebello', but are much paler; they quickly
fade almost to white with a faint blush centre, and are full
petalled with button eyes. The leaves are of fresh green, as
opposed to those of the 'Duchesse de Montebello', which are
grey-green. Early flowering. Graceful and free, growing to
4 feet. This has since proved a first-rate variety.

MARIE LOUISE, 1813. Raised at Malmaison. This rose has one of
the most sumptuous flowers of the group. It forms a rather
procumbent shrub, not only on account of lax growth, but also
because the flowers are so large and heavy. To lift up the leafy
sprays and look steadily at the fully open blooms is a revelation
—just another achievement of the rose. They carry no special
promise in their buds, but, when fully open, the uniform mauve-
pink flowers are extremely full-petalled, reflexing into a ball,
with large outer petals and pronounced button eye. 4 feet.

OEILLET PARFAIT, 1841. It is important to remember that the other
rose of this name was a striped Gallica. This variety probably

owes its compact habit to *Rosa gallica*, but may suitably be grouped here for convenience. The uniform, rounded, small leaves are of soft green, covering a 3–4 foot compact twiggy bush with mixed thorns. Flowers in clusters of two or three, opening flat and very densely packed with shell-like petals from round fat buds, borne on stiff stalks. Later they reflex into almost a ball, being of rich, warm pink, fading slightly paler. I have found this rose under the name of 'Tour d'Auvergne'.

OMAR KHAYYÁM. An interesting, true Damask Rose, which has been propagated from Edward Fitzgerald's grave at Boulge, Suffolk, where it was originally planted in 1893, having been brought as seed from Omar Khayyám's grave at Nashipur. Light green wood and dark thorns; leaves small, downy, pale green. The flowers are not large but shew distinct formation, having a pronounced button eye and folded and quartered petals, in soft light pink. **3 feet.**

PETITE LISETTE, 1817. This charming miniature variety has a few small thorns and green wood, and bears distinctly downy greyish foliage, small, rounded, and coarsely toothed. It is this cool colour which is so pleasant a complement to the clear blush pink of the neat flat circular flowers, perfectly formed, and well filled with folded petals, radiating from a pronounced button eye. 4 feet. At times I am tempted to think this is an original type of Damask Rose; it is closely related to 'Omar Khayyám', and also to the hybrid *Rosa gallica* 'Agathe Incarnata'.

QUATRE SAISONS (*Rosa damascena bifera*) (*R. rubra* × *R. moschata*). A form of Autumn Damask Rose which I received from gardens in England and Ireland, and also from California, but without a reliable name. In 1950 I was interested to find it as a sport on my 'Perpetual White Moss' (Damask) (q.v., page 161), and this same sport was recorded also at Shrewsbury by Miss Murrell in the same year. It is notable not for the shape of its blooms but for its propensity of putting forth flowers from June to October; for its particularly pale yellowish-grey-green leaves, prolifically borne; its rich fragrance and long sepals. The flowers open from shapely buds, and are of clear pink deeper in the centres, with few crumpled petals, sometimes quartered. Since this sported back from the 'Perpetual White Moss' it is presumably *the* original Autumn Damask. 5 feet. (Pls. IV, 19.) Also called the 'Alexandrian Rose'.

QUATRE SAISONS BLANC MOUSSEUX (R. *damascena bifera alba muscosa*), 1835. The 'Perpetual White Moss', 'Rosier de Thionville.' This interesting variety, recorded in *Production et Fixation des Variétés dans les végétaux* by E. A. Carrière, is undoubtedly a sport from the rose listed here as Quatre Saisons, since it reverted to that variety in 1950. The foliage is of the same colour, but bears mossy excrescences on the upper surface of the leaves on vigorous shoots. The moss on leaf, stem, and bud is brownish-green and the flowers are white with a faint blush tint on opening. Shapely buds but poor flowers. Erect vigorous bushy growth. June–October. 5 feet. (Pls. IV, 19.) See also page 208. Paul, Plate 10.
Carrière, as above.
Komlosy.

RUBROTINCTA ('Hebe's Lip', 'Margined Hip', or 'Reine Blanche'). This hybrid of unknown origin makes a pretty picture when in flower and has much charm. Fresh green, coarsely toothed leaves make a good background to the cupped semi-double flowers of creamy-white, edged with rosy-crimson. The buds are particularly beautiful. It has a rather short flowering season. 4 feet.
Willmott, Plate facing page 375.

ST NICHOLAS, 1950. This very beautiful rose appeared spontaneously in the garden whose name it bears, owned by the Hon. Robert James, at Richmond, Yorks. It forms a sturdy erect bush with hooked prickles and good, dark-green foliage. The flowers are semi-double, of warm, rich pink, paler in the centre around the circle of golden stamens. It is no less beautiful when the petals open flat and the flower becomes paler all over, and the autumn hips are very showy. 4–5 feet.

VERSICOLOR ('York and Lancaster'). A typical tall-growing Damask with the usual mixed thorns, green wood, and downy greygreen leaves of light tint. They are beautifully poised. On good soil and in cool conditions, as at Hidcote, Chipping Campden, this rose can be very beautiful, the clusters of long, stalked flowers spraying outward, in blush white and light pink, over the soft foliage. They are loosely double, and not particularly shapely, but may be entirely of the paler or the darker colour, or flaked one with the other, or distinctly parti-coloured. They are never splashed and striped as in 'Rosa Mundi'. The impression given by Redouté is by no means exaggerated; it can be a fine rose when well grown. Interesting; raised prior to 1629. Possibly this is the rose which played so prominent a part in the 'brawl in the Temple Garden', between Yorkists and Lancastrians, which factions apparently later adopted *Rosa alba maxima* and *Rosa gallica officinalis* as their emblems. 5 feet. (Pl. IV.)

Andrews, Plate 48. *Rosa damascena variegata*. Shows excellent variations.

Bunyard, Plate 23.

Lawrance, Plate 10.

Miller, Plate 221. *Rosa praenestina variegata plena*. 'York and Lancaster.'

Redouté, Vol. 1. Plate 137. *Rosa damascena variegata*.

Roessig, Plate 14. This portrait is of *Rosa gallica versicolor*.

Roessig, Plate 33. A true portrait. 'Rose d'Yorck et de Lancastre.' *Rosa nubeculis rubentibus suffusa alba*, 'York et Lancaster dicta'.

Chapter XIV

. . . .

The White Roses
(*Rosa alba*)

Then, for the truth and plainness of the case,
I pluck this pale and maiden blossom here,
Giving my verdict on the white rose side.
Shakespeare, King Henry vi

In Dr Hurst's notes it will be seen that he regards this race of roses as derived probably from *Rosa damascena* and a form of *Rosa canina*. It is a good thought that *Rosa canina*, the wild 'Dog Briar' of this and other European countries, had a part in forming what must surely be the most beautiful and refined of all the old groups of roses. Many have undoubtedly preferred *Rosa centifolia* to the White Roses, but to me there is no rose scent so pure and refreshingly delicious as that of the 'Maiden's Blush'; no half-open bloom so lovely as 'Céleste', nor foliage so good; and few rose forms can compete with 'Mme Legras' or 'Koenigin von Danemarck'. The White Roses are supreme over all the other old races in vigour, longevity, foliage, delicacy of colour (for they embrace some exquisite pink varieties), and purity of scent.

Journeying through our countryside, whether it be in Cornwall or the home counties, west of the Marches or north of the Border, or over the sea to the Emerald Isle or France, certain White Roses, specially the 'Great Double White' and 'Maiden's Blush', are encountered wherever a rose has been 'suffered' to live through the decades. Frequently they are remnants of plantings of a hundred years ago, so strong and self-reliant are they. Though sometimes crowded against a villa wall, their root run restricted by concrete pavement, or overhung by trees, or in a damp, cold, north country garden, they thrive and flower well annually. They appear to resist all diseases.

They are one of the few types of roses that can actually be recommended for north walls; *Rosa alba maxima, semi-plena,* and

163

'Maiden's Blush' give a splendid display when trained up walls and allowed to spray outward. The smallest is the compact 'Jeanne d'Arc'; 'Félicité Parmentier', 'Koenigin von Dane-marck', and 'Pompon Parfait' reach up taller, with *maxima* and 'Great Maiden's Blush' overtopping them. 'Blush Hip' is even taller and, with *Rosa gallica complicata*, and the two Moss Roses 'Jeanne de Montfort' and 'William Lobb', may be trained over hedges or into small trees, thence to grow downwards, with their flowers hanging at nose level.

Comparing them with other wild roses one notices at once their affinity with *Rosa canina*. The growth, thorns, bark, leaves, and heps of what we may term the typical form (*Rosa alba semi-plena*) are all very reminiscent of that species. But the habit is considerably more upright, and has earned them the name of 'Tree Roses'. These roses have an ideal habit for a flowering shrub. They are not so prone to make runners as the Gallicas, although they do spread slowly in that way when on their own roots, or when 'budded' plants are set rather deeper than usual. They make strong stems from the base, infrequently set with stout prickles on smooth green wood. As the years pass the stem branches more and more at the top, gradually arching over with the weight of growth, and after five or six years a well-built thicket of twigs is the result. Some of this should be removed each year after flowering, to encourage more basal growth, and this pruning will suffice when the bushes are grown as flowering shrubs in the mixed borders.

On the other hand I feel that of all the old roses these Alba varieties respond best to close pruning. This should be done in December or January, spurring back all the previous year's small wood to an inch or so, and leaving the long shoots at one-third of their length. A superb display of good blooms all well set in even array will result. The best show of this kind that I know is at Abbotswood (see Pl. 2); less formal bushes, at Mottisfont.

Alba Roses blend happily with almost any colour; typically white or pink their tone is clearer than that of many old roses, and they lack the purple shadings of many Gallicas and Centifolias. Their adoption as flowering shrubs for general use is therefore to be encouraged, and their grey-green foliage lends enchant-ment to almost any scheme. Only recently a friend decided on

Rosa alba maxima to form a hedge in a white garden, where the foliage, after the flowering season is over, will help towards that coolness fostered by cream and other 'off-white' tints.

I have for some years grown a good bushy rose, probably of Damask × Alba parentage, called 'Belle Amour', but there is no record of this name applying to a rose of this type. There was a 'Belle Aurore', but this was a blush-tinted rose. My 'Belle Amour' has the distinction of a strong hint of myrrh in its delicious perfume. The stout, prickly stems support good, green leaves, and clusters of cup-shaped, semi-double flowers in rich coral pink, shewing yellow stamens. It is unique not only in scent but also in colour. Another rose I have recently acquired purports to be 'Sophie de Bavière', otherwise known as 'Célanire'. It is a vigorous shrub with very large bunches of extremely double flowers, the petals neatly imbricated, of soft pink. This is practically thornless, and together with 'Mme Legras' and another thornless, good pink variety received from Dr J. S. Morton of Newmarket, 'Chloris', supports Dr Hurst's theory that the original *Rosa canina* parent was a thornless type. See also page 211.

ALBA ROSES

À FEUILLES DE CHANVRE (*Rosa cannabina*). The 'Hemp-leaved' rose. This is a very old form, having almost thornless stems and narrow, long, grey-green leaves supposedly like that of its namesake. The flowers are small, white, and semi-double. 3 feet or thereabouts. I believe this variety to be extinct.
Redouté, Vol. 2. Plate 47. *Rosa alba cimbaefolia*, 'Le Rosier Blanc à feuilles de chanvre'.

BLUSH HIP. Raised about 1840, this rose was described as extremely vigorous, and a rose received from Mrs Salmon at Dublin conforms to the description. I use the name with some hesitancy, as it would seem to be but another of the 'Maiden's Blush' derivatives; however, a scandent Alba variety growing to 12 feet is something of a novelty to us nowadays. The coarsely toothed leaves suggest *Rosa centifolia* as a possible parent, although otherwise it has most of the characters of 'Maiden's Blush'. The cherry-red buds open to well-formed, fully double flowers, of soft pink, with a button centre and green eye. William Paul, in 1848, mentions this rose as 'new'.

CÉLESTE ('Celestial'). A delightful rose of true 'Alba' qualities. Apart from *Rosa virginiana plena* and the earliest polyanthas like 'Cécile Brunner' I know of no rose of such exquisite charm when unfurling its petals. The bland clarity of tone in the flowers is unparalleled among pink roses. They are semi-double, of a pure, soft uniform pink, shewing rich tones in the depths of the bud. As if this were not attraction enough the plant has leaves of particularly grey tint, the perfect foil to its floral colour, and the bush itself is strong and upstanding to about 6 feet. The flowers are enhanced by a circlet of golden stamens, and Miss Jekyll observes that it is 'a rose of wonderful beauty when the bud is half opened'. Redouté, following earlier authors, decided that certain characters warranted placing this rose among the Damasks, and calls it *Rosa damascena* 'Aurora', 'Le Rosier Aurore Poniatowska'. It was apparently of Dutch origin at the end of the eighteenth century, and had become by no means common at the time of his writing. Redouté also mentions Rose Celestis, but refers this to 'Maiden's Blush'.

I had been told that 'Céleste' was the rose plucked by the men of the Suffolk Regiment after the battle of Minden, in fact I have heard it called the 'Minden Rose'. Being curious about the matter I wrote to the Officer Commanding, Depot the Suffolk Regiment, and he kindly furnished me with the following particulars:

'. . . Actually, no rose is figured in the badge of the Suffolk Regiment; but the following is an extract from *History of the 12th (The Suffolk) Regiment*:

1759

The Wearing of Roses

"All battalions of the Suffolk Regiment, on 'Minden Day' (1st August), wear roses in their head-dress, and in the event of a parade, the colours and drums are similarly decked in honour of that memorable victory.

"As regards the selection of the rose, the accepted story is that when the regiment was following up the retreating French troops, they passed through a rose garden, and each man plucked a rose, which he fastened to his head-dress. Roses are also worn by the regiment on the Sovereign's birthday, in accordance with long-established custom."

'From the above it would appear that no one particular rose was worn during the battle, though the roses now worn by members of the Suffolk Regiment on Minden Day and on the Sovereign's birthday are red and yellow roses—the regimental colours being red and yellow. . . .'

It is difficult to see how any of the *old* roses could have been in flower as late as 1st August, apart from the Autumn Damask.

Redouté, Vol. 2. Plate 41. *Rosa damascena* 'Aurora'.

Willmott, Vol. 2. Plate facing page 413. *Rosa alba rubicunda*. The description following this figure unfortunately confuses this distinct rose with 'Maiden's Blush'.

Andrews, Plate 18. *Rosa erubescens* ('Blushing' or 'Celestial' Rose).

CHLORIS ('Rosée du Matin'). Well-named 'Dew of the Morning' for its buds are only less beautiful than those of Céleste. It is a good healthy bush. The thorns are few, the leaves leathery and dark green, held horizontally and flat. In the centre of the bud is a great depth of clear pink, the outer petals rolling backwards to the finely divided sepals. When fully open it reveals a soft 'Céleste' pink all over, reflexing and shewing a button eye. A 'Maiden's Blush' type without the muddled centre. 4–5 feet.

CUISSE DE NYMPHE. Synonymous with 'Maiden's Blush'.

CUISSE DE NYMPHE ÉMUE. A name sometimes given to particularly well-coloured flowers of 'Maiden's Blush'.

FÉLICITÉ PARMENTIER, 1836. Reaching to about 5 feet, and being less upright than most of the Alba varieties, this shews a possible Damask affinity, and has light, almost yellowish-green leaves and twigs, with contrasting dark thorns. The peculiar yellow tone of the buds vanishes when they open. No other variety in this section has such densely packed buds, opening to such full flowers of clear flesh pink. The petals reflex, a fully open flower being shaped almost like a ball, and fading to cream at the edges. (Pl. 10.)

JEANNE D'ARC, 1818. Probably synonymous with 'Anglica minor'. This may be described as a dwarf version of the 'Great Double White' (*maxima*), forming a very dense bush up to 4 or 5 feet with typical, rather coarse, dark grey-green leaves. The flowers are well filled, with muddled centres, and are of a rich creamy-flesh on first opening, rapidly fading to ivory white.

KOENIGIN VON DANEMARCK ('Queen of Denmark'), 1826. Like some of the later results of hybridizing in other groups, this variety has a perfection of form almost unequalled, and may be ranked with 'Madame Hardy', 'Duc de Guiche', and a few others, to shew what the hybridizers of that day considered superlatively beautiful. The foliage is of dark blue-green, the leaves being extremely well cut and elegant; the buds are likewise perfect, and the partly opened flower reveals an intensity of vivid carmine unequalled by any other old rose. The flowers are at first cupped, but their multitudinous petals push outwards and reflex, by which time they are of a pale 'Céleste' pink, and are often beautifully quartered with a button centre. Its growth, though healthy and vigorous up to 6 feet or so, is somewhat open and spindly; wall culture would undoubtedly help. (Pl. II.)

Mr Geoffrey Taylor of Dublin tells me there was a China Rose of 1899 called 'Queen of Denmark'; but adds that Rivers in his *Rose Amateur's Guide* of 1861 and earlier says, under *Rosa alba*, 'Queen of Denmark': 'An old, but estimable variety, produces flowers of first-rate excellence as prize-flowers: so much was this esteemed when first raised from seed, that plants were sent from Germany to this country at five guineas each.' Mr O. Sonder-housen, Denmark, has sent me an amusing and exhaustive extract proving that this rose first flowered in 1816, and was first listed in Denmark in 1826. See also page 212.

MADAME LEGRAS DE ST GERMAIN. Prior to 1848. 'A superb White Rose,' says William Paul at that date. This rose has made vigorous shoots up to 7 feet, almost thornless, bearing pale-green leaves. The flowers are perfection indeed, opening from a dainty bud to slightly cupped blooms of good size, later quite flat, and filled with regular petals. They are of glistening ivory white with a distinct pale canary-yellow flush in the centre, and in this colouring they are distinct from all other Alba varieties, until the Noisettes are considered. I can give no higher praise than to state that it is undoubtedly a rival in quality to 'Mme Hardy'. Petals suffer in wet weather.

MAIDEN'S BLUSH, GREAT. Prior to the fifteenth century. One of the oldest favourites, and frequently found in cottage gardens, where its perennial good behaviour has commended it for safe keeping, in this country and on the Continent. 'La Royale', 'La Séduisante', 'Cuisse de Nymphe', 'La Virginale', 'Incarnata', and other fanciful names of free translation indicate its popularity. Specially well-coloured blooms were called 'Cuisse de Nymphe Émue'. It ranks very high among large shrub roses, having good, greyish foliage and stalwart growth up to 6 feet, thence freely branching and arching outwards to display the numerous flowers, of a delicate quality, and carrying a fragrance unequalled for pure sweetness. Its shape is informal, like that of *Rosa alba maxima*; it is a soft, warm, blush-pink on opening, and the petals reflex and fade to a pale cream-pink at the edges, the 'Maiden's Blush' remaining always in the centre. Redouté records this as *Rosa alba regalis*, 'Le Rosier Blanc Royale'. '. . . C'est la Great Maiden's Blush des Anglais, la Grosse Cuisse de Nymphe. C'est à-peu-près semblable a celle dite "La Cuisse de Nymphe Émue". . . .' This is a rose which makes a really splendid display as an informal hedge, and as a shrub has particularly good garden value. (Pl. III). See also page 213.

Redouté, Vol. 1. Plate 97. *Rosa alba regalis*.

Roessig, Plate 23. *Rosa alba rubicunda plena*, 'Rosier Blanc incarnat à fleurs doubles'. A remarkable portrait. Possibly the 'Small Maiden's Blush'. Plate 48. 'La Rose Rougissante', *Rosa rubicans*. Another excellent portrait, probably of 'Great Maiden's Blush'.

MAIDEN'S BLUSH, SMALL. With flowers only slightly smaller than the greater variety, this useful rose reaches only to 4 feet in height, but loses no charm thereby.

Bunyard, Plate 16.

Roessig, see under Maiden's Blush, Great.

MAXIMA ('Great Double White'; 'Jacobite Rose'; 'Cheshire Rose'). A noble shrub with coarse, leaden-green leaves, borne mostly at the top of the big bushes, up to 7 or 8 feet in height. It is of rather gaunt habit, and best for the back of the border or for training on walls, and has scattered large prickles. The flowers are informally double, with muddled centres, opening to warm creamy-blush, quickly passing to creamy-white. This is a noble old rose and the most common in old gardens of all the old roses. I have seen it in the east and west, and in Wales, Scotland, and Ireland, always doing well. (Pl. 11.) See also page 213.

Kingsley, facing page 37, described as 'Rugosa'; *Rosa alba*.

Roessig, Plate 15. 'Le Rosier Blanc à fleurs doubles', *Rosa alba plena*.

Andrews, Plate 12. *Rosa alba flore pleno*.

POMPON BLANC PARFAIT, 1876. A stranger to this group in several ways. It is, however, a true 'pompon' type with delightful neat rosette blooms in palest lilac-pink, produced from fat, round, little buds. These are borne over a very long period, well into July. The growth is slender and erect, with few thorns, and the small, pale, grey-green leaves are perfectly in keeping with the miniature blooms. 5 feet.

SEMI-PLENA. This is probably *Rosa alba suaveolens* or *nivea*, one of the roses grown for distilling attar at Kazanlik, where it frequently surrounds plantations of Damask Roses. Assorting well with true species roses on account of its refined air, this nearly single-flowered type may be regarded as an old form of this group, and it is one of the loveliest in growth, spraying its clusters of milk-white, golden-centred blooms over the ample grey-green foliage. In the autumn it carries a splendid crop of red heps. 5–6 feet. See also page 213.

Jekyll, facing page 14.

Bunyard, in *New Flora and Silva*, Vol. 2. Fig. 4 (The 'Maiden's Blush' Rose).

Willmott, Plate 136. *Rosa alba*.

Redouté, Vol. 1. Plate 117. *Rosa alba flore pleno*. Redouté records that the single variety has never been found wild, according to Desvaux.

Roessig, Plate 34.

Andrews, Plate 11. *Rosa alba semi duplex*.

Chapter XV

· ·

The Provence Roses

(*Rosa centifolia*)

Loveliest of lovely things are they,
On earth that soonest pass away.
The rose that lives its little hour
Is prized beyond the sculptured flower.

William Cullen Bryant

IT IS ONLY in favourable conditions that the varieties of *Rosa centifolia* can be called good garden plants. More often than not their open thorny growth is anything but elegant, but when their full gracious flowers appear we can forgive them all their faults.

As a group their growth is generally lax and open, and the gaunt thorny stems need the support of stakes or close planting. *Rosa centifolia*, and its varieties *cristata*, *bullata*, 'La Noblesse', and *variegata* are of similar habit and qualities. 'Petite de Hollande', 'Spong', and 'Unique' are much more bushy and able to stand on their own; 'Fantin-Latour', 'Blanchefleur', and 'Paul Ricault' are equally sturdy and taller growing. The two miniatures, 'De Meaux' and *burgundica*, are self-reliant also. 'Tour de Malakoff' is very prone to flop, and needs a wall or stake, also 'Robert le Diable', a smaller bush.

New shoots five feet long are not uncommon during the summer, and apart from any other pruning I think it is essential to reduce these by at least one-third or one-half in January. Otherwise, when the short flowering shoots appear during the following summer, the weight of the young growth will cause too much bending and arching, with the result that the stems will tend to become procumbent. By shortening the stems this evil may be avoided. Apart from this special treatment, pruning can be much the same as that recommended for the White Roses.

It would not do, however, to prune away all tendency to droop. Drooping is the very spirit of the Provence Roses. Their big

171

leaves droop and likewise their buds and flowers, and far from their having just a weak neck, they appear deliberately to enhance their charm by gracefully arching their stalks and causing their admirers to lift their great luxuriant blooms. The big outer petals enfold the shorter 'hundred leaves' which, not being affected generally by direct sunlight, retain a depth of colouring very telling in effect.

Let us therefore grow our Provence Roses for their nodding grace and fullness, and forget their prickly gawkiness and coarse leaves. Let us leave spring-like sweetness to the White Roses and revel in the full summer of the Provence varieties. Dr Hurst tells us that they blend the fragrance of two roses famed for their scent, *Rosa alba* and *Rosa moschata*. Little trace of the intoxicating, almost overpowering, scent of *Rosa moschata* is evident to my nose, but its carrying power is there. A sun-warmed Centifolia has a richness almost unbelievable.

Mr F. J. Lambe of Totnes once sent me a semi-double rose which I recognised as very near to, if not identical with, Redouté's portrait of *Rosa centifolia anemonoides* (Vol. 2. Plate 115). This originated apparently about 1810, and has flowers of the usual pink, but the central petals are short and give what in horticulture is usually termed an 'anemone centre'. I have lost this variety.

Drapiez, Vol. 6, page 417. *Rosier aux centfeuilles*, var. Anemone.

PROVENCE ROSES

The 'Rose of a Hundred Leaves' is also the 'Rose des Peintres' in its best form, the 'Provence' or 'Cabbage' rose, and its poise, its shape, and its colour have been immortalized in many an Old Master. Its noted forms, *Rosa centifolia bullata*, *cristata*, and *muscosa*, have the same long projecting sepals and rich drooping flowers, the same numerous petals—so closely curved round one another that the flower remains globe-shaped with a deep open centre—the same clear-pink colouring, and the delicious intense fragrance. R. *centifolia* itself is a wide-spreading, open, and tall shrub up to 5 feet in height, and its shoots, bearing prickles of mixed sizes and shapes from small spines to big hooked thorns, reach outwards to droop the next season with the weight of the big blooms, borne singly and in clusters. The large, rounded, drooping leaves are very coarsely toothed, and the whole plant has a lax air, yet it is sturdy. When wide open the flowers reveal a large button eye. The unfortunate title of 'Cabbage' Rose has led to considerable confusion, as cabbages today more nearly approximate the incurved blooms of 'Caroline Testout' or a modern Hybrid Tea Rose than the 'Rose des Peintres'. Moreover, few people today think of *Rosa centifolia* when describing a rose as 'cabbagy'—this term indeed more aptly describes the Hybrid Perpetuals, most of which have fallen out of cultivation. In fact my experience has been that people who want to plant 'cabbage roses' generally mean some coarse old Hybrid Perpetual rose of their childhood and seldom have any conception of *R. centifolia*. See also page 214.

Kingsley, facing page 38.

Willmott. Plate facing page 345. Hardly recognizable; the material available was obviously incorrectly named, as Alfred Parsons captured all the grace of the Provence Rose in the 'Common Moss Rose'.

Redouté, Vol. 1. Plate 25.

Jamain and Forney, Plate 15.

Roessig, Plate 1.

BLANCHEFLEUR, 1835. Not quite a typical form, but obviously a close relative, this rose has a vigorous open habit up to some 5 feet, with very spiny shoots and light-green leaves. The flowers have a rather cabbagy appearance, but are nevertheless very attractive in their creamy white, blushing in the centres of newly opened flowers, and with red-tipped buds. The blooms are often quartered and open flat, with rolled edges to the petals.

BULLATA, or the 'Rose à feuilles de Laitue'. This distinctive form originated about 1801, and apart from its leaves is a typical Provence Rose, with growth, buds, flowers, and scent like *Rosa centifolia*. But the leaves are remarkable and are in their way the most handsome in the genus. They undoubtedly resemble those of a lettuce—particularly 'Continuity'—in their puckered, 'bullate', and enlarged segments, hanging loosely from their stalks, and are richly tinted with mahogany while young. A rose of botanic and historic interest. 4–5 feet.

Willmott, Plate facing page 367. *Rosa provincialis bullata*.

Redouté, Vol. 1. Plate 37.

CENTIFOLIA ALBA. The rose figured under this name by Bunyard is the Hybrid Damask Rose 'Mme Hardy' (q.v., page 158). It is quite possible that 'Mme Hardy' has Centifolia parentage, but is not fit to be classed as a true *Rosa centifolia* variety, and is usually found among the Damasks in old French books.

CRISTATA, 1826. This is also called 'Crested Moss', but is, according to Dr Hurst's findings, not an approach to a Moss Rose, but rather a parallel sport. The 'wings' of the calyx are crested and enlarged to such an extent that the buds are almost enveloped in greenery. These buds are in fact of very great beauty, and impart to this otherwise typical *Rosa centifolia* a distinct charm. Fancy has added another title, 'Chapeau de Napoléon', as the winged calyx resembles a cockade. Records tell us that it was first found in 1820 in the crevice of an old wall at Fribourg in Switzerland, and may have been a chance seedling. The flowers are not quite so globular as *Rosa centifolia* itself. (Pl. II.) 4-5 feet.

Keays, facing page 52.   *Botanical Magazine*, t.3475.
Bunyard, Plate 20.   Hariot, Plate 60.
Paul, Plate 1.
Willmott, Plate facing page 351. (not easily recognizable).
Journal des Roses, Avril 1885.

DE MEAUX (*Rosa centifolia pomponia*). This miniature is a charming little plant, with erect green shoots up to 3 or 4 feet, branched and twiggy in later years, bearing miniature Centifolia leaves of light green. The flowers are not of Centifolia shape, but are those of a pompon, opening flat, from exquisite buds, and of typical pink. It is much earlier flowering than the larger Provence varieties. The form known as 'White de Meaux' ('Le Rosier Pompon Blanc') is an albino with pink centres. 'Mossy de Meaux', introduced in 1814, I have not yet found. (Pl. 14.) See also page 214.

Bunyard, Plate 28.
Willmott, Plate facing page 353.
Redouté, Vol. 1. Plate 65. *Rosa pomponia*. Perhaps.
Lawrance, Plate 31.
Lawrance, Plate 50. 'White de Meaux' ('Rosier de Pompon').

Roessig, Plate 24. 'Le Rosier de Dijon.' Perhaps.

Roessig, Plate 37. 'Rose-pompon', *Rosa pomponia*.

DUC DE FITZJAMES. Vigorous shrub up to 6 feet with good foliage and trusses of cupped blooms revealing green eyes. The petals are densely packed, shewing very beautiful quartering, and fade to a soft lilac, being paler on the reverse. An effective plant, but the blooms are rather coarse.

FANTIN-LATOUR. It is difficult to know where to class this splendid rose, as it clearly has Centifolia flowers, but the leaves shew signs of China Rose smoothness. In growth and flower, however, it nearly approaches typical *Rosa centifolia*, and as it has one season of flowering only, it seems best included under this heading. It will make a large rounded bush, well clothed in handsome, broad, dark green leaves, 5 feet high and wide on good soils, and is one of the most handsome of shrub roses, particularly when in flower. Poised with Centifolia charm the blooms have a circular, cupped shape when half open, of a bland pale pink, warmly tinted in the central folds with rich blush. Later the outer petals reflex, still leaving the centre cupped, and at this stage it is scarcely surpassed in beauty. It is a most satisfying rose in every way, and has a delicious fragrance. I found it in one garden where its name was unknown, labelled 'Best Garden Rose', and as such it is worthily named after the great French artist. So far I have been unable to trace the name in any book. (Pl. 15.)

JUNO, 1847. An arching shrub with soft, leaden-green leaves. It is grouped as a 'hybride non-remontant', and it would appear to fit this description, as it is certainly not a Hybrid Perpetual, but has some affinity with that group, although the flowers more nearly approach the exquisite form of the Provence Rose. The globular blooms of delicate blush open to a flat flower resembling 'Souvenir de la Malmaison', with a large button eye. Being lax in growth it would be very suitable for hanging over a low wall or growing as a standard. 4 feet. See also page 214.

LA NOBLESSE, 1856. This is the last of the Provence roses to flower, and has proved to be a fine shapely bush, more compact and with better foliage than the type. The flowers have the characteristic colour, shape, and scent, but are rather smaller than *Rosa centifolia* itself. 5 feet.

OMBRÉE PARFAITE, 1823. Vigorous but rather procumbent shrub, copiously clad in fresh green, folded, pointed leaves. The rather shapeless little blooms resemble those of 'Hippolyte', and show a similar remarkable diversity of tones, light-pink petals being placed next to those of intense dark maroon-purple. One of the darkest roses in my collection. 3 feet. A *gallica* derivative.

PARVIFOLIA. The 'Pompon de Burgogne' is another favourite old miniature, also known as *Rosa burgundica* and 'Pompon de St François'. Perhaps figured by Tabernaemontanus in 1590. It no doubt occurred as a mutation. The growths have few thorns, and are very erect and densely covered with dark, grey-green, acute leaves, a fastigiate mass of growth, setting off the tight rosette flowers, which are of dark Tyrian pink suffused with claret and purple, with paler centres. I have two distinct forms of this, one much more vigorous and larger in all its parts than the other. 3–5 feet. Probably of *gallica* derivation.

Willmott, Plate 120.

Lawrance, Plate 44.

Roessig, Plate 4. 'Le Rosier de Bourgogne', *Rosa Burgundiaca*.

Redouté, Vol. 3. Plate 107. *Rosa Pomponiana*. There is no doubt about this figure, but it is somewhat confusing to find that Thory makes this rose synonymous with 'Le Petit de St François', 'Le Pompon de Reims' (Remensis), 'Le Rosier de Meaux' (Meldensis), 'Le Petit Provins Violet', 'Le Rosier de Champagne'. He was evidently in error here, as Miss Willmott points out. I have been unable to determine whether the title 'Pompon de St François' should refer to this rose or to 'De Meaux'; one author states that it belongs to *Rosa arvensis*! See also page 214.

PAUL RICAULT, 1845. Like 'Blanchefleur', which it closely re-sembles, except in colour, this rose shews signs of hybridity. The rolled petals and densely packed flowers have considerable charm, and it is one of the most free-flowering among these old types. Soft, rich pink, and well scented. 5 feet.

PETITE DEᵗHOLLANDE ('Petite Junon de Hollande', 'Pompon des

Dames', *Normandica*). While 'De Meaux' and *parvifolia* are true pompons, this is just an exquisitely formed miniature Centifolia, every part reduced to scale, but of rather more bushy habit. The leaves resemble Centifolia leaves, reduced in size, but similarly coarsely toothed, and the calyx and flower are of typical colour and form, but borne with just a little more stiffness, which is the character of the bush. This imparts an air of distinction, and it is the best Provence Rose for smaller gardens. 4 feet.

This is probably the rose figured by Miss Lawrance, Plate 55.

Bunyard in *New Flora and Silva*, Vol. 2. Fig. 2.

Roessig, Plate 20. 'Le Petit Rosier à cent feuilles', *Rosa centifolia minor*.

ROBERT LE DIABLE. A very late flowering, lax shrub, whose almost procumbent 4-foot thorny stems would shew their considerable beauties to the greatest advantage when allowed to spray over a low wall. The leaves are narrow and of dark green. It is by no means a typical Centifolia, and probably has Gallica derivation. The medium-sized flowers are most beautifully shaped, the half-open blooms having bold outer reflexing petals, and later all the petals reflex somewhat except those held centrally, which remain erect and poised outwards. An amazing number of tints is held in these flowers, a dark slatey lilac-purple predominating, shaded with violet-purple and lightened by vivid splashes of intense cerise and scarlet. Many of the petals have a minute veining of the same colour, and some of them fade to pale parma violet, eventually turning to dove-grey on exposure. This rose only develops its most arresting colours in dry, hot weather. 4–5 feet. (Pl. VII.)

SPONG, 1805. This interesting little bush, a typical form of *Rosa centifolia*, and midway in size between 'De Meaux' and 'Petite de Hollande', is very early flowering, and is generally over before the larger forms are in flower. The habit is bushy and upright, much branched, with rounded leaf segments and coarsely toothed margins. The flowers are cupped, opening flat; they are not very shapely nor are they pompons, and their numerous petals stay conspicuously on the plants when the flowers have faded—an unfortunate habit of some of the older roses, but in none so objectionable as in this plant. In all other respects it is good. 4–5 feet. See also page 214.

THE BISHOP. I suspect that this may be synonymous with the old French Gallica variety 'L'Évêque'. In the evening and after a hot day, when seen against the light and in shadow, this rose more nearly approaches blue than any other. The flat flowers, of closely packed rosette-form, and not at all like typical *Rosa centifolia*, have rolled petals of cerise-magenta. They quickly turn to tones of violet and slatey grey-violet, and it is at this development that the blue shades appear so convincing. The grey tones only develop on parts of the flowers, cerise being present frequently with them. It forms a slender, rather erect bush, with neat leaves, rather polished, and shewing affinity with 'Tour de Malakoff'. 4–5 feet.

TOUR DE MALAKOFF, 1856. A very large bush of lax habit except on very strong fertile soils, where its colours and size of flower are wonderful. The smooth and rather small leaves are not in keeping with its other characters, and the tall stems, often up to 7 feet in height, should be supported, to shew the flowers to best advantage. The buds are shapely and the reverses of the petals are of light lilac-pink; in a half-open bloom, somewhat cupped and not of formal shape, vivid magenta may predominate, but when the flowers receive full sunshine and the petals reflex, some petals turn to intense parma violet with many intermediate shades. All the magenta areas are veined and flushed with violet. Eventually, before falling, a cool lilac-grey assumes predominance over the 5-inch blooms, and a bunch of flowers of all tones is a startling revelation of what a rose can do. A few stamens light the centres.

UNIQUE BLANCHE. Discovered at Needham, Suffolk, in 1775. The 'White Provence', 'Unique', or 'Vierge de Cléry' is a typical Provence Rose in growth, thorns, leaves, scent, and the texture of the petals. The buds, with long sepals, are red-flushed and almost burnished; a half-open bloom is cupped, the central petals being held together by those on the outside; later a distinct button eye is surrounded by a starry and effective display of creamy-white, glistening, transparent, narrow petals. At this stage it is arresting. On good soils can be a very pleasing plant up to 4 or 5 feet. It flowers late in the summer season.

Redouté, Vol. 1. Plate 111. *Rosa centifolia mutabilis.*

Andrews, Plate 20. *Rosa provincialis alba.*

Roessig, Plate 41. Poor.

Lawrance, Plate 4. Excellent drawing.

VARIEGATA. Introduced from Angers in 1845. This rose is found under many names in books and gardens: 'Belle des Jardins', 'La Rubanée', 'Village Maid', 'Cottage Maid', 'Panachée à fleur doubles', 'La Belle Villageoise', 'Dometil Beccard', and 'Dominic Boccardo' have been given to me at one time or another, and all have turned out to be not Gallica roses (to which these names should refer) but this old and fairly typical Centifolia. Miss Willmott, in *The Genus Rosa*, has a good portrait of it, and she wisely accords it the descriptive and safe name *Variegata*. It is a vigorous bush, producing strong thorny shoots and good dark leaves, coarsely toothed. The flowers, borne singly or in clusters, are globular, filled with thin petals which do not resist wet weather and soon drop. But who can deny the beauty and freshness of those silky, creamy-white blooms so neatly striped with pale lilac-pink? It is very free-flowering. 5 feet.

Bunyard. 'Village Maid.'

Bunyard in *New Flora and Silva*, Vol. 2. Fig 3. 'Cottage Maid.'

Willmott, Plate 122. *Rosa provincialis variegata.*

Journal des Roses, Août 1893. 'Dometil Beckart' (Beccard).

Andrews, Plate 25. *Rosa provincialis variegata,* Variegated Provence Rose. Rather highly coloured and too flat.

Chapter XVI

· ·

The Moss Roses

(*Rosa centifolia muscosa*)

> Gather ye rosebuds while ye may
> Old Time is still a-flying,
> And the same flower that blooms today,
> Tomorrow may be dying.
>
> *Robert Herrick*

IN THESE FORMS of the Provence Rose the sepals assume great importance. These green segments enclosing the buds of all roses have interested mankind for a very long time. Mr J. G. Glassford sent me the old Latin rhyme about them:

> Five brothers take their stand
> Under the same command.
> Two darkly bearded frown,
> Two without beards are known,
> While one sustains with equal pryde
> His sad appendage on one side.

The sepals are so arranged that some of their edges lie over and some under their neighbours, and they are always arranged in the same way. In *Rosa centifolia cristata* the beards are enlarged and leafy—or 'crested'—while in the Moss Roses they have the effect of moss. What really happens is that the glandular projections all over the flower stalk and sepals—which add so much to the fragrance of many old roses—are enlarged and, at the apex of each sepal, a leafy, 'winged', and mossy elongation may be present. The 'moss' is sticky and fragrant on one's fingers.

Dr Hurst's notes tell us all that we are likely to know about Moss Roses, but I would refer the reader to my own conclusions regarding the white Mosses, given under *Rosa centifolia muscosa alba*. The Mosses are really of comparatively recent occurrence, and, as they originated just when the China Rose was making its influence felt, it was inevitable that some of the later varieties should flower again, after the summer outburst is over. For these few late blooms we must be grateful, but the plants cannot really be called perpetual flowering. Direct evidence also may be found of the influence of the Damask Rose 'Quatre Saisons Blanc Mousseux' (page 161), not only regarding its perpetual flowering habit, but also in the quality of its 'moss', which is hard and prickly, and very different from the soft moss of Centifolia varieties.

Generally speaking the Moss Roses lack the exquisite quality of the true Provence Roses, except in the few that are direct sports, e.g. *Rosa centifolia muscosa* and *alba*; the variety ' À longues pédoncules'; and a few other later kinds such as 'Louis Gimard' and 'Maréchal Davoust'. These have the grace and refinement we might expect; in fact I think the two first named are undoubtedly the most beautiful, and I think that subsequent hybridization and selection did not succeed in giving us anything particularly good. This rather hard statement is, however, somewhat tempered by the thought of 'Comtesse de Murinais', 'Général Kléber', 'Henri Martin', 'Nuits de Young', 'René d'Anjou', and 'William Lobb'. These are certainly highlights among later Moss Roses.

In size the Moss Roses range from the dwarf varieties 'Little Gem' and 'Mousseline' to tall pillar roses like 'Jeanne de Montfort' and 'William Lobb', both of which are capable of reaching 8 feet. A number are really bushy, such as 'Monsieur Pelisson' and 'James Mitchell'; some have grand flowers of considerable quality, like 'Eugénie Guinoiseau' and 'Mme Louis Lévêque'; *japonica* is a unique form, with mossy stems which are very elegant in their green moss contrasting with the rich amethyst tinting of the young foliage. But for really exquisite quality one must leave these and grow only the original sports.

Since 1900 a few Mosses have been raised which embody the vigour and mossy characters with rather modern colours. 'Gabrielle Noyelle' (1933) has flowers of orange salmon with yellow base; 'Robert Léopold' (1941) is of similar colouring with attractive dark moss and brilliant green leaves. These are both good bushes up to about 5 feet, and with them we can grow the 'Golden' or 'Yellow Moss' (1930). This is rather shy-flowering. Their colours are somewhat fierce for growing with the old roses, but I feel their quality is a little lacking for inclusion among Hybrid Teas.

This proves once again that certain plants are best retained in their original state, with no attempt to bring them up to date by hybridizing. The Moss Roses fill a niche in the development of roses, and as such should be left alone, to be enjoyed with the old roses, and as period pieces particularly reminiscent of the 'cosy' Victorian era. Although they are contemporaneous with many of the best Gallica roses, the Moss Roses alone have, to me, a specially Victorian quality. A few years ago I had a Valentine sent to me—from an unknown source, of course!—on which was a wonderful spray of Moss Roses in rich Victorian style. Underneath the sender had written, 'Be my rose but not too old-fashioned'. I feel that the Rose thereby soared to great heights of period quality and also humour, and I have many times been immensely tickled by the sender's kind thoughts for me. One could so easily become old-fashioned in such a pursuit as this!

In the garden Moss Roses have the same values and qualities as the Provence Roses themselves, although on the whole they are of more robust and erect habit. Pruning will be the same as for the Provence Roses, always remembering that fairly hard spur-pruning in the winter will help to keep the more perpetual flowering varieties bushy and producing flowers through the summer.

MOSS ROSES

CENTIFOLIA MUSCOSA. A great stir was made at the end of the seventeenth century, or at least by 1727, when the Moss Rose was introduced from the Continent. This sport from *Rosa centifolia* gave rise to several other forms, but it was not until after the single pink Moss Rose occurred at Bayswater in 1807 that seedlings were raised—none of which surpass the 'Common Moss' in beauty. The fine foliage of mid-green, coarsely toothed, and long projecting calyx make a perfect foil for the lovely Provence blooms of clear pink, globular at first, opening flat, with button centre, and exquisitely fragrant. Only the white form and 'Gloire des Mousseux' have in my opinion buds which approach it in beauty. 4 feet. (Pl. 19.) See also page 215.

Kingsley, facing page 39.

Keays, facing page 52.

Les Plus Belles Roses, facing page 98.

Willmott, Plate facing page 345.

Redouté, Vol. 1. Plate 41. *Rosa muscosa multiplex*. He also shews the Single Moss, Vol. 1. Plate 39.

Lawrance, Plate 14.

Roessig, Plate 6. 'Le Rosier Mousseux', *Rosa muscosa*.

Andrews, Plate 58. Depicts the Single Moss Rose, R. *muscosa simplex*.

Komlosy.

Hoffmann, Plate 2.

CENTIFOLIA MUSCOSA ALBA. Up to the present I have found it impossible to be quite certain about the typical white Moss Roses, but there is no doubt that this rose is identical with Redouté's beautiful portrait of *Rosa centifolia muscosa alba* (Plate 87). He calls this 'Shailer's White Moss', and refers also to 'White Bath' or 'Clifton Moss', which he says is rare in gardens and difficult to propagate. As there is apparently no coloured figure of the 'Clifton Moss' I am tempted to suggest that these sports were identical; in other words that the White Moss was variously called 'Shailer's', 'Bath', or 'Clifton'; I therefore like to follow Redouté and use the botanical name.

This rose has the grace of pure *Rosa centifolia*, and is almost alone in this beauty, apart from the 'Common Moss' and 'René d'Anjou'. The growth is lax and open, the leaves of soft green, well rounded and well poised, and the graceful flower stalks bear lovely buds with long, mossy calyces. The flower is less full than *Rosa centifolia*, but has the same papery delicate quality, and the blooms are flushed with flesh tint in the centre immediately on opening, passing to pure white, and reflexing quite flat with noticeable button eye. Occasionally a pink petal is produced. A delightful rose, very fragrant, probably reaching to 4 feet.[1] (Pl. 19.) 'Shailer's' occurred in 1790.

Redouté, Vol. 1. Plate 87.

Andrews, Plate 63.

Botanical Register, 102.

Both Andrews's and the *Botanical Register* figures are less easily recognized than Redouté.

[1] During the summer of 1954 I was interested to observe a flowering shoot of this double white Moss Rose producing perfect blooms in the typical pink of the Common Moss. On the spray the central bloom was pink, and the buds on the one side white, and on the other, pink. This also occurred at Mottisfont in 1980.

ALFRED DE DALMAS. See 'Mousseline'.

À LONGUES PÉDONCULES, 1854. This extremely graceful rose, with its clusters of long-stalked flowers and pretty, neat foliage is worthy of more frequent cultivation. The leaves are of soft green, small and rounded, and the pale green mossy sheaves of buds open to small nodding pink flowers of a peculiarly soft tone of pink flushed with lilac. In spite of this lack of size it is recognizably a true Centifolia variety, and forms a vigorous plant. True Centifolia charm. 5–6 feet.

BARON DE WASSANAER, 1854. Vigorous shrub, of distinctive growth and good foliage. The buds are not conspicuously mossy, and the flowers are of globular or cupped shape, light crimson, but not very attractive. 4–5 feet. Rather modern.

BLANCHE MOREAU. A fine white Moss, raised in 1880, the parentage being given as 'Comtesse de Murinais' and 'Quatre Saisons Blanc'. The latter was a Damask Rose, but I can see no sign of its influence in 'Blanche moreau', apart from the occasional later flowers which may indicate Autumn Damask or China Rose parentage. It is a vigorous but slender, lax shrub up to 6 feet in height, with many thorns and dark, brownish-green moss; this dark colouring is noticeable on the leaf stalks also; truly a brunette among Mosses. The dark moss contrasts strongly with the small creamy-white flowers, very double, cupped or flat.

This is probably the rose on Plate facing page 349, Willmott, figured as *Rosa centifolia albo-muscosa*, which she states is the 'White Bath' or 'Clifton Moss'. The general appearance of the flower is so far removed from *Rosa centifolia* that her material was presumably wrongly named.

Journal des Roses, Septembre 1885.

CAPITAINE BASROGER, 1890. Vigorous and suitable for a pillar, or can be pruned to a bush. Very thorny, and the bulging buds are scarcely enveloped by the green mossy calyx, which has practically no wings at all. The flowers are not of classic shape, but have an intense, purplish-crimson colouring, and are cupped and reflexed. Produces a few late blooms. 6 feet.

CAPITAINE JOHN INGRAM, 1856. A vigorous but dense bush up to 5 feet, with neat, dark leaves and many fine thorns. The blooms are pompon-like, opening flat and compact from tight slightly mossy buds; the first colour is an intense, dark purplish crimson shaded with maroon. This gives way to softer tones of purple, mottled with a variety of tints, and when fully open the button eye reveals the lilac pink of the reverse of the petals. This is the darkest and most velvety Moss Rose I have seen except 'Nuits de Young'. (Pl. VI.)

CATHERINE VON WURTEMBURG, 1843. A slender, erect Centifolia bush reaching to about 6 feet, with small thorns, red-brown moss, and reddish young leaves, neat and pointed. The flat blooms are not particularly attractive; they are of soft, lilac pink, with muddled centres.

CELINA, 1855. This is a name which crops up now and again; the rose I grow has crimson and purple shades in each flower, clouded with maroon, and is semi-double. It gets mildew very badly, and is not a worthy variety.

COMTESSE DE MURINAIS, 1843. A very beautiful and very vigorous white Moss. Long shoots up to 6 feet bear light-green leaves, curiously ribbed, and the moss is green and hard to the touch. The blush-white of the half-open flower fades, leaving a milk-white, well-formed bloom with a pronounced button eye. The petals open flat and are sometimes quilled or quartered. A superlative bloom. Probably of Damask Moss derivation. (Pl. 17.)

CRESTED MOSS. See *Rosa centifolia cristata*, page 174.

CRIMSON MOSS. May be described as a fairly typical Centifolia, mossy, and crimson, with broad leaves. The flowers are so enveloped by their dark, maroon-purple outer petals that in all but the best weather they do not open properly. In the centre of the flower there is a rich mixture of crimson and purple. An unworthy variety. 5 feet.

DEUIL DE PAUL FONTAINE, 1873. A noted variety, but not of great garden value. It was originally described as very vigorous, but has obviously lost some of its vigour. Very hard prickly moss on the buds and globular flowers, very double, shewing all tints from dark Tyrian rose through purple and maroon, to almost black, often with brown shadings. Quartered. 3–4 feet. June to October.

Journal des Roses, Août 1882. The portrait lacks the purple tones and is hardly 'nuancé acajou', but is otherwise excellent, if a little overdone.

DUCHESSE DE VERNEUIL, 1856. One of the brightest and most effective of Moss Roses for the garden. It bears a close relationship to 'Général Kléber', in its pointed leaves of good green, and has flowers of a similar shape and purity. The clear, bright-pink petals are paler on the reverse and show this diversity in the button eyes. A delightful, bright, and healthy rose. 5 feet.

EUGÉNIE GUINOISEAU, 1864. Tall, erect bush up to 6 feet in height bearing very few real thorns. The leaves are rounded, dark, and rather shiny, and give a good effect in contrast to the large, full, velvety blooms. They are cupped on opening, reflexing with rolled edges, making a broad, rounded flower. Tints vary from the early vivid cerise-magenta, to soft grape-purple, fading to soft lilac-purple, but frequently maintaining a rich claret colouring in the centre. Produces blooms through the summer and autumn.

Journal des Roses, Novembre 1884.

FÉLICITÉ BOHAN. A pleasant shapely bush bearing very neat, small leaves of rich green edged in a young state with brown moss. The flowers are of medium size and of delicate flesh-pink, warming to rose in the centre, quartered and with button eyes, reflexing with age. 4 feet.

GÉNÉRAL KLÉBER, 1856. A most desirable variety. It is the only Moss Rose I have seen which bears any resemblance to the clear and refined beauty of *Rosa alba* 'Céleste'. The double blooms are wide and of great quality, fragrant, in soft pure pink. A vigorous and attractive bushy plant, and the foliage and copious moss have a lettuce-green freshness. 5 feet.

GLOIRE DES MOUSSEUX, 1852 ('Mme Alboni'). A most attractive shrub, with sturdy growth and characteristic light-green leaves; likewise the moss is light in colour and, in keeping with the name, abundant, especially on the long sepals. Midsummer sees the only display of blooms, but they are enormous, full-petalled, opening well and reflexing, of clear bright pink, fading to paler tones, and long lasting. 4 feet.

HENRI MARTIN, 1863. A particularly graceful plant, with wiry shoots bearing leaves and flowers of a dainty perfection. The foliage and rather scanty moss is of clear green. The flowers are by no means full, but are of the clearest and most intense shade approaching crimson among the Moss Roses that I know, fading to a deep rose shade. The petals are rounded and flat, and reflex with a camellia-like precision. I have seen this rose with flowers of gorgeous quality on a north wall, growing in moist deep soil. 5–6 feet.

JAMES MITCHELL, 1861. Vigorous plant of bushy, yet wide spraying habit, with neat, pleated, bronzy leaves. The browny-green moss on the dainty little buds creates an exquisite picture and, when the whole bush is covered with the flowers borne singly or in clusters, a very fine garden plant is apparent. The intense magenta-pink of the buds fades to a soft lilac-pink in the flat, open flowers, each with a neat button eye. The flowers are small for the size of the bush, but their numbers and pompon-shape compensate for this. 5 feet. (Pl. V.)

JAPONICA ('Moussu du Japon'). A slow-growing and interesting shrub whose young shoots are enveloped in clear green dense moss for their entire length; the moss spreads to the leaf stalks and the surface of the pointed leaves, and is, of course, on the buds. The young foliage is frequently of metallic lustre, lilac and coppery hues appearing together. The magenta-rose flowers quickly reflex and fade to a soft grey-lilac, and are not unlike those of 'William Lobb', but are smaller and less intense in colour. 3 feet.

JEANNE DE MONTFORT, 1851. Perhaps the most vigorous Moss Rose, apart from 'William Lobb'; the bronzy mossy stems have shiny leaves and bear large clusters of flowers. The buds are very mossy, with long sepals covered with brown moss, in pleasing contrast to the clear warm pink of the blooms. They open well, are not over-filled with petals, and are lit with yellow stamens. An altogether pleasing rose where there is room for it. 6–8 feet. Occasional late blooms.

LITTLE GEM, 1880. A pretty little rose, which grows to 4–5 feet, well covered with small neat leaves. The buds are not very mossy, and enclose tightly packed blooms of light crimson, opening to flat pompon blooms. The colouring is uniform. Also grown under the name of 'Validé'.

LOUIS GIMARD, 1877. Very hard, densely packed, cabbage-like buds open to rich lilac-cerise flowers, flushed and veined with lilac, flat with muddled centres, the petals being rolled at the edges. Neat, dark green pointed leaves. First-class shapely blooms of rich appearance. 5 feet.

MADAME DELAROCHE-LAMBERT, 1851. Purplish-rose flowers, of good size and vivid colouring, with beautifully rolled petals, centres muddled. The buds are particularly beautiful, with their green moss and long foliaceous sepals. The moss on the stems is brownish, and the leaves are soft, green, and rounded. A highly desirable plant whose flowers appear intermittently until the autumn. 4–5 feet.

MADAME LOUIS LÉVÊQUE, 1873. A remarkable variety of stiff, upright habit, long-pointed, bright green, copious foliage, and little moss. The flowers are larger than any others I have seen, and have probably been bred from a Hybrid Perpetual, for it is very markedly of 'remontant' habit. In wet weather the flowers are inclined to ball, but in dry, sunny times a large globular flower emerges, very fragrant, reflexing slightly, but at all times remaining a uniform pale pink. Bears some resemblance to 'Mrs John Laing' (H.P.). 4–5 feet.

MARÉCHAL DAVOUST, 1853. This is a first-rate bush up to about 5 feet, with attractive pointed leaves. The buds, of perfect shape, have brownish moss, and on first opening shew intense, deep, crimson-pink, with paler reverses. The petals reflex and have a button eye and green centre, retaining their colour well, a suffusion of cerise and purple mingling with the softer tones. This is particularly free flowering and gives a rich general effect. 4–5 feet.

MARIE DE BLOIS, 1852. Vigorous and bushy plant with most attractive young shoots, the spines and moss being flushed with red among the fresh green leaves. The blooms are shapeless, but freely borne through summer and autumn, bright pink, frilled and muddled. 5–6 feet. A bush for garden effect, dense and floriferous. Suitable for hedging.

MONSIEUR PÉLISSON. Although there appears to be no authority for this name, I have come across this rose in several gardens so named and believe it to be worth recording. The plant I grow is notable for its coarsely toothed yet small leaves; its vigorous, dense, bushy habit; and for its symmetrical, very flat, fully double flowers, with fine button centres. In colour they are at first bright deep pink, fading paler, and at all times attractive. Greenish-brown moss in average quantity. 4 feet. A fine hedging rose. 1848. See also page 215.

MOUSSELINE, 1855. It is difficult to decide whether this name or 'Alfred de Dalmas', under which this variety is also sometimes found, should be used. The old writers are not definite in their descriptions. This variety makes an extremely compact bush up to 4 feet or so, with many short twigs and distinct spoon-shaped leaflets; it flowers from June to October. The creamy-blush blooms are cupped and well filled with high centres. Very free flowering, few thorns, but not conspicuously mossy. This variety seems to me to be obviously related to the Damask 'Quatre Saisons Blanc Mousseux', perhaps through the Portland Roses themselves. (See page 155.)

NUITS DE YOUNG, 1851. One of the most famous Mosses, and justly so, on account of its distinct habit and foliage, and the size and colouring of its flowers. It forms a wiry, thin bush up to 5 feet or so, with sparsely disposed leaves, small and dark, yet beautifully burnished with maroon and metallic tones. The small flowers are of intense maroon purple, dark and velvety, lit by a few golden stamens. They are not very full, but reflex prettily and do not fade much. A gem. Midsummer flowering only.

Mr Selwyn Duruz, in his book *Flowering Shrubs*, points out that a yellow flower creates a most satisfying contrast. See also page 215.

REINE BLANCHE, 1857. Foliage fresh, light green, making a pleasing contrast to the white flowers, which have a creamy-lemon intensity. The moss is copious and bright green, the sepals long and foliaceous. The flowers are fully double, inclined to nod, and have pronounced button centres. 4–5 feet.

RENÉ D'ANJOU, 1853. Exhibiting the beautiful poise of the typical Centifolias, this variety has most charming buds, with brownish-green moss, opening to soft, warm, pink flowers, passing to light lilac-pink, veined and crinkled and with muddled centres. Bronzy young foliage; bushy growth, probably to 5 feet. At all times beautiful.

SALET, 1854. A fairly perpetual flowering, sturdy, reliable bush. The flowers are not of the very first quality, but are well filled with narrow petals, often quartered, with a muddled eye, and reflexing; clear pink, not very mossy. Soft, light-green leaves and few thorns. 4 feet.

SOUVENIR DE PIERRE VIBERT, 1867. Very near to 'Capitaine Basroger', but slightly less double, and less coarse in all its parts. The flowers are of fairly regular shape, rich magenta-crimson, quickly flushing with purple and maroon. Dark foliage and moss. 5 feet.

STRIPED MOSS. Quaint little flowers of pale pink, striped and particoloured with vivid crimson, fading to softer tones. Not very sturdy growth; inferior to other striped roses. 3–4 feet. See also page 215.

WILLIAM LOBB, 1855 ('Duchesse d'Istrie'). The 'Old Velvet' Moss. An amazing piece of colour. The freshly opened blooms, large and semi-double with muddled centres, have petals of dark crimson-purple with pale lilac-pink reverses; they fade the next day to a uniform lavender grey, lightened by the nearly white bases of the petals. The heavily green-mossed buds are borne in large clusters, on exceptionally strong shoots, reaching to 8 feet. Foliage small for the size of the plant, dark leaden-green. Best grown in a big group so that the branches of neighbouring plants interlace; or it can be trained up poles or on walls, or mixed with other vigorous roses. At Kiftsgate Court, it is used to great advantage with the rambler 'Albertine', which is of warm coral and salmon-pink tones.

Herr Wilhelm Kordes of Germany sent me 'Park Jewel', a moss rose of his raising ('Independence' × a red moss rose, 1950). The big, strong, arching branches clothed in copious light-green leaves bear clusters of great, fully double, rich pink blooms. This is growing well with me, and I hope to see it become popular. About 4 feet and flowering freely at midsummer.

Chapter XVII

. . . .

The Bourbon Roses

(Rosa bourboniana)

The cowslip is a country wench,
The violet is a nun;
But I will woo the dainty rose,
The queen of everyone.

Thomas Hood

IT WOULD NOT BE surprising if the Bourbons were excluded from this book, as they are hybrids of *Rosa chinensis*, which was the species that destroyed the floral perfection of the old roses. The Bourbons were the roses which eventually gave rise to the Hybrid Perpetuals, and these undoubtedly are far from the old roses in style and quality. The older types of Bourbon Roses, however, have often the charm of flower found in the old roses, and in consequence I feel they merit inclusion. The varieties of the China Rose, on the other hand, though equally old or older, do not conform to the old pattern, and I have therefore omitted them, sorely tempted as I am to include two, 'Fellemberg' and 'Hermosa'. 'Hermosa' is actually a reverted Bourbon, as Dr Hurst tells us on page 83, but it very nearly approaches the China Rose in general characters.

NOTE TO PLATE 19. SPORTING OF MOSS ROSES

The top spray was cut from *Rosa centifolia muscosa alba*, and its lowest bud was pure white. The top buds and the main terminal flower were pink. It had reverted to R. *centifolia muscosa*.

The roses on the right of the picture are of the 'Perpetual White Damask Moss' or R. *damascena bifera albo-muscosa* ('Quatre Saisons Blanc Mousseux'); it has reverted twice in the author's experience to the 'Perpetual Damask Rose' or R. *damascena bifera* ('Quatre Saisons'), which is shewn in the lower left portion of the photograph.

The difference between the long harsh 'moss' of the Damask variety and the short soft 'moss' of the Provence variety can be plainly seen; the long receptacle of the Damask is also very evident.

Practically all the Bourbon varieties I am describing flower more or less through the summer, and they give the old rose garden a little colour at an otherwise dull time. Fortunately their colours blend happily with all others mentioned in this book.

In view of their gradual development as so clearly described by Dr Hurst, it was inevitable that many types of habit and flower were evolved, and I therefore cannot dispose of them as a class in a few words. Every now and again through the years a 'new' Bourbon rose is raised; such as 'Adam Messerich' (1920), a flaunting beauty in warm Tyrian rose and admirable for a wall or pillar; the showy red 'Parkzierde' (1909), a martyr to 'black spot'; and the more famous and useful 'Zigeuner Knabe' (1909) or 'Gipsy Boy'. This is a great bush bearing hundreds of rich purple roses at midsummer, and is a useful and showy shrub for general planting. But these new varieties have not inherited even the rather diverse and indeterminate characters of the more authentic varieties. They lack the true Bourbon's floral qualities and charm.

For the old Bourbons have, all of them, much charm; the lovely shape of the old roses coupled with the silky petal of the China Rose puts them high in the floral delights of the genus. Two roses often classed as Hybrid Perpetuals can very well be grouped with the Bourbons, as they so nearly approach them in all characters. They are 'Reine des Violettes' (1860) (Pl. 13) and 'Souvenir d'Alphonse Lavallée' (1884). They are both fine, large shrubs up to 5 or 6 feet with good foliage, that of the former having a greyish sheen, assorting well with the flowers, which at times I place first among the purple roses. My pen will not do justice to the regular and beautiful arrangement of the incurved petals forming a wide, flat, quartered flower with button eye. From a pale blush-mauve centre the petals flush to a rich parma violet, with a touch of cerise and purple here and there. Against these 'Souvenir d'Alphonse Lavallée' gives extra velvety, dark wine-red flowers, whose colour intensifies with age to darkest maroon.

These two shrubs, together with the true Bourbons like 'Honorine de Brabant', 'Variegata di Bologna', both growing to about 6–7 feet high and wide, the smaller 'Boule de Neige' and the great 'Mme Ernst Calvat' and 'Mme Isaac Pereire', can produce superlative blooms in August and September. In fact, these roses do their best at that time of the year, the earlier blooms frequently being of poorer quality. The slender 'Mme Pierre Oger' and 'La Reine Victoria' are most suitable for putting among other roses, where on good soil they will grow to 5 or 6 feet, taking up surprisingly little room, especially if staked. It is sad that the superlative 'Mme Lauriol de Barny' flowers only in early summer.

'Mme Hardy du Thé'—sometimes called 'Mme Melon du Thé'—is a strange little rose which may be an early polyantha or a dwarf Bourbon. I have not been able to trace its name in any book so far. Occasionally it produces, in really warm weather when the soil is moist, blooms of such exquisite charm, shewing a depth of pink in their centre surrounded by blush-white serried petals, that one is tempted to think it is a good rose. As the conditions are not usually so favourable, balled wet-papery blooms are more often the rule, and, in spite of Miss Willmott's story about its having been brought from France by the émigrés, one feels like putting it on the rubbish heap. (See also page 216.)

This brings me to pruning. It will be obvious that these roses need rather different attention from the old roses, as they flower on the current year's growth as well as on that produced the previous season. Pruning away all short, twiggy growth as soon as it has flowered will again be beneficial, as it will help to encourage fresh flowering shoots to appear. But some thoughtful winter pruning must also be done, much in the same way as is advocated for modern roses, although these Bourbons are all vigorous bushes, and it is little use trying to keep them down. In December all small wood can be spurred back to three eyes, and long vigorous shoots reduced by one-third of their length. The best blooms will be produced on really vigorous shoots which grow up after the first flush of flower is over.

BOURBON ROSES

BLAIRI NUMBER TWO. Mr Blair, of Stamford Hill, raised his No. 1 and No. 2 seedlings in 1845, and although both are still at Hidcote I have not grown No. 1, as I have not considered it really worthy. No. 2 is a most beautiful climbing rose up to 15 feet, and is admirable on a wall or pillar, the long, arching shoots bearing elegant mahogany-tinted foliage. The flowers are very large, fully double, retaining the rich pink centre, while the outer petals develop a paler tone, the fully open flower being of rare beauty, richly veined. Excellent for planting among shrubs through which its long shoots can thread their way. Little pruning is needed.

BOULE DE NEIGE, 1867. A vigorous erect bush reaching to 4 feet or so, constantly thrusting fresh shoots of bold, leathery, dark foliage, and bearing from June to October heavy blooms in small clusters. The buds are hard and round, tinted with crimson, and open to flowers of the old perfection, densely packed and formal in shape, of creamy white. They reflex almost to a ball. This is a rose to plant among those of lower bushy habit, for it is slender and erect in growth, although I have known old compact heads on standards. See also page 215.
Nestel's *Illustrierte Rosengarten.* Plate 5.

BOURBON QUEEN, 1835 ('Reine de l'Île Bourbon'). An old cottage favourite, still seen up and down the country, displaying its semi-double magenta and pink flowers mainly in June. They are cupped and loose, and the petals are crinkled and beautifully veined with a darker shade. Reaches some 10 or 12 feet as a climber, but can be pruned to a shrub. The leaves are leathery, mid green, and distinctly toothed. Judging by a portrait of this rose in Komlosy I have doubts about my plant being true to name, but it is well established in various collections in this country. See also page 215.

CHAMPION OF THE WORLD, 1894. This high-sounding variety is quite a meek little rose! It belongs to the more refined 'Louise Odier' type, of rather dainty bearing, with light-brown thorns and small, light-green, neat leaves. The crimson buds expand, giving medium-sized, reflexed blooms of soft pale-pink with a faint lilac tinting. It would appear to be similar in growth to 'Louise Odier', and is constantly in flower during summer and autumn. 5 feet.

CHARLES LAWSON, 1853. A vigorous plant, needing some support; useful for fences and pillars. The flowers only appear at midsummer, and are large, loose, of soft pink shaded with a darker tint. 6–8 feet.

COMMANDANT BEAUREPAIRE, 1874 ('Panachée d'Angers'). This is one of the most spectacular of striped roses, containing in its flowers tones of light carmine-pink, splashed and striped with rose-madder, carmine, and purple, and an occasional blazing scarlet splash on the inner surfaces. It has an elegant growth and the arching shoots often display a score of blooms open at one time, when their glorious colours need to be seen to be believed. The flowers are round and cupped. In marked and delightful contrast to the flowers, the leaves are long-pointed, undulating, and of a peculiarly light yellowish-green. Thorny. The flowers appear at midsummer. Only careful and selective pruning will prevent it from becoming an overcrowded mass. 5 feet. (Pl. V.)

COUPE D'HÉBÉ, 1840. Of rather coarse growth; bright green leaves on tall, pale-green shoots, reaching to about 8 feet. The flowers are of soft pink, borne in clusters, and have a somewhat modern appearance. They are sometimes slightly quartered, and fade very little. Best on a pillar or with other support. Midsummer only.
Paul, Plate 6.

GREAT WESTERN. (The *Great Western* was the first transatlantic steamer in 1838.) A free and vigorous variety rather lacking in quality. Large rounded flowers, well quartered, of vivid magenta-crimson, flushed with purple. It has only one season of flowering. 5 feet. See also page 216.

HONORINE DE BRABANT. An extra vigorous, well-filled shrub up to some 6 feet, shewing a relationship with 'Commandant Beaurepaire', but larger and coarser in all parts. Green wood, with a few large thorns and good foliage of mid green, large and leathery. The main crop of flowers is borne at midsummer, but it is seldom out of flower, and the later blooms retain their colour better. Their shape is informally cupped and quartered, of pale pink daintily spotted and striped with much darker tones, varying from mauve to violet.

KATHLEEN HARROP. See under ZÉPHIRINE DROUHIN.

LA REINE VICTORIA, 1872. This variety has achieved much fame through giving rise to the lighter coloured sport 'Mme Pierre Oger', which has acquired much greater popularity. Both make slender erect bushes to about 6 feet in height, constantly sending up fresh shoots which bear flowers from June to October. They are borne well aloft, over elegantly poised leaves of soft green. The flowers are full and very rounded, retaining their cupped shape until the last; each petal is like a thin shell, of intense rose-madder where the sun lights upon it, but far paler within and at the base. I know of no other roses with more delicate charm. They are unique period pieces. (Pls. III, 12.) 'La' should be omitted in the name of this rose. See also page 216.

LOUISE ODIER, 1851. A most valuable rose, being of vigorous growth up to about 6 feet, and fresh green in leaf, and bearing a constant succession of flowers from June to the end of October. This is a Bourbon with the old-world perfection of shape; each half-open bloom shews a flat face which appears to be made up of circles, so closely and so truly are the petals laid together. The warm pink, shaded softly with lilac, is delightful. See also page 216.

Hariot, Plate 16.
Journal des Roses, Juin 1883.

MADAME ERNST CALVAT, 1888. This very vigorous pillar rose can be pruned to encourage bushy growth if required. It is unique among roses in the rich, crimson-purple of the leaves on the strong shoots. This colour makes a wonderful foil for the globular cabbagy blooms, which appear constantly through summer and autumn, of warm flesh pink, with darker reverses. The blooms are frequently and characteristically quartered. Of rare beauty in many ways. 7–8 feet. In view of the dates of introduction of this rose and 'Mme Isaac Pereire', and the fact that the latter has recently occurred as a sport on the former in Father Curtis's garden near Dublin, it would seem that 'Mme Ernst Calvat' was originally a sport from 'Mme Isaac Pereire'.

MADAME ISAAC PEREIRE, 1880. Possibly the most powerfully fragrant of all roses; the flowers are enormous, of intense rose-madder, shaded magenta, bulging with rolled petals, quartered, and opening to a great saucer-face. Big, bold foliage on a fine big bush up to 6–8 feet. It can also be trained upon supports with advantage. The blooms are produced in several bursts; those appearing early are frequently misshapen, but the September blooms are unbelievably fine and large. When it is well grown, on good deep soil, it has no peer.

Journal des Roses, Avril 1893.

Jekyll, facing page 6.

Hariot, Plate 44.

MADAME LAURIOL DE BARNY, 1868. For several years I have had a rose called 'Lauriol de Barny', but I have been unable to trace it satisfactorily in old books. Singer states that the name applies to a 'currant-red' Hybrid Perpetual, but I find he also lists 'Mme Lauriol de Barny' with flowers 'rose charmant'. I think this must be our rose, which I trace back to the Bunyard collection; it is one of the most beautiful, producing early in the season, but seldom later, large fully double blooms of light silvery pink, rather after the style of 'Mme Isaac Pereire'. With the smooth foliage they are set along the arching stems. It is a first-class variety, suitable for growing as an open bush up to about 5 feet, or as a pillar rose, 6–7 feet.

MADAME PIERRE OGER. This favourite variety originated in 1878 as a sport from 'Reine Victoria', and has become more popular than its parent, although it is identical in every respect except colour. When first open on a cool day 'Mme Pierre Oger' is of a soft, warm, creamy flesh, and in dull weather may remain so; in sunny weather the sun warms the petals or the portions of them that it touches to a clear rose, and in very hot weather a really intense colour develops. These two roses have petals of shell-like beauty, and are of a dainty and formal perfection unique among roses. Dark thorns. 6 feet. June–October. (Pl. III.) See also page 216.

Bunyard, Plate 17.

Hoffmann, Plate 14. Shewing rich colouring from hot sun.

PRINCE CHARLES. A vigorous, nearly thornless rose, and a counterpart to 'Bourbon Queen' in its growth and the veined and crinkled quality of its flowers. Big, broad, dark-green leaves are well disposed, and the flowers are borne in the usual clusters or singly, but I have not known flowers to appear after mid-summer. They are loose and not very double, dark madder-rose on opening, quickly attaining maroon tinting, and fading to lilac-magenta, when the veining of crimson-purple becomes more noticeable. These rich tints are accentuated by the pale, almost white, bases of the petals. 4–5 feet. (Pl. VIII.)

SOUVENIR DE LA MALMAISON, 1843. A climber, 10–12 feet in height, and with handsome large leaves and thorns; when in bud this notable variety might be taken for a vigorous, modern, climbing Hybrid Tea Rose. The big, strong shoots need some support, but it can also be pruned and kept to neater proportions; indeed, during its long years in cultivation a bush form has appeared which does not reach more than a few feet in height. The half-open flowers are cup-shaped, expanding later to very large flat flowers some 5 inches across, distinctly and regularly quartered. The colour is a very soft flesh-pink, fading to paler tints on exposure, and the flowers have a peculiarly soft and unusual perfume, probably derived from a Tea ancestor. Its flowers are produced in two large crops at midsummer and in September, with a few blooms in between. As with so many roses of more than one flowering season, the flowers produced in the cooler weather of September are unsurpassed for quality and colour. Kingsley, facing page 124 (bud only). (See also page 217.)
Paul, Plate 15.
Hariot, Plate 16.
Curtis, Vol. 2. Plate 17.
Komlosy.

SOUVENIR DE ST ANNE'S. This originated in the late Lady Ardilaun's garden—St Anne's, near Dublin—and has been carefully preserved by Lady Moore at Willbrook House, Rathfarnham, Dublin, for many years. A nearly single sport of 'Souvenir de la Malmaison', it has all its characteristics, except the full, quartered blooms. The petals are slightly deeper on the reverse side, and have a very rich quality in their delicate tints and beautiful sculptured shapes. Lady Moore suggested the name for this rose, and I have so far found no reference to any such sport in old books. It makes a bushy plant up to 7 feet, slowly building up its branches. Prior to 1916.

VARIEGATA DI BOLOGNA, 1909. This comparative newcomer has all the attributes of the older Bourbon Roses. On deep, good soil it will reach up to 8 feet in height, producing strong shoots with neat, narrow, pointed foliage, but is much less vigorous on poorer soils, where it is subject to 'black spot'. I believe it would do well on a north-west wall where a cool root run would probably help it. There is no doubt that it is a most spectacular rose when in flower, and fortunately it produces a few blooms through late summer and autumn, apart from its midsummer crop. The blush-tinted, almost white, petals are numerous and unfold, making a rather globular flower, very neatly striped with vivid crimson-purple. A yard-long spray of blooms makes a striking picture when placed next to 'Commandant Beaurepaire', the shapely buds and blooms of each are so different in every way. Fortunately like other Bourbons it can be kept as a bush by pruning. (Pl. 18.) This has sported to what was presumably its original, a dark crimson-purple rose, but I have not yet found its name.

ZÉPHIRINE DROUHIN, 1868. This has been the most popular of the Bourbon Roses over many years, partly on account of its thorn-free branches and partly, no doubt, due to its vivid cerise-pink flowers, very sweetly scented, borne for so many summer and autumn months. It is best classed as a climber up to some 15 feet, but is suitable for use as a large bush if kept within bounds by pruning. The beautiful leaves are of rich green, and of coppery-purple tint while young, and the flowers have a loose, semi-double formation. The sport 'Kathleen Harrop' occurred in 1919, and is in my experience not so vigorous, but makes a very pleasing bush with flowers of bright, light pink, the petals being much darker on the reverse side, and beautifully marked with transparent veins. It is reported that this rose was found wild in Turkey.

9. A rose introduced in 1832, 'Madame Hardy', a Damask of superlative quality and period charm, shewing characteristic quartered
blooms and green carpels in the centres.

10. Few of the Alba Roses have more beautiful buds and more exquisite blooms than 'Félicité Parmentier'. The grey-green leaves act as a soft foil to the blush-pink of the open flowers. Introduced in 1836.

11. *R. alba maxima,* the 'Great Double White' or 'Jacobite Rose', a noble shrub in grey-green and creamy white, which is found in gardens all over these Islands, thriving often in complete neglect and in the worst of conditions.

12. A fine bush of 'Reine Victoria' (1872), photographed in September at the Manor House, Hemingford Grey.

13. A Hybrid Perpetual, 'Reine des Violettes' (1860), which gives the old shape and colour – parma violet – with the perpetual flowering habit. Good flowers when fully open may be as much as 4½ inches in width.

14. One of the miniature Provence Roses, 'De Meaux', which bears flowers of clear pink about the size of a florin.

15. 'Fantin Latour', a rose which unites vigorous growth and handsome foliage with a free and showy display of blush-pink blooms with neat 'button eyes'.

16. 'Général Kléber', an excellent soft pink Moss Rose of 1856. The general was in Napoleon's Nile campaign.

17. A two-year-old bush of 'Comtesse de Murinais', a Moss Rose which shows marked Damask affinity. Introduced in 1843.

18. One of the most distinctly marked of the striped roses, the Bourbon 'Variegata di Bologna', crimson-purple on white.

19. Sporting of Moss Roses. (See page 192.)

20. The Gallica rose 'Gloire de France', 1828. A typical arching spray; flowers of warm lilac-rose fading to paler tints around the circumference.

21. 'Stanwell Perpetual', found as a seedling in a garden at Stanwell, Middlesex, prior to 1838, and presumed to be a hybrid between the Burnet Rose and the Autumn Damask. It flowers from midsummer until autumn; blush pink and very fragrant.

Chapter XVIII

· ·

Notes on the Old Yellow Roses and a few Others

The rainbow comes and goes
And lovely is the rose.

William Wordsworth

IT WILL HAVE been noticed that the roses described in this book have colours ranging from white through pink to Tyrian rose, lilac, purple, and maroon. The yellow and flame colourings, bringing with them all the multitudinous shot shades, the salmons and oranges, coppery tones and lemon-white, have arisen because the Tea Rose and the Austrian Briars have infused their colours into the older groups of roses. This is made abundantly clear in Dr Hurst's notes.

In the old days *Rosa hemisphaerica*, the Sulphur Rose, was the only large, double yellow rose known, and was introduced before 1625; it seldom opens its globular well-filled flowers properly in our climate, except in extremely hot weather. It may be seen in many old pictures, resembling a cabbage rose, in brilliant yellow. We may judge, therefore, of the delight to gardeners when *Rosa foetida persiana*, the Persian Yellow, was introduced in 1837 from Western Asia. Here was a good garden plant making a shrub up to 5 or 6 feet, and giving a splendid display of vivid buttercup-yellow, globular, fully double blooms of medium size. It is today still the most striking rose of its kind. The rich parsley green of its leaves and the rounded leaflets, distinctly serrate, and the smooth brown twigs and grey thorns are characteristic of the race.

Rosa foetida itself, the Austrian Briar, is a single-flowered rose of a similar brilliant colour. It is also known as *Rosa lutea*. The Austrian Copper is the dazzling two-toned rose, named *Rosa foetida bicolor* or R. *lutea punicea*. For sheer brilliance it is hard to find anything to compete with it among flowers, and a spray well studded with half-open blooms of intense coppery orange-red, shewing their yellow reverses, is certainly unequalled among roses. It occasionally reverts to the yellow type, and branches bearing both colour forms are not uncommon.

These three roses make shrubs up to 5 feet or so, rather open, but very free-flowering early in the rose season, and they delight in full sunshine, although it must be admitted that they do not thrive everywhere. The sun's rays turn their fragrance—by the botanists termed 'foetid'—into an acceptable warm aroma. This strange scent can be traced through many of the progeny of these remarkable plants. The term 'Austrian' is misleading, as *Rosa foetida* is a native of western Asia, although it has been found naturalized in Austria.

Crossed with *Rosa spinosissima*, the Austrian Rose has produced *Rosa harisonii* (1830). This has the upright habit and numerous small thorns of the Scots Rose, but the union has intensified the colour to a brilliant clear yellow. The rather gaunt bushes up to 6 feet present a really fresh and delightful piece of colour, the flowers being small, double, and shapely, and rather more sweetly scented than those of the Austrian. The double yellow Scots Briar is also possibly a hybrid. I well remember big shrubs of this in Lady Moore's garden near Dublin, loaded with blossom, a sight of rare beauty until marred by the dead flowers, whose petals seem loth to leave them. The bunch of green carpels in the middle of the flower distinguish it at once from *R. harisonii*.

Here, then, are the old yellow roses. A few other rare kinds were also grown, such as *Rosa hardii*, and also numerous forms of *Rosa spinosissima* with pale yellow flowers. But this represents the sum total of old roses giving yellow colour to the rose garden. Most of these yellows are, however, of a harsh strident tone and cannot be recommended for inclusion with a planting of other old roses, whose soft colours blend so well together; fortunately most of them are usually going over before the Gallicas and other groups begin to flower.

The numerous forms of *Rosa spinosissima* recorded in old books —Paul lists seventy-eight—bring home once again how the old growers loved a long catalogue of names irrespective of their individual merits. Very few are the dwarf plants that anyone might expect who has seen these little Burnet Roses growing in thickets on some of the sand dunes around our coasts. Many of the garden forms will grow to 5 feet. They are pretty, ferny-leaved bushes, mostly of very dense habit, needing no pruning except the occasional removal of old wood. For colonizing waste areas in poor soils they are admirable, although the fresh and dainty charm of their numerous little fragrant flowers is rather short-lived, in May and June. Their habit is to run, and run vigorously they will, especially in sandy soils. In the autumn their foliage often assumes rich maroon colouring, while their maroon-black shining heps have considerable attraction, although not from the display point of view. In flower they vary from white to pale yellow, pale pink to dark pink, and lilac-pink to wine-crimson and maroon. Many are paler on the reverse, and many are mottled, veined, or marbled. Extremely few authentic names remain today, but I hope that when the numerous forms which I have collected have settled down I may be able to match them with descriptions of a hundred years ago. A handful of distinct forms would be well worth preserving, especially the true dwarfs, and the exquisite double white so redolent of lily of the valley, and the valuable 'Stanwell Perpetual'. This is one of the isolated hybrid roses one finds here and there in the genus; a hybrid which has made no mark on roses owing to its sterility. At Hidcote it reaches 5 feet or more in height, a gracious bush bearing the double, flat, flesh-pink blooms freely among the dainty greyish foliage from midsummer onwards. They are all deliciously fragrant.

Apart from several colour forms which I have under descriptive names I believe the following Burnets to be correctly named in my collection:

Bicolor. Rosy-lilac, reverse palest lilac-pink, fading to palest lilac-white. Yellow centre. Semi-double. 3–4 feet.

Falkland. A beautiful, soft, 'Celestial' pink, fading to a paler tone. Base of petals yellow. Greyish leaves. Rather open habit. Double. 4 feet.

Mrs Colville. Vivid crimson-purple, white eye, strong grower. Single. 4 feet.

Myriacantha. Very dainty foliage and innumerable dark thorns. Single. White flowers, nearly black heps. Is this extinct?

Ormiston Roy. Large, single yellow flowers, beautifully veined. 3–4 feet.

Purpurea plena. Rich 'old rose', fading to light lilac-pink. Reverse of petals palest pink. Centre creamy yellow. Double. 3–4 feet.

Townsend. Blush-pink, cream-pink reverse; fading to cream, base of petals yellow. Double. Vigorous, bushy plant to 5 feet.

William III. Double, vivid lilac-crimson on opening, fading to dark lilac-pink; centre yellow. Reverse of petals light lilac-pink, marbled white. Small growth to 2 feet.

R. *spinosissima altaica* (R. *grandiflora*) and R. *s. lutea maxima* are two very beautiful large-growing varieties, creamy-white and bright yellow respectively.

White is not over abundant among the old roses, and I find its presence in large quantities necessary to serve as a contrast to the pinks and purples. Among whites one of the very finest is 'Madame Plantier'. This is often classed as a Noisette, although it flowers only at midsummer. At Sissinghurst Castle it is trained up old apple-trees, giving them a curtained crinoline of white blooms for fully 12 feet. (Pl. 20.) It is usually grown as a sprawling bush some 4–5 feet high and wide, and is one of the very best roses for adding freedom and grace to a collection of Gallica and other old roses, making a wonderful contrast with the purple varieties. The neat, soft-green leaves are nearly hidden beneath the showers of medium-sized, well-filled flowers, opening with a creamy-yellow flush in the centre and rapidly turning to pure white. Every flower has a characteristic green point in the centre, enhancing its purity, and their fragrance, rich and sweet, is carried well on the air.

With such a subject as roses it is difficult to bring a book to a close. I might go on selecting other individuals in the great wealth of strange roses, such as the exquisite 'Rose d'Amour' or 'St Mark's Rose' (R. *rapa* or R. *virginiana plena*), probably a hybrid of R. *virginiana*; the rare double form of *Rosa microphylla,* and the old double forms of the Sweet Briar, R. *rubiginosa* 'La Belle Distinguée' (light crimson) and 'Manning's Blush'.

But this book has really been written to shed light on the principal old groups. The genus has numerous cherished varieties and forms which remain in isolated distinction, never having linked themselves through hybridization with the main groups. With the magnificent group of *Rosa rugosa* forms and hybrids, and some of the splendid species, there is a great wealth of good shrubs untouched by this volume, and it is my hope to write another volume embracing all these other shrub roses; bringing out of retirement old favourites and putting forward the claims of new races such as the Musks and Herr Kordes's new hybrids of *Rosa spinosissima*, *macrantha*, and *rubiginosa*, the *rugosas*, the best species together with Hybrid Perpetuals and China Roses.

By that time some of the several old roses now on trial may have proved their worth or been given their rightful names, and these will then rank for inclusion in the new volume. I will, therefore, lay aside my pen and prepare to enjoy the flowering season in the hope that what I have written may give help and pleasure to all those who grow the old roses, and may even stimulate others with a new interest in flowers.

I cannot help remarking again, as my mind wanders through the exquisite species, refined and graceful, to their man-made progeny, the old and new florists' roses, or good garden climbers and prolific ramblers, and the tiny miniature Lawranceanas, that indeed the Rose provides varieties for every taste. In this fact lies its ubiquitous popularity.

The sequel to this book, *Shrub Roses of Today* (revised edition, Dent, 1980), has now appeared and all roses mentioned briefly in this chapter, together with hundreds of others, are fully discussed in its pages.

Further Gleanings

Wanted: a refuge for the old roses where they
may be found again when tastes change.

George Paul, R.H.S. Journal, 1896.

THAT THE old roses were in danger of being lost so early as the
end of the last century may come as a surprise to many. All the
more famous writers on roses during the last 100 years have
echoed this plea for preserving the old roses. Mr George Paul,
who was a nephew of Mr William Paul, the great rosarian, wanted
to find some place where the roses depicted by Redouté could be
assembled, together with roses of other old groups. But we had to
wait until they were in danger of extinction before they were
again collected. How often have I wished that I could have gone
to some botanic garden and found the lot! And yet the quest
would not have been so interesting, and considering how they
were neglected it is remarkable how many have survived, and it
can only be put down to their toughness and their unequalled
fragrance.

The continued demand for this book has warranted the preparation of a revised edition. A few small discrepancies that crept
into the first edition (1955) were corrected in the third impression
in 1957, and now a thorough revision has been made. Several
dates have been added or corrected, reports on various untried
varieties have been stated and dimensions adjusted where necessary. All this applies to the body of the book, but a much greater
amount of information has come to light than could comfortably
be included in a reprint, and hence this additional chapter.

In it are numerous citations of illustrations extra to the first
printing and a collection of varied notes, arranged in the same
sequence as in the preceding chapters. I take pleasure in having

this opportunity to thank all those kind correspondents who have sent me reports of the behaviour of their roses, and various notes and details for inclusion. The quest continues. I have found two very old-type Damasks and a pink version of the Red Rose of Lancaster, but further research is required before I can feel sure of their names.

THE FRANKFORT ROSE, ROSA FRANCOFURTANA. Under this name I have described (page 139) a rose which had become known, without any published validity, as 'Empress Josephine'. Redouté's portrait is very near to if not identical with it and probably both his plants and mine were hybrids of either a form of R. *francofurtana* and R. *cinnamomea* or the latter and a double R. *gallica*. At any rate, as Mr Gordon Rowley pointed out to me, the botanical R. *francofurtana* recorded in old books (apart from Redouté) refers to a much less double and impressive rose. Plate I.
Jacquin, *Horti Schoenbrunnensis*, Plate 415. A thorny type, semi-double.

THE ROSE OF PROVINS

R. GALLICA PUMILA. Jacquin, *Flora Austriaca*, Plate 198, shews a very similar rose.

DUC DE GUICHE, 1835. Synonym 'Senat Romain'.

OFFICINALIS
Andrews, Plate 45. 'Officinal or French Red Rose'. Fanciful.
Lawrance, Plate 16. R. *officinalis*.
Donnaud, Plate 14. Too dark.
Duhamel, Vol. 7. Plate 8.
Komlosy. R. *damascena rubra*. Poor.

TRICOLORE DE FLANDRE
Revue Horticole, 1847, Fig. 3. Poor colour.
Journal des Roses, Octobre 1881. Unrecognizable.
Flore des Serres, Vol. 11. Plate 155. Unrecognizable.

VERSICOLOR. 'Rosa Mundi', a name possibly signifying 'Rose-mouth' (Andrews, 1805). Sir Thomas Hanmer in his *Garden Book* of 1659 states that it also occurred, as a sport in Norfolk 'a few years since'.

THE DAMASK ROSE

BOTZARIS. A very pleasing little rose, probably owing its whiteness and distinct fragrance to R. *alba*; the hep is not of true Damask shape. Very double, opening flat, creamy white, even lemon-white in the centre, quartered and with button eye.

DUC DE CAMBRIDGE. A rich dark crimson-tinted Damask with purple flush.

MADAME HARDY was one of Dean Hole's favourites, with a reservation: 'a true white, and a well-formed Rose, but alas! "green-eyed" like "jealousy"—envious, it may be, of Madame Zoutman, who, though not of such a clear complexion, is free from ocular infirmities'. Personally I think the green eye is an additional charm.

OEILLET PARFAIT
Journal des Roses, Novembre 1879. I have not seen this striped rose. Although classed as a Damask, it has a rounded hep, and its colour distinguishes it from the pink Gallica of the same name.

QUATRE SAISONS BLANC MOUSSEUX. The figure in Komlosy referring to R. *alba menstrualis* 'Mousseuse Blanche' does not match this rose so well as one captioned 'Princesse Adelaide'.

AUTUMN DAMASK ROSES

Portraying these perpetual Damask roses was indulged in more often than the Summer Damasks, which is understandable, considering the esteem in which they must have been held before the advent of the China Rose.

DAMASCENA BIFERA. The Autumn Damask. Mr Gordon Rowley

finds the present name invalid and proposes the use of the earlier *R. damascena semperflorens.*

Jamain et Forney, Plate 31. 'Rose de Quatre Saisons.'

Roessig, Plate 8. 'Le Rosier de tous les mois.' *Rosa omnium calendarum.*

Roessig, Plate 42. *R. bifera rosea persiana.* A good portrait.

Lawrance, Plate 5. *R. damascena,* the red monthly rose.

Revue Horticole, 1865, page 151. Quatre Saisons Ordinaire et Q. S. Mousseux Blanche ou 'Rose de Thionville'; growing on the same branch.

Duhamel, Vol 7. Plate 9. *R. damascena semperflorens.* 'Le Rosier de tous les mois'.

Andrews, Plate 51. *R. saepeflorens alba.* 'The White-flowered Monthly Rose.' This I have not seen but I mention it here as it may again occur as a sport from this rose or from 'Quatre Saisons Blanc Mousseux', from one of which it no doubt originated.

THE PORTLAND DAMASKS

On page 86 Dr Hurst gives a few brief notes on the Portland Rose, an historic link, presumably, between the Autumn Damask and the Hybrid Perpetuals. For some years I have been growing a rose given to me by Mrs L. Fleischmann, and also by Captain Robert Berkeley, and have at last identified it with Redouté's portrait of 'Le Rosier de Portland'. It makes a low bush with erect twiggy growth, armed with small bristly thorns, and bright green foliage, rather reminiscent of the Red Rose of Lancaster. The flowers have the 'high shouldered' arrangement of the Autumn Damask, and are borne in erect clusters at the top of every shoot. They are bright crimson, rather darker and more intense than the Red Rose of Lancaster, but much smaller, and semi-double, in shallow cup formation, opening well and shewing yellow stamens. In hot dry seasons there is a long pause without flowers after the first flush at midsummer, but with good cultivation and reasonable moisture there are further flowers in autumn. It is not very strongly scented. Heps long, of true Damask shape.

This is *Rosa paestana,* or 'Scarlet Four Seasons'; its colour distinguishes it from all the old Autumn Damask variants, which were never more than pink.

Redouté, Vol. 1. Plate 109. *Rosa damascena coccinea.*
Andrews, Plate 49.
Lawrance, Plate 5.

The Portland Roses received from the Roseraie de l'Haÿ some years ago have proved to be sturdy, erect little plants and very free-flowering throughout summer and autumn. Some did not survive and are apparently no longer available in the Paris garden, but the following have grown well. They are briefly described on page 155, but further testing enables me to give fuller details. They bear the rich old-rose fragrance and are doubly welcome.

ARTHUR DE SANSAL, 1855. A hybrid of 'Géant des Batailles'. A satisfactory sturdy plant with good dark green leaves. Erect growth, producing large heads of bloom in late summer, but in more or less continuous production from midsummer. Pretty buds of darkest maroon purple. They open completely flat, very full of short petals, quartered, and of deepest maroon-purple-crimson, fading to a rich grape-purple. Probably 4 feet.

BLANC DE VIBERT, 1847. Yellowish green soft Damask foliage. The cupped, double blooms are pure white with a hint of lemon in the centre when half open, becoming pure white. **4 feet.**

COMTE DE CHAMBORD, 1860. This is a first-class plant, always in flower, of sturdy erect growth, well clothed in pointed light green leaves. Most beautiful buds, opening with rolled petals to a densely filled flat flower, sometimes quartered, but always with reflexed and rolled petals around the edge. A full rich pink with lilac tones. Intense fragrance. 4 feet. Plate I.

JACQUES CARTIER, 1868. Compact and erect habit with plenty of light-green leaves, the terminal leaflet exceptionally long and narrow. Sepals often pronouncedly foliaceous. Flowers similar to those of 'Comte de Chambord', very full, quartered and with button eyes. Very fragrant. 4 feet.

MABEL MORRISON. According to *Modern Roses V* this occurred as a sport from 'Baroness Rothschild' in 1878, which had been a sport from 'Souvenir de la Reine d'Angleterre'. It is classed as a Hybrid Perpetual. 'Baroness Rothschild' bore large flowers in, as far as I remember, the typical Hybrid Perpetual shape and style. 'Mabel Morrison' on the other hand seems to have reverted to some inherent Damask influence, and conforms most nearly to the characters of the Portland Roses, having greyish leaves, neat erect habit, and the typical Damask hip and 'high shouldered' habit. The flowers are comparatively small for a Hybrid Perpetual, cupped, of a delicate blush pink becoming white, deliciously fragrant and borne recurrently. This rose was sent to me by Mrs Dorothy Stemler, who carries on so well the collection started by my old friend the late Will Tillotson in California, and I regard it as a most valuable addition to the all-too-few Portland Roses. 1878.

PANACHÉE DE LYON, 1895. This is supposed to be a sport from the 'Rose du Roi'. It has small, pleated, flat flowers variously flaked or particoloured with pink and crimson. An erect rather spindly plant; recurrent, but not prolific.

PERGOLÈSE, 1860. Mid-green leaves, a small upright plant. Comparatively small flowers opening quite flat and filled with petals, quartered, and often with a green pointel in the centre. Bright cerise to magenta purple when freshly open, taking on dark purple shadings like 'Duc de Guiche'. 4 feet.

Two varieties I have not seen are depicted in Jamain et Forney, 'Madame Boll' (Plate 39) and 'Marie de St Jean' (Plate 36). The latter in particular shews the 'high shouldered' character of this group. 'Madame Boll' is also in the *Revue Horticole* for 1865, page 111.

THE WHITE ROSES

BELLE AMOUR. Referred to on page 165, but I have still found no authority for the name. I was given this rose by Miss Lindsay, who had found it in an old convent at Elbœuf. In 1959 I saw it on the front of a cottage in Norfolk: an old-established bush, which must have been there for many years. This is the only rose in the old groups with such a salmon-tone to its pink colouring, and I suspect the influence of 'Ayrshire Splendens', an old rambler of the R. *arvensis* group, for not only is it precisely the same colour but has also the scent of myrrh; 'Ayrshire

Splendens' was also known as the 'Myrrh Scented Rose'. This
theory may seem far-fetched but it has a parallel in that the
only other Old Rose with a hint of salmon—'Belle Isis'—has
been used as a parent by Mr David Austin and one of the seedlings has a pronounced myrrh scent. This most lovely seedling
we had the honour of naming after the late Mrs Constance Spry.
It is, I feel, a fitting tribute to one whose help and influence were
so great in re-establishing the Old Roses in popular favour.

KOENIGEN VON DANEMARCK. The French synonym about 1900 was
'Naissance de Vénus'. I must add a note regarding the origin of
this rose from Mr O. Sonderhousen of Denmark; this contri-
bution arrived too late to be more than mentioned in the 1957
impression of this book. Mr Sonderhousen kindly sent me a
full account of an argument by the raisers and Professor
Lehmann, Director of the Botanic Gardens at Hamburg; the
pamphlet was published at Altona in 1833 'in aid of the poor'
and was written by John Booth. The complainants were James
Booth & Söhne.

Under the motto *Nemo me impune lacessit* Booth states that a
seedling of 'Maiden's Blush' flowered for the first time in his
nursery at Flottbeck in 1816; that at first it was called the 'New
Maidenblush' and as such distributed on a very small scale from
about 1820–1. After building up a good stock it was entered in
their catalogue for 1826 as 'Königen von Dannemark' at a
price of 12 marks. He obtained permission from the king to
name it after the queen (i.e. the Danish queen, as in those days
Denmark stretched down into Germany).

Then in 1828 Professor Lehmann claimed, in a list of plants in
the Hamburg Botanic Gardens, that a rose named 'Belle Courtisanne', a cross between *R. centifolia* and 'Maidenblush' and
mentioned already in 1806 in a French catalogue, had been
offered for sale recently under the name of 'Königen von
Dannemark'.

On being tackled about this by Booth, Lehmann gave evasive
replies, saying the rose was generally known in France and had
been depicted by Redouté. Booth wrote thereupon to all the
well-known rose breeders and Redouté, and their answers,
quoted in full in the pamphlet, proved that nobody had ever

heard of a rose called 'Belle Courtisanne'. The remaining pages Booth devoted to a considerable crowing over Lehmann. Booth adds that 'even the probably best-known Rose collection in England in those days, viz. that in Hammersmith [Messrs Lee & Kennedy], eight years ago paid three guineas per plant for it before it had been entered in our catalogue, and mentioned it in their garden list in 1830 as "Queen of Denmark"'.

'Koenigen von Danemarck' was undoubtedly a peerless rose then, as it is now, and it is not surprising to find the raiser standing up for himself in such circumstances.

MAIDEN'S BLUSH. Mrs Gore, page 269, gives the following synonymy:

'La Royale' = 'Cuisse de Nymphe'.

'Cuisse de Nymphe Émue' = 'Cuisse de Nymphe' with glossy ovary.

Small 'Cuisse de Nymphe' = alba rubigens.

Lawrance, Plate 32. 'Great Maiden's Blush Rose.' Buds excellent.

Andrews, Plate 16. 'Rosa Bella Donna', 'Maiden's Blush Rose'; good portrait but too much colour.

Plate 17. Ditto, var. flore minor; 'Maiden's Rose', small-flowered variety.

MAXIMA. Sported to R. alba semi plena, 1959. This was called the 'Common White Rose' in the Florists' Vademecum, 1882, and must have been a double as the author compares it with 'Maiden's Blush', this 'being the same, but blush'.

Duhamel, Vol. 7. Plate 16. R. alba; this is R. alba maxima.

Lawrance, Plate 25. Rosa alba β, 'Double White Rose'. This is R. a. semi plena.

Plate 37 shews the single R. alba (5 petals only).

Andrews, Plate 40, under the name of Rosa glabra, has a thornless double white rose, like 'Mme Plantier' and 'Mme Legras de St Germain'.

Andrews, Plate 10. R. alba, single white type; 'is in very few collections'; 5 petals only. This occurred at Mottisfont, 1980.

SEMI PLENA. This occurred as a sport on R. alba Maxima in 1959 in my own garden and at Sunningdale.

THE PROVENCE ROSES

CENTIFOLIA. The genuine R. *centifolia* can be traced in *European Flower Painters* by Peter Mitchell (A. & C. Black, 1973) to the early 1620s, such as by Balthazar van der Ast. While similar roses occur in yet earlier paintings, they appear to be of a related type, but not true R. *centifolia*.
Komlosy. Fair.
Duhamel, Vol. 7. Plate 12. A good portrait.
Andrews, Plate 15. Poor.

'ROSE DES PEINTRES'. I have always considered simply as R. *centifolia*, but some of the old writers praise it considerably, apparently as a separate variety.
Choix des Plus Belles Roses. Plate 29. 'Rose des Peintres.' Raised by Verdier.
Donnaud, Plate 48. *Roses et Rosiers*, par des Horticulteurs et des Amateurs de Jardinage, Paris, 1872. Plate 48. 'Centfeuille des Peintres.' 'Cette magnifique varieté fleuri de Juin à Aôut.' It does sometimes linger in flower until August in cool districts.

BULLATA. Andrews, Plate 28. Poor.

DE MEAUX
Step, *Favourite Flowers*, Vol. 1. Plate 78. R. *centifolia pomponia*; de Meaux.

DE MEAUX, WHITE. The figure and description in the *Botanical Magazine*, 5. 407, probably apply.

JUNO. This has proved a vigorous bush, not necessarily procumbent, but graceful, and I place it in the front rank of Old Roses.

PARVIFOLIA
Botanic Register, Vol. 6. Plate 452.
Andrews, Plate 56. R. *parvifolia*.

SPONG
Andrews, Plate 27. R. *provincialis hybrida*. Hybrid Provence Rose. 'It is commonly known by the appellation of the "Spong Rose" from having been first raised in quantities by a gardener of that name.'

THE MOSS ROSES

William Paul, in his 9th edition, quotes the French raiser of roses M. Laffay as having said in 1847 'from the moss roses we shall soon see great things'. During the next forty years or so numerous varieties were introduced, running into several hundreds. Today but a handful remains and none has quite as much beauty as the Common Moss; none achieved high distinction but they are treasured because of their mossy buds and also, I need hardly repeat, their scent.

CENTIFOLIA MUSCOSA. Niedtner, page 24. A pleasing portrait.
Jamain et Forney, Plate 45.
Botanical Magazine, t.69. Beautiful drawing.

CRIMSON GLOBE. An unsatisfactory, very dark crimson variety, often remaining 'balled'.
Paul (catalogue) 1890. Very grandiose.

LANEI, 1845. A remontant moss which is occasionally seen. It is rather a coarse variety with big round buds and deep mauve-pink very full blooms. Extremely vigorous lax growth. Not very mossy.
Journal des Roses, Mai 1880.

For 'MONSIEUR PÉLISSON' please read 'Pélisson', 1848.

NUITS DE YOUNG. Raised 1845, not 1851. Presumably named after 'Night Thoughts' by the eighteenth-century English poet, Edward Young.

STRIPED MOSS, 'Oeillet Panaché'. As will be seen on page 120 et seq., several striped mossy roses occurred at different dates.
Andrews, Plate 64. An excellent drawing.
Miller, Plate 221. The Striped Moss is depicted but the description does not apply.

BOURBON ROSES

BOULE DE NEIGE
Jamain et Forney, Plate 32. Poor.
Hariot, Plate 59. *Journal des Roses*, Octobre 1902. I wish mine grew so magnificently.

BOURBON QUEEN. Sometimes known as 'Souvenir de la Princesse de Lamballe'.

COMMANDANT BEAUREPAIRE AND PANACHÉ D'ANGERS
Journal des Roses, Mai 1882. A poor and exaggerated portrait lacking the purple colouring. The specimen was given the former name in error.

FERDINAND PICHARD. Tanne, 1921. I have been unable to ascertain whether this was raised from seed or occurred as a sport. It is obviously closely related to 'Commandant Beaurepaire', but is of more compact growth, with similar light green though more pointed leaves. The flowers on freshly opening are clear pink heavily dotted, splashed, striped and flaked with vivid crimson; on the next day the pink turns to blush and the crimson to purple. Cupped and fairly double. The most important point is that it constantly produces flowers through summer and autumn, after the first glorious flush is over. Probably 4–5 feet.

GREAT WESTERN. The details I gave on page 196 are not quite correct. This ship was the second mail steamship to cross the Atlantic. She arrived only a few hours after the *Sirius* which had left four days earlier, so our rose is duly honoured.

KRONPRINZESSIN VIKTORIA. This sport of 'Souvenir de la Malmaison' is recorded in August Jäger's *Rosenlexicon*, Leipzig, 1960, as originating with Vollert, and being introduced by the nurseryman Späth of Berlin in 1888. It has recently come to light, having been treasured in the garden at Smallhythe, Kent, a property of the National Trust. It makes a compact bush, and is in effect a pure white sport showing lemon tinting in the bud and half open flower and thus is unique in bringing this tint to the Bourbon Roses.

LOUISE ODIER. 'Madame de Stella.'
Jamain et Forney. Plate 50. Poor.
Choix de Plus Belles Roses, Plate 40.

MADAME HARDY DU THÉ and MADAME MELON DU THÉ. Names without foundation for a rose which has turned out to be 'Clotilde Soupert'. See page 149 in my *Shrub Roses of Today*, revised edition 1974.

MADAME PIERRE OGER

Rosenzeitung, 1889.

Journal des Roses, Juillet 1885.

MRS PAUL. Paul & Son, 1891. (Not to be confused with 'Mrs William Paul' (1863), a dark maroón-crimson Hybrid Perpetual—see *Florist & Pomologist*, 1863, p. 121.) A seedling from 'Mme Isaac Pereire', raised by Mr George Paul of the Old Nurseries, Cheshunt. Occasionally, usually in September, I have seen blooms as good and large as those depicted in *The Garden* but in the summer they are not up to the standard of 'Mme Isaac Pereire'. A vigorous rose with good foliage, and very free flowering; needs the support of a stake or a wall, and of similar growth to 'Mme Isaac Pereire'. It makes a good trio with its parent and 'Mme Ernst Calvat', and is equally fragrant. Pearly white suffused pink and a soft peach shade; best in the autumn.

The Garden, 1890, page 484.

Jekyll, facing page 128 (photograph).

SOUVENIR DE LA MALMAISON. The date 1843 refers to the introduction of the bush, and original, form. I saw this at La Malmaison very appropriately occupying a bed on the lawn. During the hot summer of 1959 this rose excelled itself in several gardens, producing enough flowers to make a Floribunda wilt. The climbing form originated in 1893. Mr Roy Shepherd tells us that it was the Grand Duke of Russia who, obtaining a plant for the Imperial Garden at St Petersburg, gave it its name. The climbing form, which originated in Australia, is not quite so free as the bush variety, as would be expected, but will reach 15 feet in height on a wall. There was a pink variety which is illustrated in Verschaffelt: *L'Illustrations Horticole*, 1860; perhaps this was a sport and may occur again.

Choix des Plus Belles Roses, Plate 2.

Hoffmann, Plate 4. Very good.

Note for 1979 Edition

ROSA CHINENSIS is not in cultivation. The species is a native of central China and is a tall climbing rose, leaves with 3–5 leaflets, flowers single, usually crimson, sometimes pink, produced in summer only. In this book—and many others—the R. *chinensis* usually quoted is one of four hybrids that were introduced to Europe around 1800, particularly 'Parson's Pink' which is now usually called 'Old Blush'.

BIBLIOGRAPHY

ANDREWS, Henry C., *Roses,* 1805–28.
BEAN, W. J., *Trees and Shrubs,* 1949.
Botanical Register, 1816.
BUNYARD, Edward A., *Old Garden Roses,* 1936; also in *The New Flora and Silva,* Vol. 2.
CARRIÈRE, E. A., *Production et Fixation des variétés dans les végétaux.*
CRANSTON, John, *Cultural Directions for the Rose,* 1875.
CURTIS, Henry, *Beauties of the Rose,* 1850–3.
DRAPIEZ, P. A. J., *Herbier de l'Amateur de fleur,* 1828–35.
DUHAMEL DU MONCEAU, H. L. *Traité des arbres et arbustes, nouvelle edition,* 1804–9.
DURUZ, Selwyn, *Flowering Shrubs,* 1952.
GERARD, John, *The Herball,* 1597.
HARIOT, Paul, *Le Livre d'Or des Roses,* 1904.
HARVEY, N. P., *The Rose in Britain,* 1951.
JAMAIN, Hippolyte, and FORNEY, Eugène, *Les Roses,* 1893.
JEKYLL, Gertrude, and MAWLEY, Edward, *Roses for English Gardens,* 1902.
Journal des Roses, 1877–1914.
KEAYS, Mrs Frederick Love, *Old Roses,* 1935.
KINGSLEY, Rose, *Roses and Rose Growing,* 1908.
KOMLOSY, *Rosenalbum,* 1868–75.
LAWRANCE, Mary, *A Collection of Roses from Nature,* 1799.
MCFARLAND, J. Horace Company, *Modern Roses,* IV, 1952.
MOLLET, Claude, *Théâtre des plans et jardinages . . .,* 1663.
NESTEL'S, *Illustrierte Rosengarten.*
NIEDTNER, T., *Die Rose,* 1880.
PARKINSON, John, *Paradisi in Sole Paradisus Terrestris,* 1629.
PAUL, William, *The Rose Garden,* 1848, 1872.
REDOUTÉ, P. J., *Les Roses,* 1817–24.
REHDER, Alfred, *Manual of Cultivated Trees and Shrubs,* 1947.
RIVERS, Thomas, *Rose Amateur's Guide,* 1837, 1877.
ROESSIG, D., *Les Roses,* 1802–20.
SHEPHERD, Roy E., *History of the Rose,* 1954.
SIMON, Léon, and COCHET, Pierre, *Nomenclature de toutes les Roses,* 1906.
SINGER, Max, *Dictionnaire des Roses,* 1885.
Société Nationale d'Horticulture de France, *Les Plus Belle Roses au début du vingtième siècle,* 1886.
THOMAS, H. H., *The Rose Book,* 1913.
WILLMOTT, Ellen, *The Genus Rosa,* 1910–14.
WYLIE, A. P., in *Journal of the Royal Horticultural Society;* Vol. LXXIX, p. 555 *et seq.,* December 1954.

Index